New Language Learning and Teaching Environments

Series Editor
Hayo Reinders
Department of Education
Unitec Institute of Technology
Auckland, New Zealand

New Language Learning and Teaching Environments is an exciting new book series dedicated to recent developments in learner-centred approaches and the impact of technology on learning and teaching inside and outside the language classroom. The series aims to: Publish cutting-edge research into current developments and innovation in language learning and teaching practice. Publish applied accounts of the ways in which these developments impact on current and future language education. Encourage dissemination and cross-fertilisation of policies and practice relating to learner-centred pedagogies for language learning and teaching in new learning environments. Disseminate research and best practice in out-of-class and informal language learning. The series is a multidisciplinary forum for the very latest developments in language education, taking a pedagogic approach with a clear focus on the learner, and with clear implications for both researchers and language practitioners. It is the first such series to provide an outlet for researchers to publish their work, and the first stop for teachers interested in this area.

More information about this series at
http://www.springer.com/series/14736

Robert Vanderplank

Captioned Media in Foreign Language Learning and Teaching

Subtitles for the Deaf and Hard-of-Hearing as Tools for Language Learning

Robert Vanderplank
Centre for the Study of Lifelong Language Learning
Kellogg College, University of Oxford
Oxford, United Kingdom

New Language Learning and Teaching Environments
ISBN 978-1-137-50044-1 (hardcover)   ISBN 978-1-137-50045-8   (eBook)
ISBN 978-1-349-69884-4 (softcover)
DOI 10.1057/978-1-137-50045-8

Library of Congress Control Number: 2016943309

© The Editor(s) (if applicable) and The Author(s) 2016, First softcover printing 2018
The author(s) has/have asserted their right(s) to be identified as the author(s) of this work in accordance with the Copyright, Designs and Patents Act 1988.
This work is subject to copyright. All rights are solely and exclusively licensed by the Publisher, whether the whole or part of the material is concerned, specifically the rights of translation, reprinting, reuse of illustrations, recitation, broadcasting, reproduction on microfilms or in any other physical way, and transmission or information storage and retrieval, electronic adaptation, computer software, or by similar or dissimilar methodology now known or hereafter developed.
The use of general descriptive names, registered names, trademarks, service marks, etc. in this publication does not imply, even in the absence of a specific statement, that such names are exempt from the relevant protective laws and regulations and therefore free for general use.
The publisher, the authors and the editors are safe to assume that the advice and information in this book are believed to be true and accurate at the date of publication. Neither the publisher nor the authors or the editors give a warranty, express or implied, with respect to the material contained herein or for any errors or omissions that may have been made.

Cover illustration: © Olivier DIGOIT / Alamy Stock Photo

Printed on acid-free paper

This Palgrave Macmillan imprint is published by Springer Nature
The registered company is Macmillan Publishers Ltd. London

For Sirpa, but for whom I might never have watched a programme or film with captions

Acknowledgements

I thank Jason Cole, Cristina Mariotti and Annamaria Caimi for their helpful and valuable comments on reading the manuscript of this book.

The author and publishers acknowledge the following sources of copyright material and are grateful for the permissions granted.

Extract and facsimile from K. Price (1983), by permission of MATSOL and Karen Price. Extract from R. Vanderplank (1988a) by permission of Oxford University Press. Extract from R. Vanderplank (1990) by permission of Elsevier. Extracts from R. Vanderplank (1994a) and (2015) by permission of Peter Lang. Extracts from R. Vanderplank (2010) and (2016) by permission of Cambridge University Press.

Contents

1 Introduction   1

2 Some Essential Themes in Building the Case for
   Captions in Language Learning   7

3 The Value of Closed Captions and Teletext Subtitles
   for Language Learning   43

4 The State of the Art I: Selected Research on Listening
   Comprehension and Vocabulary Acquisition   75

5 The State of the Art II: Selected Research on Other
   Issues in Watching Captioned TV, Films and Video   105

6 Focus on Genres: The Practical Uses and Limitations of
   Different Types of Programmes   149

7 The EURECAP Project   187

8 The Developing Environment for Language Learning:
   A New Audience and the Revised Model of Language
   Learning with Captions   223

9 Conclusion   245

References   251

Index   265

List of Figures

Fig. 3.1	The Price and Dow study	46
Fig. 3.2	The central role of attention	63
Fig. 3.3	"Paying attention to the words" model	64
Fig. 8.1	The basic model	238
Fig. 8.2	Attention with selection and grading factors	238
Fig. 8.3	The original 1990 model of "paying attention to the words"	239
Fig. 8.4	A cognitive-affective model of language learning through captioned viewing	240

List of Tables

Table 7.1   Films with captions watched during the project   190
Table 7.2   Film and viewer factors in watching captioned films   217

1

Introduction

1.1 Why a Book on Captioned Viewing and Language Learning?

Welcome to the world of watching television programmes and films with subtitles in the same language, or captions, as I shall call them in this book. If a reader who has never watched a programme or film with captions thought that captioned viewing was a simple matter, rather like watching a foreign film with translation subtitles, he or she needs to think again and try and watch a few programmes with captions. The many over-simplistic experimental studies on foreign language learning with clips from captioned programmes that are published in journals may conceal the richness and variety of the world of captioned viewing, a world in which both language and culture are made accessible to those who have normal hearing but who are "hard of listening" in the foreign language.

The reader may well wonder why there should be a book on foreign language learning with such a simple device as captions intended to enable the deaf and hard-of-hearing to enjoy television programmes, films and DVDs. It really ought to be pretty obvious, oughtn't it? After my first article was published back in 1988, I also thought that would be the end of the argument, so obvious was it to me that they were a boon to language learners and to second language users with normal hearing. But no, questions and issues have been raised for over thirty years about their value, the advantages and downsides, how they work (or not) at different levels of proficiency, whether keywords and summaries would be better than those produced by captioners for the deaf, their relationship with translation subtitles and their availability in different languages.

With regard to the last point, until relatively recently, captions were rare in languages other than English, and it has only been through the pressure from deaf associations and through legislation that we now see captioning of TV programmes and DVDs in many countries and languages. I had thought about writing a book on captions and language learning some years ago but put it aside, as I wanted a book that would open up the world of captioned programmes and films to a global, multilingual audience, not just the English language learning and teaching audience. With captioning now widespread in Europe and elsewhere in the world, as well as in North America and the UK, we can say that significant progress has been made, albeit very slowly and not without reluctance on the part of some countries. It is in this context of widespread and growing multilingual captioning, together with the growth in informal language learning fuelled by the sophisticated multimedia use of independent learners worldwide, that this book has been written.

While this book will, I hope, be of interest to a wide readership of teachers as well as students and researchers in applied linguistics and second language acquisition, the message is also for all those who wish to learn a foreign language, especially those who choose to learn independently. If there is one thing that has come out quite conclusively over the years, it is that to gain benefit from watching TV programmes and films with captions, the learner-viewer needs to have choice and control of the viewing and to put effort into watching. The paradox of using television programmes and films to help learn a language is that our very viewing habits work against us taking it seriously and gaining much apart from fleeting enjoyment and entertainment.

1.2 Chapter Outlines

This book has a thesis and a narrative, which I build through the chapters. I begin in Chap. 2 by outlining what captions are and the basic principles of captioning. I also provide information on the current state of captioning in Europe and elsewhere before moving on to talk about television and video in foreign language learning. If asked what sort of medium television is, most people would probably say that it is a visual medium, or possibly an audiovisual medium. It is almost a reflex to call it a visual medium, yet, as I shall argue, television has its roots in radio and is very much a verbal medium. This reflex is especially true in foreign language teaching and learning where "recipes" for teachers about using audiovisual material in language teaching have stressed the visual side of TV and films from the 1950s to the present day. I acknowledge that such a position is entirely understandable given the fast and fleeting nature of speech on television and in films, but in focusing on the visual, we have been missing out on a fantastically rich source of language input for our learners. However, learning from television is not without its special problems and conceptual issues; I draw on the work of Gavriel Salomon and Albert Bandura to tease out why it is not enough to just "open the box" by providing captions, for it requires motivation, effort and a positive "can-do" attitude on the part of the learner-viewer, as evidenced by recent research in France and Brazil.

While Chap. 2 serves to set the conceptual and functional scene, Chap. 3 takes us through the pioneering of Karen Price and Anne Dow at Harvard in the early 1980s and my own *Teletext 888 Project* in the 1980s and 1990s. Readers may well be surprised to find that so much was achieved by Price and Dow in their large-scale study, yet the study has often been overlooked in the research literature. In my case, the project occupied ten years of my professional life before I decided that, at the time, there was little more I could do, as I had come up against some paradoxical issues affecting my own learners' ability to exploit captions for language learning.

In Chap. 4, I use the pivotal meta-analysis of research into the benefits of captioned viewing for language learning by Maribel Montero-Perez and her colleagues to review key research studies, especially those that focus on listening comprehension and vocabulary acquisition. I also describe in some detail the key study by Holger Mitterer and James McQueen, comparing viewing with captions and viewing with translation subtitles. I close by suggesting that the scale and nature of the research justifies captioned viewing having its own space quite separate from video and language teaching on the one hand, and translated subtitles on the other.

I continue to review research in Chap. 5, covering themes such as "keyword" captioning, learners' strategies, longitudinal studies and literacy development with captions. I highlight how there is one area of research that remains underdeveloped, namely, how learners may develop their listening skills and strategies through watching captioned TV programmes and films over time and the complex matrix of factors at work. I also outline the theories and ideas that have been advanced for how captions appear to work or not with language learners.

The following chapter, Chap. 6, looks at the richness and variety of the language in TV programmes and films, how the language can be exploited and the positives and negatives that arise from using such a linguistically rich medium. I discuss the "flipped classroom," which may be the only feasible way of exploiting extensive watching of audiovisual material, and consider genres such as comedy, news, documentaries, lifestyle programmes, culture and drama. We may make programmes accessible through captions, but if a comedy programme contains discourses that are constantly shifting in topic, style and content, how can a learner possibly make either sense or use of the language. Similarly, what should a teacher or learner focus on when watching a documentary? A documentary is a sophisticated and often complex product containing a narrative thread, which may be disrupted by case studies and highly engaging talking heads. We may easily become so absorbed in a programme that we retain little in language learning terms.

In Chap. 7, I describe my recent EURECAP pilot project, the first longitudinal study of how informal learners watch and make use of captioned films in DVD format in four languages, namely, French, German, Italian and Spanish. While there are obvious limitations to this pilot project, the results underline the complexity of the interactions between the nature and the quality of the film watched; the viewer's proficiency, strategies, confidence and mental set; the tasks and setting and the quality and perceived value of the captions. I analyse the diary feedback of the participants in terms of their self-perceived relationship to a captioned film, their confidence, the degree of self-regulation, the value they place on the activity in terms of language learning, the amount of effort they appear to invest and their attitude to captions.

In Chap. 8, I provide evidence for the new environment for captioned viewing by learners outside formal learning in the classroom. I describe a large-scale survey reported at the "watershed" conference at the University of Pavia in 2012, which identified informal captioned viewing as an important and growing phenomenon among Europe's expatriate and immigrant communities. I outline some studies that also capture how independent learners in informal contexts are exploiting captions to further their goals to substantial effect. This leads me to consider the changing roles of the learners and technologies, and how both formal and informal independent learners have become active agents in accessing and using foreign language audiovisual material in novel ways. We have moved from a position where we look at the "effects of technology" to one where we need to think of the "effects with technology" and also "effects through technology," together with the implications for teaching and learning with captions. I end the chapter by revisiting my earlier model of language learning through watching captioned programmes and films to arrive at a reformulated model, which takes not only the research evidence into account but also the perceptual, cognitive and affective complexities of captioned viewing for language learning. The model is intended not only to capture the processes of captioned viewing but also to provide a source of future research questions.

In the final chapter, Chap. 9, I provide a brief overview and look forward to what more is needed in global terms to help the spread of captioning. While informal language learners may already be making good use of captioned viewing, the potential for teachers and learners in drawing on captioned TV and films in the classroom remains largely unfulfilled. This book is intended to help teachers and researchers understand the challenges and potential of using captioned TV programmes and films and provide ideas and a framework for developing their benefits in our classrooms and research studies.

2

Some Essential Themes in Building the Case for Captions in Language Learning

2.1 The Pavia "Watershed"

The conference, "Subtitles and Language Learning," held at the University of Pavia in September 2012, brought together, on the one hand, translation researchers and professionals and, on the other hand, those of us who have spent years promoting same-language subtitles or "captions" for deaf and hard-of-hearing people as a valuable aid to foreign and second language learning. It marked not only a watershed but also a "coming out," as captioning has now spread beyond the UK and North America, and has the backing of the European Union (EU) as a multilingual means of supporting its accessibility and equality agenda beyond deaf and hard-of-hearing people. We also heard about the findings of a large-scale survey (reported in detail in Chap. 8), which confirmed the importance of captions for second language viewers, especially migrant workers and adult expatriate learners of host country's languages. While the recognition by the EU that captioned viewing may help to bring the reality of a multilingual Europe a step closer for millions of its citizens, the history of captioning, particularly outside North America and the UK, is relatively short, and the nature and value of captions for second language users and learners is still not widely appreciated despite the large research literature on the value of captioned viewing worldwide. In this chapter, I shall try to build a unique position for the captioned viewing of TV programmes and films between the two large and well-established professional areas: those involved in translating films and TV programmes, and those who specialise in language teaching using TV and video.

2.2 A Captioned Revelation

During the two years I lived in Finland in the mid-1980s, I spent a lot of time watching TV programmes and films in English that were subtitled in Finnish. I found this helped me a lot in picking up useful Finnish expressions, grammar and vocabulary, and even in tuning in to Finnish after a while. I also learnt a lot of Finnish from advertisements on TV. Additionally, I observed that many Finns benefitted with regard to their English proficiency from watching English language programmes (soap operas, comedies, detective series and films subtitled in Finnish or Swedish). Friends and family also confirmed the value of watching, even with translation subtitles. While in Finland, I heard about English language subtitles for deaf and hard-of-hearing people available on broadcast TV on page 888 of the *Teletext* system in the UK, so when I returned to Britain in 1985, I was keen to explore their nature and potential. I was surprised (and thrilled) at the quality of the captions, and my Finnish wife, with native-user ability in English, was delighted at the support that these captions offered, especially when speech was fast or in an unfamiliar accent. These subtitles were not summaries of what was being spoken but, as far as possible, were accurate verbatim text of the spoken word. I was also amazed how they shifted the viewer's focus onto the language being spoken and raised one's awareness of the language. Running, real-time captions on news broadcasts were inevitably so out of sync with the spoken word that they were very distracting and offered much less potential for language learners.

2.3 What Are Captions for the Deaf and Hard-of-Hearing?

So what exactly are these captions? How did they come about? I do not intend to go into technical detail, as it can be easily found on the Internet and is not of great importance in this book. Nonetheless, I think it is important to grasp that in having the use of captions as an aid to watching films and TV programmes, foreign language learners with normal hearing and, of course, non-native speakers living in a country where captioning is provided, gain from a technological add-on designed to be of benefit to deaf and hard-of-hearing people.

Over the years, several different terms have been used to describe these same-language subtitles. The standard term in North America is "closed captions" (often seen as CC on media such as *YouTube*), since they do not appear in vision but can be revealed through the closed caption decoder built into the television set. In translation circles, I have often seen and heard them described as "intralingual subtitles" in contrast to "interlingual subtitles." In the UK and some other countries, they were known as Teletext subtitles, as they were broadcast through the Teletext information system. In non–English-speaking countries, they tend to be called the equivalent of "subtitles for the deaf and hard-of-hearing" (e.g., in France, "sous-titres pour les sourds et malentendants"). In this book, I have chosen to call them captions for simplicity and consistency.

A complaint frequently made about captions by language learners and teachers concerns their quality, in particular, that captions are not verbatim replications of the language spoken. In my opinion, we can really have no complaints; we are just fortunate that those with a disability have provided us, who are merely 'hard-of-listening' in a foreign language, with a wonderful resource not only for making films and TV programmes accessible to us but for helping us improve our reading, listening and speaking skills.

In the UK, the Teletext information system, providing news and information via television through numbered pages, was developed in the early 1970s (it was known as CEEFAX on BBC and ORACLE on ITV [Independent Television]), and televisions with built-in decoders were available in the late 1970s. Around this time, Teletext was also adopted as world standard and remains so today, although CEEFAX and ORACLE have disappeared in the UK. The first captions for the deaf (called Teletext subtitles and available on page 888) appeared in 1975 on the CEEFAX system. Basic principles were quickly developed through consultation with organisations for deaf and hard-of-hearing people, and through research projects such as the one based at the University of Southampton (Baker, 1985; Baker, Downton, & Newell, 1980), which asked the following questions:

- Where should subtitles be on the screen?
- What kind of background should be used for subtitles?
- How many words should be transmitted in each subtitle?
- Should we use short, uncomplicated sentences or every word that is spoken?
- How far can we edit the speech without losing too much information?

From the responses, it became clear that summary captions were considered patronising; deaf viewers wanted to have the text language as close to the spoken language as time and space on the screen would allow. The notion of "shot to shot" was followed as in translation subtitling, whereby the subtitle text should, as far as possible, refer to the shot in which it appears, and not to shots before or afterwards (an issue which plagues live captioning).

One drawback in the early days of captioning was that they could only be watched on broadcast television through a special decoder and could not be recorded on standard household VHS recorders. By the late 1980s, almost all televisions in the UK were equipped with Teletext decoders, which could show broadcast captions, and manufacturers such as Philips were producing VHS recorders, which could record programmes with captions fixed in vision (you could not switch them on and off as you can now on DVD players and hard drives).

2 Some Essential Themes in Building the Case for Captions

Minimum amounts of captioning for broadcast programmes were established by law in the UK in 1990, and editing standards were steadily refined in the 1990s. A key guide to caption editing was published by the now-defunct regulator, the Independent Television Commission (ITC), in the UK in 1999 (Independent Television Commission, 1999), which offers valuable insights, applicable to foreign language learning in many respects, into the thinking behind captioning. As the document says:

> Subtitle editing is different from most other forms of text editing. Not only is the medium more dynamic than most others, but also the target audience is not a homogenous group. Although the common voice of deaf and hard-of-hearing people is that they require access to television, they vary in terms of literacy, hearing loss and socio-economic factors. With the increasing size of an aged population, the preferences of the elderly in particular should be taken into account.
>
> The following are some of the factors which contribute to the distinctive nature of subtitling:
>
> (i) Comprehension and enjoyment of normal text are enhanced for the reader by the ability, if necessary, to re-scan the article. Comprehension of a television programme, however, is typically gained only at the time of viewing.
> (ii) Readers normally have only text to absorb. By contrast the user of subtitles must take in simultaneously the action within the television image as well as the information provided by the subtitling.
> (iii) The pace of programmes sometimes means that subtitles cannot reasonably be expected to convey the full range of information contained in the television image. However, deaf and hard-of-hearing people naturally expect to receive as much as possible of the information which is available to the general audience.
>
> Careful and sensitive editing is therefore needed in order to produce subtitles which will suit the intended audience, while still conveying the full meaning of the dialogue or commentary within the limitations set by the pace of the programme.

Subtitling Priorities

The priorities for effective subtitling can be summarised as follows:

1. Allow adequate reading time.
2. Reduce viewers' frustration by:
   (a) attempting to match what is actually said, reflecting the spoken word with the same meaning and complexity; without censoring
   (b) constructing subtitles which contain all obvious speech and relevant sound effects; and
   (c) placing subtitles sensibly in time and space.
3. Without making unnecessary changes to the spoken word, construct subtitles which contain easily-read and commonly-used English sentences in a tidy and sensible format.
4. In the case of subtitles for children, particular regard should be given to the reading age of children. (pp. 4–5)

In addition to valuable guidance on editing for maximum ease of reading, the document also makes recommendations for such matters as timing and synchronisation, and shot changes. My earliest memories of obvious and striking editing involved changes where a less frequent word was used in the caption text. For example, in an episode of a very popular American series called *Thirtysomething* in the late 1980s, the speaker said "for thousands of years." To keep to the line limit, the captioner shortened the phrase to "for *millenia.*"

Obviously, captioners were told to ensure that captions were displayed for a sufficient length of time for viewers to read them. The normal maximum caption presentation rate for pre-recorded programmes was not to exceed 140 words per minute, and only in exceptional circumstances was the higher rate of 180 words per minute permitted. The most common case of fast speech these days is certainly on some news broadcast where reporters rush to get their words in the number of seconds allowed. A maximum of three lines of text is also recommended.

As the document says, presentation rates will depend on the programme content, so some real-time captioned current affairs programmes where the speaker is not on screen, or chat shows that have a higher text complexity than drama, may have far more text and higher presentations rates than, say, a soap opera or practical skills programme such as cookery demonstrations.

Captioners were early users of eye-movement research and took into account that deaf and hard-of-hearing viewers made use of visual cues from the faces of television speakers in order to direct their gaze to the caption area. It was found that if there was no caption, the resulting "false alarm" at missing something important caused considerable frustration. They also drew on research that found that hearing-impaired viewers followed a specific pattern:

1. Change of caption detected
2. Read caption
3. Scan picture until another caption change is detected.

Therefore, caption appearance needed to coincide with speech onset. Caption disappearance was to coincide roughly with the end of the corresponding speech segment, since captions remaining too long on the screen were likely to be reread by the viewer, producing another kind of "false alarm."

The advice also stresses that captions that are allowed to over-run shot changes can cause considerable perceptual confusion and should be avoided. It was recognised that, in practice, the frequency and speed of shot changes in many programmes presented serious problems for the captioner. A caption should, therefore, be "anchored" over a shot change by at least one second to allow the reader time to adjust to the new picture. Since shot changes normally reflect the beginning or end of speech, the captioner was to try to insert a caption on a shot change when this was in synchrony with the speaker.

Most captions are pre-recorded, but there are also real-time or running captions on many news programmes and live broadcasts. These captions usually rely on specially trained and highly skilled captioners, who work like court stenographers, to enter the captions on the screen as they are spoken, minimising the time lag as much as possible.

Captioning for the deaf in the UK has undergone regular scrutiny since the 1999 document. For example, in 2005, the successor to the ITC, Ofcom, published a report on how comprehension and enjoyment of different types of programmes were affected by the speed of the words on the screen—a topic of obvious interest to those involved in language learning with caption-aided viewing. As the report makes clear, there are a number of interacting variables: degree of deafness, age, reliance on captions and literacy level. For those with some hearing (and many second language viewers), captions are often just a useful reference point if they miss a word. For others, reading speed is much more of an issue, as a viewer who cannot keep up will literally lose the plot.

The research reported in the document (Ofcom, 2005) found that speed was not a main concern, and, in fact, the major concern was that increasing captioning speed would reduce the enjoyment of deaf viewers and alienate those with lower literacy skills. The research brought out other issues such as editing, spelling, speaker identification and the need for captions to faithfully mirror the action (I have seen captions in dubbed foreign films where they are very different from the spoken, lip-synced scripts, as they have been copied from the original translation subtitles).

In general, respondents found that clips that had speeds of between 160 and 180 wpm were "a bit too fast." Again, it is worth bearing in mind what this means for those with normal hearing or non-native speaker viewers. My own experience is that it is not until they have reached the age of about ten years that native speaker children with normal hearing are comfortable with keeping up with captions on many adult programmes, and then only if they are at the upper range of reading ability. They may be fine with cartoon captions at a slightly younger age, but most adult programme captioning will be too fast for them to read comfortably. The same is the case for non-native speaker viewers who require a higher level of reading ability (around C1/C2 on the Common European Framework of Reference for Languages (CEFR) scale) to follow programmes subtitled at 180 wpm. In addition, the report noted that deaf and hard-of-hearing respondents who had used captions frequently for five years or longer found that their reading speeds had increased over time—the higher the quality of the captions, the easier they found it to follow them. Familiarity with different programme genres (e.g., soap operas) where characters were familiar and dialogue and action could be interpreted caused fewer problems with speed. The report also questioned whether the criterion of words per minute was the best means of evaluating captioning speed, since the speed of speech might vary greatly within any one programme or sequence-burst of speech followed by silence.

2 Some Essential Themes in Building the Case for Captions

Recently, interest in captioning in Europe has grown, especially since a directive was passed by the EU in 2010, which included the following in paragraph 46:

The right of persons with a disability and of the elderly to participate and be integrated in the social and cultural life of the Union is inextricably linked to the provision of accessible audiovisual media services. The means to achieve accessibility should include, but need not be limited to, sign language, subtitling, audio-description and easily understandable menu navigation.— (DIRECTIVE 2010/13/EU OF THE EUROPEAN PARLIAMENT AND OF THE COUNCIL of 10 March 2010)

The amount of captioning in each member country still varies enormously, as do the laws passed by each state (or not passed). France, for example, currently captions a large proportion of broadcast output after a law was passed in 2005, requiring all major broadcasters to caption programmes within five years; in Germany, captioned programmes are still a relatively small proportion of broadcast output. In Italy, captioning has increased steadily in the past ten years, and by now, the three main broadcasters caption approximately 70 % of their output. Some reports have suggested that this may be to do with whether a country has been used to dubbing foreign language programmes (both France and Germany), while another may be used to providing translation subtitles (Scandinavian countries); however, this does not appear to be the case, and its seems likely that local politics and the political influence of deaf communities are more important as governments pass anti-discrimination legislation. For example, in Germany, all producers of German films that have received local or federal subsidies are required to produce a copy with captions for deaf and hard-of-hearing people.

The audience for captions and multilingual subtitling has grown significantly over the past 10–15 years, just as the number of broadcasting channels has increased exponentially globally. In 2011, a report commissioned by the European Federation of Deaf and Hard of Hearing People (EFHOH) on the state of captioning for deaf and hard-of-hearing people went well beyond the usual physical impairments to full access to TV programmes, with a list that included age and languages in the scope and challenges of accessibility. For example, children of immigrants and refugees who can read, even teenagers and young adult refugees, who have problems following a television programme if captioning is not available were included. For languages, the challenge was identified as linguistic accessibility, ensuring that as many citizens as possible can understand programmes. For these non-native speakers, listening, rather than reading, is often the liberating language skill.

The development of captions in the USA (called closed captions there, as they were only made visible if specifically selected using a decoder) closely paralleled their development in the UK. The first broadcast TV programme with captions according to the National Institute for Deafness and Other Communication Disorders (NIDCD) was a cookery demonstration of a chicken recipe by Julia Child in 1972, broadcast by WGBH, Boston. The Decoder Circuitry Act, passed in 1980, required manufacturers to include closed captioning decoders in television sets, while the establishment of the National Captioning Institute (NCI) provided the means of engaging with programme producers to put captions on broadcast output. Initially, approximately 36 hours of programmes were captioned. It was quickly realised that the use of closed captions went beyond the deaf and hard-of-hearing community to the very large population of second language speakers in the USA. These days, according to the NIDCD, following legislation to require programme producers and broadcasters to include captions in their output, more than 2000 hours of entertainment, news, public affairs, and sports programming are captioned each week on network, public, and cable television.

Currently in Europe, where matters are much more complicated, an updated report from the EFHOH (2015) indicated that in the three years since the first report, most EU countries for which they have data, had demonstrably improved their captioning provision, with relatively few exceptions. The report is also notable for highlighting how new services such as "on-demand" providers (e.g., *BBC iPlayer, Sky, Netflix*) vary greatly in the provision of captions. At the time of writing, *YouTube's* auto-generated closed captions tend to be rather error-prone and more of a hindrance than a help, but undoubtedly they will improve with time and further development.

Indeed, the absence of accurate captions on Internet sites such as *YouTube* has meant an explosion in amateur captioning, resulting in the spread of "fansubs" or subtitles and captions produced by fans, "fansubbers," often collaborating in groups internationally. For example, in a fascinating article, Benson and Chan (2010) report how fansubbers produced and discussed online both translation and pinyin captions for *Beijing Welcomes You*, the Chinese song produced for the Beijing Olympic Games in 2008 and available on *YouTube*.

Fansubs grew out of an interest in the Japanese animated series called *anime* in the 1970s and 1980s and the need to subtitle it in English. Over the past few decades, fansubbing of *anime* has grown from a "cottage industry," producing poor quality VHS or Betamax copies in small quantities, into a worldwide phenomenon. However, as producers have steadily released DVDs with captions, the legal position of fansubbers in breaching copyright through distributing their fansubbed copies of *anime* has become increasingly precarious.

Fansubbers who join captioning and subtitling groups such as the *Amara* network (www.amara.org) are at less risk of being sued, though I would not downplay the skill needed to produce good quality captions and the time it requires to do so. I visited the *BBC* captioning unit in Glasgow some years ago and observed at first hand the truly impressive speed and skill of professional captioners. I recommend that readers should try captioning *YouTube* video clips using the *Amara* software to experience the skill needed to do captioning well.

2.4 TV as a Verbal Medium

In the 1990s, I was asked to write a short *Encyclopaedia of Linguistics* entry on captions and subtitles (Vanderplank, 1994b). The research sent me delving into the nature of what is assumed to be a predominantly visual medium. For 50 years or so, writers of television and video language learning programmes have stressed the visual element in broadcast and recorded programmes and have emphasised the relevance and value of the visual element to language teaching. From the start, Pit Corder (1960), writing about the characteristics of an audiovisual language teaching programme that will produce good learning and comprehension, lists five key elements, all of which are primarily visual: (a) movement, (b) diagrams and visual aids, (c) the visible presence of the speaker, (d) coordination of visual and verbal material and (e) concreteness of material. Such opinions have been regularly reinforced during the intervening years by many writers, and the reinforcement has continued right up to the present by authors such as Keddie (2014) and Goldstein and Driver (2015). Indeed, the notion that television is primarily a visual medium for foreign language teaching still appears to be quite uncontroversial. For language learning video programmes, the images themselves provide the sense of realism and direct appeal which are attractive to learners. What is emphasized above all is a visual reality rather than a verbal reality.

Taking a completely different view are historians and analysts of film and television such as Roy Armes (1988) and Dennis Lowry (2014) who have long stressed that television has its roots neither in the photograph nor in the cinematographic film, where the image so clearly predominates. The real roots of television lie in sound radio, in the verbal message. Most television programmes and advertisements actually contain the key messages in words, not in images. News programmes, as Lowry (2014) reports, are still spoken reports supported by pictures, not vice versa. TV drama and comedy are largely about words, even if looks, gestures and body language contribute significantly at times. A documentary without the voice-over or presenter would present no case, no argument and little meaningful information. While it may seem that sports programmes are, self-evidently, visual, even a live football match without the running commentary might lack an element essential to ignite interest among viewers. Rarely is there an advertisement on television that is without a verbal message, spoken or written. When a company wants to get its message across in a TV advertisement, it gives it in captions as well as in sound. Take *Coca Cola*, for example; the key message, such as "*Open happiness*" in the advertisement featuring polar bears, is given in text in the last shot of the iconic bottle. Alternatively, consider Honda and its caption: "*Honda The Power of Dreams*." Lowry uses the term "dominance" (p. 245) to describe the relationship between the verbal and the visual in news programmes. This term may usefully be used to describe the balance of the verbal and visual in other genres, too. Words dominate in dramas, soap operas and sitcoms and in most documentaries and lifestyle programmes, whereas the visual dominates in natural history programmes and sport. In foreign language learning, teachers and learners are mainly concerned with teaching and learning, respectively, a verbal code rather than visual conventions. An emphasis on the visual element must inevitably restrict the value of the medium to that of being a stimulus and primarily a visual support rather than a language resource on which to draw.

One effect of the "visual" view of television has been to largely limit discussion of television as a verbal medium and resource among language professionals. I have strong memories from the 1970s of the hopes and expectations that the new Video Cassette Recorders (VCR) would unlock the verbal element of television programmes through the greater control offered. Such hopes remain largely unfulfilled not only because adapting video programmes is still so time-consuming but also because controlling sound is inherently difficult. You cannot freeze sound, you only replay it, and replaying segments of video material can be frustrating for both teachers and learners. Although there have been technical improvements, the problem of presenting and exploiting verbal messages in clips from TV programmes, DVDs, films or *YouTube* videos remains much the same: the language comes too quickly, there is too much of it, it is too colloquial and it is culturally bound much of the time.

My argument throughout this book is that captions provide a simple means of controlling the verbal element of audiovisual material without substantial teacher preparation and also provide crucial support for learners in informal and independent settings. However, opening the box, that is, making television and films accessible to those for whom it might remain an unattainable goal of language learning creates a new and different set of challenges connected with the very notion of using television and films as educational resources. If learners are able to watch as native speakers do, and as they might watch television in their first language, do they bring attitudes and mental sets which work against an educational goal? Under what circumstances can television and films thrive as language learning resources?

2.5 Television and Video in Language Learning and Teaching

In 1993, I wrote in an article for the now defunct *TESOL Journal* that for many language teachers, the serious study of television and foreign language learning remained a contradiction in terms. At the time, television was barely recognised as a resource or an object of study in second language acquisition or bilingualism. To me, this was particularly ironic. Although the focus of language teaching goals and practices had already shifted from the printed word and knowledge of the language system to the use and communicative value of the spoken language in everyday settings, the most important conveyor of popular culture, language, values, beliefs and attitudes, namely television, barely received a mention in the vast literature of language teaching, except in special books dedicated to providing teachers with "recipes" for exploiting recorded programmes and films clips. The same is largely true today, with some notable exceptions. Although English language teaching had become and still is populist, for the most part, it still fails to recognise its most populist and popular resource. Even 20 years on, by failing to recognise the importance of television and its potential in the language teaching and learning process, however, we are still missing important instructional opportunities. The potential of television has always seemed enormous, particularly when combined with the choice and control offered by video recording.

For many years, I have held the view, mantra-like, that no teacher or classroom can offer the range of situations and settings, the knowledge of and insights into target language attitudes, values and behaviour that television programmes can. There is no doubt that television, film and video have already contributed indirectly to the development of language learning and teaching in the past 50 years. In English as a Second Language (ESL) and English as Foreign Language (EFL) contexts, the perception of value and uses of television programmes, broadcast or recorded, has developed in parallel with general trends, from Pit Corder's (1960) situational/behavioural approach to the interactional, communicative and humanist approaches of the 1990s (e.g., Cooper, Lavery, & Rinvolucri, 1991; Stempleski & Tomalin, 1990) and the recent eclectic "how to" books focusing on online and digital video (e.g., Keddie, 2014; Goldstein & Driver, 2015). In one sense, the impact of television on language teaching has been similar to its impact on society as a whole, influencing our views and attitudes about the status of the spoken language. We are not content to read reports of debates when we can watch them live or recorded. The sound bite of the televised media event becomes the material on which elections are believed to be won or lost.

2 Some Essential Themes in Building the Case for Captions

What has always struck me is that so many of those who write about TV, video and language learning rarely watch television themselves and hardly have a good word to say for it. Jack Lonergan, for example, who had almost celebrity status at conferences following the publication of his best-selling book *Video in Language Teaching* (1984), was certainly dismissive of the medium in my conversations with him. Perhaps, not surprisingly then, there is no mention of closed captions or teletext subtitles in his state-of-the-art review for *Language Teaching* in 1991, although they had been available in the USA and UK for over 10 years, and there was already published research on the benefits of captioned viewing. Even the future for video that he maps out in this article has no place for captioned viewing of TV and films. He sees developments in the use of TV for language learning only in training teachers in how to exploit audiovisual material and in language testing.

I understood a very long time ago that I have been treading on the toes of those with a vested interest in NOT using captions. In the mid-1990s, for example, the spotlight was on authors such as Susan Stempleski and Barry Tomalin who had produced a best-selling book of "recipes" for using video in language teaching called *Video in Action* (1990). This book and others, such as John McGovern's edited collection *Video applications in English language teaching* (1983), had much to recommend them, but it was striking that they all tended to avoid focusing on the language of the programme to any great extent and used the video clips as stimulus to stimulate students to speak, interact and generally do things. *Satellite Television in the Classroom—A Guide for Language Teachers* (Fisher, Lynch, & Allen, 1995), a book considered to be a model of good practice in the 1990s, recommended that short video clips of programmes should be used as visual aids or "moving flashcards" to stimulate learners to produce language; programmes recommended are adverts, game shows, cartoons, weather forecasts and short news flashes **with captions** (!). Clips of documentaries should be shown only to advanced level learners.

Has much changed today? The two recent publications mentioned earlier, one by James Keddie (2014) and the other by Ben Goldstein and Paul Driver (2015), seek to exploit the variety and flexibility of digital and online video for language teaching and learning. Goldstein and Driver's *Language Learning with Digital Video* traces its roots back to a chapter by Jane Willis in the McGovern collection on key roles for video in the language classroom, which suggests four roles: language focus, skills practice (mainly listening and speaking), stimulus (engaging interest and as a catalyst for tasks) and resource (as a source of information and content for tasks). My own recollection of our attempting to follow these principles and make use of video in the 1980s was that it was extremely time-consuming and ultimately the benefits were often just not worth the effort. The authors reveal just how little has changed in reality when they list the different task focuses for learners to carry out while they watch a video and afterwards. There are nine areas of focus: images/objects, cinematic elements, cultural aspects, text, inference ("what do you think the characters are thinking judging by their body language?"), character types, sound, genre, narrative (e.g., say what's happening and predict what's going to happen next). Only one of the nine focuses on the language of a video, a position which marginalises the verbal element at the heart of most TV and film. Most revealing is the fact that in listing sources, the "viewing and sharing" section contains only sites such as *YouTube* and *Vimeo*, though the lists for Content provide a rich resource and include *BBC iPlayer*.

In Keddie's *Bringing Online Video into the Classroom* (2014), which highlights video as an accessible and interactive medium for expression, he considers that video has now been reinvented, thanks to digital and online video, a position I wholeheartedly agree with. This is a very different book from Goldstein and Driver's and takes the novice teacher or learner through the hardware and software options, and then makes countless suggestions for clips, which will provide monologues, dialogues, chats, interviews, reports and sketches. Keddie makes a useful distinction between explicit video texts, which include spoken texts and subtitle texts, and implicit video texts, which are the texts that teachers and learners make in response to the video. However, only one chapter is devoted fully to explicit spoken texts, while other chapters cover much the same ground as Goldstein and Driver's book, albeit very thoroughly. It is truly an inventive and inspirational book for teachers who wish to take advantage of the huge potential of digital video for language teaching.

2.6 Research on Television, Video and Language Learning: An Under-Investigated Field?

In my state-of-the-art review, "Déjà vu? A decade of research on language laboratories, television and video in language learning" (2010), I reported several studies on the use of television and video programmes for language learning and teaching. There are, of course, many practical articles on using different programmes and video clips in the language classroom as well as many excellent series available online or on DVD, but overall there is little that can be called research on television, video, films and language learning and teaching.

What is usually stressed is that to be successful, there has to be a large amount of integration involving the teacher, and, already in the 1990s, Brett's (1997, 1998) studies involving Computer Assisted Language Learning (CALL) programmes indicated a possible overloading of media options for students, which was later confirmed in a study by Brett (2000). Shea (2000), on the other hand, reports how a well-designed interactive video application, fully integrated with the cooperation of teachers, could motivate learners, save time and help address learner weaknesses, especially for those most in need of assistance. In addition to increasing both learner motivation and learning efficiency over time, the programme helped the least able with the means to better understand and respond to foreign language discourse. Weaker learners in the experimental group performed beyond their apparent ability levels and the experimental group was able to complete tasks more quickly without sacrificing accuracy. Additionally, both the teachers and the learners were positive about working with the technology.

It is worth mentioning that there are several studies that underline how difficult it may be for learners to get much out of watching videos, whether for simple comprehension or content. Mills, Herron, and Cole's (2004) study comparing teacher-assisted and individual viewing of foreign language videos stresses the value of training learners in how to use videos in self-access mode. We may think that because our learners have watched us hone our video skills, such as pausing, rewinding, re-playing and freeze-framing, they have absorbed strategies for their own exploitation. As the Mills et al. study shows, learners can be quite lost without guidance and feel much less effective than when supported by a teacher. They compared 53 beginning French university students' comprehension of a French video in a teacher-assisted viewing (TAV) classroom environment and an independent viewing (IV) computer-based setting. All students watched four videos in the TAV condition and four in the IV condition in the language laboratory followed by tests with recall and interpretation questions.

Students performed equally well on comprehension measures in both the TAV and IV conditions. With regard to their own perceptions of their success, however, students felt significantly more confident in their ability to comprehend video in the TAV than in the IV condition. Levels of engagement significantly predicted students' comprehension performance while working independently, but were not a significant predictor of comprehension in the TAV condition. There were considerable individual differences, too. The authors suggest that there is a need for increased exposure to self-directed learning tasks in beginning for learning (FL) classrooms to improve self-efficacy toward independent activities, and for student exploration during TAV tasks to improve engagement.

Bird's (2005) description of how he developed a hybrid mixture of an entertainment DVD (*Lord of the Rings*) with educational tools in Brunei reinforces the concerns I have expressed on many occasions about learners bringing leisure habits to watching video programmes, with associated strategies. Bird's approach is to begin with highly entertaining core materials and then to build generic language learning software and content around the core, using the captions of the DVD as the bridge from the movie to the learning system. Several key issues related to his study emerged from the student feedback. There were two distinct groups, those that used DVDs for learning and those that did not, and the two groups showed significantly different interaction preferences when presented with the "edutainment" system. While both for learning (FL) and not for learning (NFL) groups reported that the system would be useful for learning, NFL users tended to prefer features that allowed learning to be deferred until after viewing, that is, they wanted to "do the learning" later. The author concludes that an edutainment system attempting to enforce simultaneous viewing and learning effort will be more likely to create a negative impression on such users and hence lead to the danger of reduced use and less learning generally. By contrast, the FL group were learners who reported liking to study and attempting to learn at the time of entertainment viewing. Considering that both groups had the same English proficiency level, it appeared that those in NFL group were not simply less interested in or able to learn per se, but that they had a different learning strategy, which drove their preferred interaction with the system. Bird's feedback reports are supported by Cole's (2015) recent research with autonomous and classroom-based learners reported in Sec. 2.9 of this chapter.

Cross (2009) provides us with a rare empirical study looking at whether listening strategy instruction can improve learners' ability to understand news videotexts. In his study, 7 adult, advanced-level EFL learners formed an experimental group (EG) and were given strategy instruction as part of a 10-week, 3 hours a week, Current Affairs course, while a comparison group (CG) of 8 participants followed the same course, but without strategy instruction. The groups were self-selected convenience groups. For 8 of the 10 weeks, they watched a 2–3 minute news clip from the *BBC*'s Internet news service. Both groups received 30 minutes of pre-listening using website material. Then the EG received 90 minutes of strategy instruction in areas such as prediction, self-monitoring and selective attention, while the CG did a 60-minute listening task with the same news clip. Both then carried out a 30-minute post-listening task.

Predictably, both groups made significant gains over the period of the study, as measured by pre- and post-tests. Variation between participants in both groups was very large, and there was no significant difference between the final test scores of the two groups; according to the author, this could be due to individual differences in the small groups, especially with regard to pre-existing preference for top-down processing in the CG, and the cycle of viewing and tasks, which may have been enough to ensure significant gains for both groups. Learners were probably able to adjust their own strategies as they went along. He also considers that fewer strategies and more input and practice might have been preferable, especially as the low mean scores indicated that the news clips and tasks were rather challenging for the learners, suggesting that gains from strategy use may have been negated through lack of linguistic proficiency.

Not surprisingly, some authors have promoted television and video as ideal means of showing not only authentic language but also the culture of the language being taught, both high culture (sometimes called big C culture or cultural products) and low culture (daily customs and practices, lifestyles, sometimes referred to as little c culture). Claire Kramsch and Roger Andersen (1999), for example, provide a very useful analysis of how audiovisual multimedia technology can be used to teach language in its authentic cultural context. They argue that this represents a double challenge for language learners and teachers. On the one hand, the computer gives learners access to authentic video footage and other cultural materials that can help them get a sense of the sociocultural context in which the language is used. On the other hand, CD-ROM and DVD multimedia textualise this context in ways that need to be "read" and interpreted. They provide an insightful analysis of the interaction of text and context in a multimedia Quechua language programme, and make some practical suggestions for teaching foreign languages through multimedia technology.

One of my favourite pieces of research involving uncaptioned video is Joseph Weyers' (1999) well-designed, longitudinal study conducted in two university Spanish classes. Weyers emphasises that, with the right guidance from the teacher, television programmes can provide valuable language input when it forms part of a structured class activity. Intact control and experimental classes met daily for 60 minutes, for a total of 8 weeks. The control group followed the established curriculum for second-semester Spanish, without alteration. The experimental group watched two episodes per week of the Mexican telenovela, *María Mercedes*. Before viewing, the experimental group received a list of ten questions, written in Spanish to ensure engagement, to answer while watching the programme. All participants took two pre- and post-tests in listening comprehension and oral production. An ANOVA indicated a significant difference in favour of the experimental group in listening comprehension. In oral production, the experimental group outperformed the control group in the number of words they used in discourse, in their confidence in generating output and the scope and breadth of their discourse. The results also threw up some interesting differences between learners, especially with regard to the transfer of native speaker language skills.

Carol Herron and her colleagues investigated whether learners at low levels would be overwhelmed by the language and images, or whether they could actually gain cultural knowledge from viewing. Herron, Cole, Corrie, and Dubreil (1999a) looked at how much cultural knowledge students would gain during a semester from viewing the ten videos as part of the *French in Action* beginning French multimedia course. Scores on both little c culture and big C culture increased significantly from pre-test to post-test, though there were also differences, which showed that students were better at recalling the social patterns of daily living, such as that the French eat pigs' feet, than the achievements and institutions of French culture. One of the most interesting findings was that the video series levelled differences in cultural knowledge between those who had been to France (approximately 36 %) and those who had not (approximately 64 %). The authors considered, too, that the higher scores for social pattern and behaviour reflect the students' practical concerns and functional priorities. They cared more about shopping, visiting friends and eating in restaurants than visiting museums or knowing about historical events.

A similar study (Herron, Dubreil, Cole, & Corrie, 2000) involving students in their first semester, but with an additional oral testing component, found some differences between the first semester and the second semester studies, such as no difference between the big C and little c quiz scores only with first semester students. Not surprisingly, the authors suggest that growing familiarity with both language and culture accounted for the difference between the scores of the first and second semester groups. As in Herron et al. (1999a), students perceived that they had learnt more about daily life in France than about the achievements and institutions. A weakness of both studies, acknowledged by the authors, was that they used specially designed instructional materials with videos, which were explicitly intended to teach both language and culture in a structured way. In this sense, the studies were not so much a test of the learners but of the materials, a situation far removed from learners trying to gain cultural knowledge from watching authentic broadcast programmes.

This point is emphasised by the findings of Herron, Dubreil, Corrie, and Cole's (2002) later study into the role of background knowledge in developing cultural knowledge in which intermediate-level learners of French watched 8 videos of 5–6-minute-long segments consisting mainly of interviews with French-speaking people from France, Canada and the French Antilles. As before, post-test scores were significantly higher than that of pre-test scores. The increase in scores, however, was associated with the level of French background. The difficulty of the video clips seemed to prevent those with less background knowledge from benefiting as much as those who had background knowledge on which they could build.

As Herron, York, Corrie, and Cole (2006) say, even though over twenty-five years have passed since the publication of the first complete video-based foreign language programme, there are few experimental classroom studies with a CG on the effectiveness of these instructional packages to improve students' language skills. The key question with comparative studies is always whether one of the approaches has to be deliberately restricted in order for there to be a comparison. Herron et al. (2006) compared a story-based video instructional package with a feature-length film as its focus, to a text-based course with supplementary video material, aiming to assess the effectiveness of each approach in improving the listening and grammar performances of intermediate-level college French students. The main difference (besides content) between the courses was that a tourist video supplemented the text with enrichment material, while the feature film was the vehicle by which students were introduced to all new and review structures. Students in the film-based course significantly improved their listening skills and grammar knowledge, while for the text-based group, students did not significantly improve in listening, but they significantly improved in grammar. For grammar only, the increase in mean scores for the film-based group was significantly higher than the increase in mean scores for the text-based group. Of course, it could be argued that using the DVD as the listening test rather biased it in favour of the video-based course group, but this would not explain their better performance on the grammar test.

There has been relatively little research on the viewing behaviour of learners who watch television programmes broadcast specifically for language learning. In my review (Vanderplank, 2010), I reported on an audience survey (Vanderplank & Dyson, 1999) of viewing behaviour and attitudes to *Italia 2000*, a topic-based Italian video series (intended for students in higher education) centred around news broadcasts by *RAI* and *Teletna* (Sicily), broadcast at night as 30-minute programmes on the *BBC*'s *The Learning Zone*. The article on the audience survey now reads like a lost and forgotten world, because of the changes that have happened regarding access to foreign language broadcasts worldwide since 1996–1997. At the time, not a great deal had changed since Stephanie Rybak (1993) wrote of the issues of isolation for adult distance learners of foreign languages and the need for contact and support. Now, for independent or informal language learners, the world is a global village, and contact may be no more than a click away.

Published in the same year, Umino's (1999) well-designed and insightful study provides an excellent reminder that much of what was valued in the past still holds true today for independent language learners. The author reported a questionnaire study of 138 university students (mainly women) in Japan, most of whom made use of self-instructional broadcast (SIB) language programmes. The findings of the study stressed the importance of selection and structure for many distance learners. SIB materials were highly valued for the exposure they gave to native speakers, since there were limited opportunities for practice in many of the languages in their learning environment. Respondents' answers also clustered around the length and organisation of programmes. They could easily watch a 20-minute programme broken down into well-structured chunks. They liked songs, comedy sketches, stories and dramas, and the serials seemed to be one way of reducing drop-out. Interestingly enough, many also liked the broadcast, fixed time of programmes and did not record them. This external determination of timing and pace provided welcome regular study for learners. The relaxed context of home viewing, ease of access and low cost were also important factors. The "materials-centred" nature of this form of self-instruction was perceived by many informants to be advantageous, enabling them to persevere with learning; experts had already taken the key decisions. In contrast, the same limitations on users' control over learning could cause problems, such as the time not being convenient, potentially leading to non-completion of courses. The advantage of easy access to programmes also could become a downside—just as it is easy to start SIB materials, so it is easy to stop since there is no pressure to study. However, informants reported using various strategies to overcome these limitations, such as establishing routines and buying the textbooks. The findings on the uses of SIB materials revealed that they were not necessarily as passive or directed as might have been expected, and learners used materials in ways not expected by the designers. Did designers of online video games ever expect that their games would become major vehicles for English language learning globally (Sockett, 2014; Vulchanova, Aurstad, Kvitnes, & Eshuis, 2015; Cole, 2015)?

2.7 TV Programmes and Films as Comprehensible Input

The opening up of television and films through video recording coincided with the paradigm shift in language learning and teaching to one in which Stephen Krashen's (1985) comprehensible input hypothesis came to dominate. From the beginning, TV, film and video have been seen by Second Language Acquisition (SLA) researchers (including myself) as an excellent potential source of comprehensible input, since they fulfil Stephen Krashen's idea of exposure to natural language, which provides the opportunity for the i + 1 principle to be activated (i.e., the input from TV is just one level above the learner's proficiency level and the learner may use context, extra-linguistic information, current level of competence and prior world knowledge to understand) and for the learner to make progress. TV and video also provide a large amount of redundancy in the input as well, tending to create a low affective filter among viewers (i.e., there is little anxiety and pressure in TV watching, so there is a greater likelihood of the input being processed and taken in). Krashen saw comprehensible input as "the essential ingredient for second language acquisition. All other factors work only when they contribute to comprehensible input and/or a low affective filter" (1985:4). Krashen (1985) notes that "the Input Hypothesis makes the plausible prediction that television can be helpful if it is comprehensible" (p. 34).

In other respects, as Michael Rodgers (2013) suggests in his research on incidental vocabulary learning and attitudes towards captioned viewing in a Japanese university context, TV programmes also meet conditions,

2 Some Essential Themes in Building the Case for Captions

which make them suitable as input for language learning by providing suitably large quantities of input for processing together with familiar and interesting content for learners. However, as the (short) history of TV, video and language learning has shown, the positive potential benefits of audiovisual material for language learners may be largely negated by the nature of the medium as a complex, dynamic, fast-paced resource.

In the past few years, though, with the greater choice and control of the input offered by online viewing of films and TV programmes, the hopes which I expressed some years ago appear to have been fulfilled, at least, in informal learning contexts. The work published by Geoffrey Sockett and his associates with French students at the University of Strasbourg (Sockett, 2014; Kusyk & Sockett, 2012; Sockett & Toffoli, 2012) has confirmed what many of us know about the informal viewing activities of young people around the world from our own experiences. For example, Kusyk and Sockett (2012) found in their study on television viewing that nearly 50 % of Information Technology (IT) students watched English television weekly (p. 51). The researchers attempted to corroborate television viewers' beliefs that they acquired vocabulary while watching television for leisure purposes. Their fascinating study of 45 IT students compared frequent viewers of English language television with non-frequent viewers in their knowledge of commonly occurring four-word strings (4-gram) on television. The authors used a specially designed corpus (the HHOLD corpus) made up of the transcripts of one season of episodes for five different television series, representing a range of genres, that had been found to be popular in earlier surveys of student viewing habits (Toffoli & Sockett, 2010). The corpus corresponded to 70 hours of television viewing a year, a number that previous surveys on viewing habits had shown to be typical. Participants listened to contextualised recordings by native speakers of the 50 most common 4-word chunks. Using the Vocabulary Knowledge Scale (VKS) developed by Paribakht and Wesche (1993), participants reported how confident they were that they knew the item. If participants indicated they were sure they knew an item, they then had to translate the sentence into French. If the translation was correct, they were judged to have acquired the item. There was a highly significant difference between two groups' knowledge of the most common chunks, with frequent viewers more likely to have acquired the commonly occurring chunks.

A follow-up study using the same corpus asked liberal arts students to write fan fiction based on a favourite show. Corpora of these writing samples by frequent (more than one show per week) and non-frequent (less than one show per week) television viewers were then compared statistically with the corpus. The study found that there was a statistically significant relationship between frequency of television viewing and use of the 50 most common chunks in the corpus. While chunks in the fan fiction written by frequent viewers appeared at frequencies similar to their frequencies in the corpus, this was not the case for the non-frequent viewers.

More recently, in ground-breaking empirical research, which in many respects has finally validated Krashen's (1985) acquisition-learning distinction, Jason Cole (2015) identified substantial numbers of autonomous, naturalistic learners (or fully autonomous self-instructed learners [FASILs]) who were making extensive use of online English language TV programmes and films in achieving very high levels of English language proficiency. As with the French informal learners in Strasbourg, the way forward for the extensive use of audiovisual media appears to lie with independent learners who can exercise choice and control over their viewing. In comparing the group of FASILs with a matched group of classroom-trained learners (CTLs), Cole found that while both groups were well motivated with positive attitudes towards learning English and the use of films and TV programmes, the defining difference was that when FASILs sought to engage in valued activities in English, one of which was the viewing of English language TV programmes, they focused on the linguistic elements of the programmes more actively and attentively than did the CTLs.

2.8 Lessons from Student Engagement with Television at the Open University

The model of films and TV programmes as input for language learning is certainly in need of updating, and it is probably a truism to say that we have been in the middle of a media revolution for about a decade as far as learning in general, and foreign language learning in particular, are concerned.

2 Some Essential Themes in Building the Case for Captions

For example, a document by the Open University (OU, the national university dedicated to open and distance learning in the UK), published recently (Sharples et al., 2014), highlights the innovative changes driving forward the OU as it expands ever further into the global marketplace for education and lifelong learning. It lists blended learning, Massive Online Social Learning, the flipped classroom, learning design guided by sophisticated analytics, personalised dynamic assessment, event-based learning, threshold concepts and the so-called bricolage learning where you keep trying out different ways of doing things as you learn.

This is a far cry from the earlier research by those at the Institute for Educational Technology at the OU in the 1970s, 1980s and 1990s, where the focus tended to be on programme content and how far programme makers needed to adjust content so that OU students would not lapse into watching in the same way as they did for leisure and entertainment. While programme makers are undoubtedly more sophisticated and have years of experience to guide them, little has changed in the way our attitudes to television as a leisure and social medium shape our viewing behaviour. There are interesting comparisons to be made and insights to be gained from early research into native speaker use of TV and video programmes for learning at the OU. Already in the 1970s (Gallagher, 1978; Thompson, 1979), it was being reported that there was a conflict between the values of "good television programmes" and programmes that produced useful learning. OU students enjoyed programmes and rated them "good," "useful" and "interesting," as they might have rated programmes in their everyday viewing experience. They found that many students were seeing what they wanted to see in programmes and were remaining untouched and unchallenged by what was actually being presented in programmes. Gallagher found that in watching documentaries, "the more students were involved and interested in the material, the less they were able to relate the empirical content with the related theory." (1978:205). Thompson characterised the viewing experience of many students as "comforting, familiar, like a hot bath" (1979:169).

In the following decades, more research at the OU indicated that they were still facing many of the same problems. Diana Laurillard (1991), for example, reported a study of 126 OU students watching five 25--minute social science programmes in which she compared the intended messages and content of programmes with the learning outcomes achieved by students. For three of the five programmes, only half or fewer students achieved the intended learning outcomes. The main finding was that successful mediation of the intended message and content of a programme depended largely on preserving the image-argument synergy. Not only must words reinforce the images and vice versa, but the linearity of images must not mask the hierarchical structure of the verbal discourse. That is, the discourse structure might consist of a general statement of the main point, followed by component points, each of which might have several examples, while the images might form what appeared to be a simple narrative. Good television tries, above all, to tell a good story.

The OU stopped broadcasting its academic programmes late at night in 2006; for many years, it has taken a far more interactive approach to how it uses its mix of audiovisual media, recognising the limitations of the broadcast, non-interactive model where many native speaker viewers may not be too concerned about whether they are picking up intended verbal messages or not, even when a broadcast is intended for specifically educational purposes. As long as viewers feel they "learn a lot" and find programmes interesting, there is a high degree of satisfaction. Therein lies both a challenge and a paradox for both television and learning and television and language learning, a theme I shall now develop.

2.9 TV Is Easy, Print Is Tough: Paradoxes in Using Television as an Educational Resource

We usually think of TV as a medium for entertainment and information which takes little effort on the part of the viewer (at least, the native speaker viewer). Where does the idea that TV is a shallow and easy medium come from? What are the consequences in education and language learning terms of such perceptions? Much of my thinking on television as a medium for language learning has been influenced by the writings of Gavriel Salomon, the Israeli psychologist, who was pre-eminent in the 1980s and 1990s for identifying issues of learning from

2 Some Essential Themes in Building the Case for Captions

televisual resources and worked as consultant to the OU (1983a). In 1981, he published a seminal paper discussing his concept of amount of invested mental effort (AIME) as a key factor in learning (or not learning) from television.

Salomon offers AIME as a way of explaining apparently contradictory findings in the relationship between media, mental effort and learning. He defines AIME as "the number of non-automatic mental elaborations applied to a unit of material" (Salomon, 1981a:92) and, as such, it reflects a voluntary allocation of effort that can be reported by the individual. According to Salomon, people will invest greater effort in processing material (and hence learn better) when they encounter complex, ambiguous or new material that cannot be easily fitted in to their existing mental schema. The other side of this is that AIME may be expected to decrease when people perceive (regardless of whether it is actually easily understood) that the material encountered is easy and requires little investment of mental effort on their part. According to Salomon's model of learning from different media (1981a, 1981b, 1984), individuals base their perceptions of different material largely on past experiences with the material. The model has four main components: perceived demand characteristic (PDC: how much effort people think they need to put in and the perceived easiness of the task or information), perceived self-efficacy (PSE: "…one's belief in one's ability to perform certain activities" (Salomon, 1981b:135)), AIME and learning.

Television, according to Salomon, is perceived as an "easy" and minimally demanding medium (though potentially just as demanding), as people are used to watching it without effort for entertainment compared to print, which is seen as less "easy," as it requires effort for minimal understanding. Print media, therefore, generally have a higher demand characteristic. For self-efficacy, Salomon gives the example of children who have greater PSE for television than for print (although much research suggests the contrary, and they have a long way to go before they fully master complex plots and relationships on screen).

Salomon's general argument is that "…learning from different sources greatly depends on the differential way in which these sources are perceived, for these perceptions determine to an important extent the mental effort expended in the learning process" (1983b:42). Individuals' perceptions (PDC and PSE) "jointly" affect AIME, which, in turn, affects learning (1983b:47). Several variables may affect the AIME, and this leads to the interesting paradox that, while it might seem self-evident that an "easy" medium would produce better learning than a more difficult medium, as Salomon proposed, the easy medium may not always be the most effective one. Firstly, the perceived demand characteristic of a medium may be negatively correlated with perceived self-efficacy, so the more effort a person thinks a particular message, medium or situation demands, the less confident they will be in meeting those demands. Secondly, the correlation between perceived self-efficacy and the amount of invested mental effort may be such that if an individual's perceived self-efficacy is very low, or approaching zero, their amount of invested mental effort will likely also be very low (i.e., if you feel it is a waste of your time trying, then you won't try hard). In more complex terms, "… when ability is held constant, AIME is a function of people's preconceptions of the relevant class of materials, the task, and their self-efficacy, and is a good predictor of performance that is based on effortful processing" (Salomon & Leigh, 1984:120).

In a study comparing learning from print with learning from television, Salomon (1984) found that children learned less from television because they perceived television to be "easy" and print to be "hard." He concluded that perceiving a medium as being easy, as in the case of television, led to people investing less mental effort in the activity, resulting in less learning. A particularly striking finding was that children identified different attributes for failure and success of learning for television and print materials. Children attributed their failure to comprehend television programmes to their own "dumbness" but those who were asked the same about print mentioned the difficulty of the print materials. In another study, involving 64 children in Year 6, half of whom watched a 13 minute TV story while the other half read an identical print version of the story, Salomon and Leigh (1984) hypothesized that AIME in TV would correlate mainly with children's perception of how much TV enables one to recall the material, a less demanding function, while effort in print would correlate mainly with how much it enables one to generate inferences, a more demanding function.

The findings of this study tended to support Salomon and Leigh's hypotheses: children's general preconceptions of the mental demands required by TV and print were reflected in the amount of effort they reported expending when they encountered a specific TV story or its comparable version in print. Investing effort in TV appeared to guard children against failures of recall, while effort in print was expended to serve inference generation. Accordingly, children appear to rely more heavily on their abilities when reading than when viewing television. The different patterns were more pronounced among high-ability children, who were more likely to dismiss TV as undemanding, expend less effort in processing its story and learn less from that story. These children treated print material more seriously, and thus learned more from it. Low-ability children, on the other hand, performed rather poorly with the print story and quite well with the televised one, a finding that suggests that the print story used in the study was difficult for them.

In a further test, with obvious relevance for language teaching, Salomon and Leigh hypothesised that one of the easiest ways to change the perceived demand characteristics of a task was to change people's perception of the task. In this study, 87 children in Year 6 were randomly assigned to groups to watch or read the same story as in the earlier test. These groups were further divided into subgroups and were instructed to watch or read for fun (so, low PDC) or watch or read to see how much that could learn from the story (so, high PDC). According to Salomon and Leigh, the former condition represents typical television viewing, and the latter represents a condition in which viewers perceive TV more seriously. They found that the children exerted more mental effort in both TV and print stories under learning/high PDC conditions. Setting the learning task facilitated greater expenditure of effort on TV, encouraged the children to mobilise their abilities more and generated more correct inferences.

In a recent insightful article (2012), drawing on Salomon's work and the concept of AIME, Soo Young Rieh, Yong-Mi Kim and Karen Markey looked at the amount of invested mental effort people put into online searching. Subjects in their study perceived the Web as being easy, and the University Library system as being difficult. They seemed to have strong preconceptions about the academic library system searching in which library resources were of limited scope, for example, for "homework, papers, and projects" or "scientific journals". They perceived Web searching was easy because it contained all kinds of information, and they could "just put the keywords" and "narrow it down from broad search topics a little bit more easily". In a striking parallel with the studies comparing TV and print materials, when they could not find Web-based information, they blamed themselves, not the search engine. They perceived the library search to be difficult, and were more active searching the library system, clicking more, entering more words, reformulating more queries and using more advanced features, though they did not recognise these actions as investing greater mental effort and considered library searching as "complicated," "overwhelming," "confusing" and "hard to understand."

As the reader will have noted, Salomon draws on the concept of self-efficacy in developing the whole picture of whether, and to what extent, people invest effort in tasks involving viewing or reading. The name most associated with self-efficacy and the effects of our beliefs and perceptions about how efficacious we may be at a particular task is Albert Bandura (1995, 2001). As Bandura puts it, "Perceived self-efficacy is the belief in one's capabilities to organize and execute the courses of action required to manage prospective situations. Efficacy beliefs influence how people think, feel, motivate themselves and act" (1995:2). Bandura also links self-efficacy and self-regulation:

> Efficacy beliefs play a central role in the self-regulation of motivation through goal challenges and outcome expectations. It is partly on the basis of efficacy beliefs that people choose what challenges to undertake, how much effort to expend in the endeavour, how long to persevere in the face of obstacles and failures, and whether failures are motivating or demoralizing. The likelihood that people will act on the outcomes they expect prospective performances to produce depends on their beliefs about whether or not they can produce those performances. (2001:10).

In other words, people do not usually embark on things that they do not think they can do.

Of relevance to this book, Bandura has turned his attention to how technology has increased the potential for human beings to exercise agency, particularly in education:

2 Some Essential Themes in Building the Case for Captions

Information technologies are altering educational systems. Students can now exercise substantial personal control over their own learning. In the past, their educational development was dependent on the quality of the schools in which they were enrolled. Students now have the best libraries, museums, and multimedia instruction at their fingertips through the global internet for educating themselves independently of time and place. This shift in locus of initiative involves a major reorientation in students' conception of education in which they are agents of learning not just recipients of information. (Bandura, 2002:4).

How does the work of Bandura and Salomon translate into issues of watching today's audiovisual materials in a foreign language (online, TV, film, DVD, etc.)? All these media still assume low effort by viewers and that they are "easy" media compared to print, since print required training in decoding and reading skills. L1 viewers perceive themselves as highly efficacious viewers. We turn on the television or go to the cinema with an assumption of being able to follow and (usually) understand. This is one of the attributes of being an adult native speaker. However, for foreign language learners, being able to understand a foreign film confidently or watch foreign language TV with an assumption of understanding is, for most, an (almost) unattainable goal compared to reading literature or technical texts in that language. As Salomon shows in his experiments with children and students on delivering information via print or TV, the attributes of TV and the perception of users mean that less effort may be put into learning from TV than from print, especially, paradoxically enough, if they grasp that their perceived self-efficacy and their ability to follow and understand are low. Yet, this does not have to be the case if one considers the greater choice and control offered by media and by different platforms today, as well as the finding by Salomon and Leigh that task demands may affect viewing and reading behaviour. Added to this must be the factor of the viewer's motivation in viewing.

In the present multimedia context of watching film and TV, we do not, as yet, have much research evidence to draw on which contrasts more and less attentive and effortful viewing of foreign language programmes and the different effects of such viewing behaviour combined with perceived self-efficacy. In his analysis of interviews with autonomous learners (FASILs) and class-based learners (CTLs) in Brazil, Cole (2015) draws on Salomon's work to explain the success of the FASILs compared to the CTLs in drawing on TV programmes and films as a language resource rather than simply as entertainment. FASILs are willing to invest time and effort into learning from TV programmes and films in order to be able to take part in valued activities such as joining international discussion forums and fan groups. They are also able to see the need to improve their self-efficacy as a challenge worth time and effort.

A major difference between the 34 FASILs and 48 CTLs regarding television use was the level of engagement with language that participants in each group reported. FASILs were more likely than CTLs to mention that television led to learning. They more often discussed the learning of vocabulary, with several FASILs mentioning specific vocabulary they learnt while watching television. Both CTLs and FASILs mentioned the positive effect of repeated viewing of scenes or whole films, but, again, it was FASILs who went into more detail about this process, describing the level of engagement with language that they were capable of. CTLs rarely reported specific aspects of engagement with language.

Cole also found that a much larger percentage of FASILs than CTLs mentioned that they used English subtitles or captions (depending on the language of the film) and the specifics of how and why they used them, for example, as a means of understanding specific language that they had not understood on first viewing. What I hope to show in this book is that while the presence of captions does not guarantee that learner-viewers will put in the necessary effort to learn language and develop listening skills consciously from watching captioned programmes, the accessibility provided by the captions will at least increase their perceived self-efficacy and encourage the investment of greater effort.

The key point from both Sockett's and Cole's work is that the choice and control offered to informal learners these days has the potential to greatly increase their self-efficacy, a key component in whether and to what extent people will put effort into an activity that they value, regardless of whether they are reading, watching audiovisual material, video gaming or doing anything else.

2.10 Coming of Age: Positioning Captioned Viewing for Language Learning

In this chapter, I have tried to cover the major themes that I consider essential to understanding the factors behind successful captioned viewing for language learners and for teachers. I hope that readers will now be better informed about the nature of captions for deaf and hard-of-hearing people and will also see how captions can be of real educational and linguistic benefit to language learners, making otherwise inaccessible resources accessible to them. I also hope that I have explained sufficiently clearly the paradoxes lying behind the use of both uncaptioned and captioned viewing, and why we often appear to come against brick walls, using TV and video for language learning when learners behave in the unhelpful, but understandable, ways, which Salomon describes.

Through the brief description of what captions are and how they are now considered an essential part of the equality and accessibility agenda for second language users in many parts of the world, together with the outline of past and current approaches to treating audiovisual material in language teaching, I have attempted to position captioned viewing for language learning and teaching as occupying an environment that is distinct from either watching professionally subtitled TV programmes and films or using uncaptioned TV, video and films in formal language learning, inside or outside the classroom. In the following chapters, I shall try to reinforce the claim for captioned TV and films to occupy their own place in the current media and language learning environment by reporting research that supports this claim and by drawing further on theorists from different disciplines.

3

The Value of Closed Captions and Teletext Subtitles for Language Learning

3.1 Setting the Context

At the Pavia conference in 2012, I used the opportunity to talk about the milestones in thirty years of caption research, the key findings of research into the benefits and principles of captioned viewing and the challenges we still face in promoting the use of captions in the new environment for language learning (Vanderplank, 2015). In this chapter, I continue to build my case for captions by going back to the start and revisiting the pioneering work of Karen Price and Anne Dow and my own *Teletext 888 Project*. So much research in the past ten to fifteen years has been largely confirmatory and has failed to build on early findings. I hope that by setting out this research, future work will be able to move forward to seek the answers to the many questions which remain.

We begin with the context in the early 1980s. Cheap and reliable video recorders using VHS or Betamax videotape have been available since the late 1970s and are greeted with huge enthusiasm by language teachers the world over. However, within a few years, the initial enthusiasm among language teachers has cooled as it became clear that learners were unable to follow the language of most popular programmes and films and teachers found that making good use of recorded material meant lengthy preparation (think IT these days). It is often easier and simpler to abandon the verbal in favour of the visual. Demand for recipe books on using video is being met by publishers. In the UK, we have *Video in The Language Classroom*, a collection edited by Marion Geddes and Gill Sturtridge (1982), and in the same year, *Active Viewing* by Mike Lavery. Despite these guides, in 1983, Frances MacKnight is writing in John McGovern's edited collection *Video applications in English language teaching* (1983) that showing films and programmes on video has become a "Friday afternoon treat" with little real pedagogical value.

But just at around the time when this cooling off was taking place, the first video recorders that could record optional captions intended for deaf and hard-of-hearing people, produced through the Teletext system (on page 888) in the UK and the closed caption system in the USA appeared. If you recorded a programme with these captions, they were fixed in the recording and could not be turned on and off as they can these days on all digital sources of video, whether broadcast, DVD, streaming or catch-up. Some countries with analogue rather than digital broadcasting systems still use their equivalents of the Teletext system.

No doubt, there were many ESL teachers in the USA who realised the potential of the closed caption system to assist ESL viewers and learners in gaining access to TV programmes that were beyond their ability to follow and understand, but the honour of publishing the first account of an experiment to demonstrate the value of captions for second and foreign language learners goes to Karen Price and Anne Dow.

3.2 The Price and Dow Study (1983)

It is now over 30 years since the pioneering work with closed captions at Harvard University. Ever since then, we have known that captions provided for deaf and hard-of-hearing people can provide access to foreign language films and TV programmes, which would otherwise be virtually incomprehensible to non--native-speaker viewers and may help with language acquisition. The key distinction, and one which, of course, was one of the main sources of the great disillusionment with video recorders, is that while programmes may be available, they are not necessarily accessible either to the deaf or to L2 viewers in any meaningful sense.

Price and Dow's work will be unfamiliar to many readers. The short article written by Karen Price was published in the *MATSOL Newsletter* and is available at http://www.matsol.org/assets/documents/Currentsv18no2Fall1991.pdf. To my knowledge, this is the only article they produced on the study, so there are few details to go on, though both spoke at conferences and led workshop on using captions.

Price begins the article with the following questions:

- Increasing comprehensibility should facilitate language acquisition but would learners be helped or hindered by the closed captions? Would it be possible for foreign viewers to process the audio and visual input and attend to the captions without being bogged down?
- Does exposure to captioned video significantly improve or impair viewing comprehension as measured by a carefully constructed video post-test?

She continues, "Therefore, it is reasonable to assume that if captions assist the learner to understand a message expressed in a foreign language at a level a little beyond his usual level of comprehension without assistance, they may actually contribute to language learning" (p. 1).

The study was ambitious in scale: 500 students from 20 language backgrounds at Harvard, profiled for educational level and language background, took part in the study. Half saw the four video excerpts with captions, the other half without. Half of each group had one viewing, the other half two viewings. Students were randomly assigned to groups after controlling for English language level and length of stay in the USA. Unfortunately, no details are given of the "carefully controlled video-post-test," but they found that all those who saw the captioned film benefited significantly from captioning even with only one viewing, regardless of educational level or language background. There were

NEWSLETTER

VOL. 12, NO. 2

Massachusetts Association Of Teachers Of English To Speakers Of Other Languages

FALL, 1983

The Intensive Method: New Life for Suggestopaedia
by Tom Garza

In 1971, Bulgarian psychiatrist Georgi Lozanov outlined the method and results of a 24-day course of foreign language instruction which he designed and had conducted with his colleagues in Sofia. The method was based on suggestopaedic "mind-liberating" techniques in the classroom, such as extensive role play, intonational text readings, and passive listening concert sessions.

Among the results of the course, Lozanov cited the assimilation of more than 90% of the 2000 lexical items included in the materials, the ability to speak within the framework of the whole essential grammar, and the accessibility of any written text with the aid of a dictionary.

By the time quantitative materials on the "Lozanov Method" reached the West in translated form, much neurolinguistic research on right/left brain hemisphere participation in language learning had given considerable theoretical support to Lozanov's suggestopaedic approach to learning. Hence, in 1975, the Los Angeles-New York conferences on suggestopaedic instruction provided a strong forum for new western proponents of the Lozanov Method to demonstrate the appropriateness of the method for American foreign language classrooms.

Unfortunately, while the West was only beginning to apply suggestopaedic techniques along the lines of the Lozanov Method, results in the Soviet Union and Eastern bloc countries were already revealing serious flaws and deficiencies in the method in terms of grammatical competence, pronunciation, and language retention of the students. By 1976, language specialists were already calling the Lozanov Method inappropriate for language teaching.

While many pedagogs simply shunned the method as a failure, several methodologists at Moscow State University saw the solid neuro- and psycholinguistic bases of the method — particularly in the realm of developing oral skills — and felt it needed serious reworking, but certainly not abandonment.

In Moscow, Galina Kitajgorodskaja, Tat'jana Kirsh and their colleagues began
(Continued on page 12)

CLOSED-CAPTIONED TV: AN UNTAPPED RESOURCE

Michael Caine in a closed-captioned scene from "California Suite"

The following article is based on a study of the potential of closed-captioned TV for English language learning conducted by Karen Price and Anne Dow at Harvard University, with funding from the Exxon Educational Foundation.

by Karen Price

Did you know that some of the most popular programs on television can be seen with captions (English language subtitles)? Situation comedies, movies, dramas, children's programming, and selected miniseries can all be viewed with captions at normally scheduled times.

The National Captioning Institute, (NCI), began captioning TV broadcasts for the hearing-impaired in March 1980. By the Spring of 1981, researchers at Harvard were trying to determine if non-native English speakers could benefit from these same captioned materials. Would captioned video materials help or hinder foreign students as they watched video? Would it be possible for foreign speakers to process both audio and visual cues and attend to captions without bogging down? If so, would captioned materials be helpful for all of the ESL population, or just part of the ESL population?

To see the regular broadcasts with captions, all one needs is a special decoder connected to a TV set. (Decoders can be purchased at Sears for a one-time charge of $279.) The decoder evolved because it was assumed that hearing people don't need captions to enjoy TV and wouldn't want to be bothered with captions popping up all through their favorite TV programs. For those without decoders, the captions don't appear on the screen. The National Captioning Institute, the major source of captioning, provides a minimum of 38 hours a week of captioned programming. Captioned programs produced by NCI are called "closed-captioned," and are identified in TV program guides by the symbol "CC", "C", or "CC".

The experimental study at Harvard in-
(Continued on page 8)

MATSOL Spring Conference
April 6-7
Bunker Hill Community College

Fig. 3.1 The Price and Dow study

benefits in terms of not only language acquisition through increased comprehension but also exposure to the "cultural script" shared by native American peers.
Price concludes

Since most of the 23 million Americans who speak a Language other than English in the home probably have easy access to televisions and since general programming far exceeds in technical and artistic quality most budget-conscious educational productions as well as providing the authenticity of situation and language so badly needed for language learning, we strongly recommend that ESL learners be made aware of the valuable resource through the these decoders in the classroom setting. Increased exposure to "mainstream" TV programming at home as well as in the classroom will facilitate language acquisition, not only by improving comprehension of language but also by enabling the ESL viewer to acquire more of the cultural script shared by native American peers. (p. 8)

The three decades following Karen Price's research was a period in which significant progress was made in our understanding of the principles and good practice of captioned video, especially in the UK and North America, where captions enjoyed official support through legislation. As mentioned earlier, broadcasters were required to produce a certain percentage of their programming with captions for deaf and hard of hearing people, while caption decoders or Teletext systems became standard in televisions.

Research quickly followed supporting captions, which were as complete and verbatim as time and space would allow (given the basic principle of "shot-to-shot," in which captions must not go over from the shot to which they refer to another shot). Summary captions were roundly rejected by the deaf community as patronising, depriving them of a full understanding of the verbal material. In contrast to the USA and the UK, the situation remained very limited for captioning until relatively recently in mainland Europe. For example, on a trip to France in the 1990s, I was told that there were captions in French on some French programmes using the *Antiope* system, but I could not find anyone who had even seen or used them, and failed to find a programme with them myself.

3.3 The *Teletext 888* Project

I set up the project at Heriot-Watt University in Edinburgh in 1986, drawing on students from the large exchange programme as my subjects and continued working on a variety of aspects of captioned viewing until 1996 when I left Edinburgh for Oxford. It soon became clear that there were a number of issues to be overcome. Teletext decoders were not widely available and it was initially impossible to find a VHS video recorder that would capture the captions broadcast through the two teletext information systems on TV in Britain, CEEFAX for the *BBC* and Oracle for ITV. Eventually, I found a *Radofin* decoder, which would capture and fix the captions on a normal VHS recorder for later playback. Once recorded, they could not be switched on and off as they can these days on DVDs and hard-drive recorders. Later in the project, Phillips kindly gave me a new recorder that could be time-set to record programmes with captions fixed in vision. Copyright for recording broadcast programmes and films was still an unresolved issue at the time, and I approached the *BBC* for permission to record their programmes and use these in my research. After some negotiation, permission was granted.

I published a number of articles based on the findings of the project, covering not only the benefits and downsides of captions, but also the value of specific content, teaching approaches, issues arising from programme discourse and what learners did with the technology. Two of them are still cited regularly (1988a, 1990), the first more than the second. I thought it would be worthwhile including material from the project, as over the ten years of its existence, I came to understand more and more the potential and limitations of captioned viewing for language learning. Already, from the first two studies (1988a, 1990), it became clear that captions were not quite the "Holy Grail" of language learning, and even with the support of captions, it took more than simply effort to gain much in terms of language from captioned programmes.

Research with a wide variety of genres (e.g., sitcoms, soap operas, documentaries, news and current affairs, direct address or "lifestyle" programmes such as decorating, consumer affairs and cookery demonstrations) followed, as I tried to build up an understanding of strategies used by learners to maximise the benefits of watching with captions, their attitudes and motivation, the cognitive and affective processes at work when watching and what teachers could do to exploit captions (See Chap. 6 and 1993, 1994a, 1996a, 1999).

3.3.1 Study 1 ("The Value of Teletext Subtitles in Language Learning", *ELTJ*, 1988a)

My first attempt at showing my exchange students a captioned programme was probably one of the great moments of my life as a teacher. Most of the students knew that they could only get the gist of popular broadcast programmes and had enormous difficulty in following the details of what was being said. At the same time, being able to watch and follow British TV was one of their most desired goals while in Edinburgh. I chose to show them the whole of one episode of *Yes, Prime Minister*, a very successful comedy about an ineffectual British Prime Minister and his all too effective senior civil servant (it was said to be one of Mrs Thatcher's favourite programmes). For the fifteen students in the group, the experience was a revelation. To put it simply, they could follow what was being said, even the rapid exchanges of dialogue, and could laugh in the right places for the right reasons.

I continued to show a captioned programme every week for the term, and the findings of the term-long experience were reported in *ELT Journal* (Vanderplank, 1988a). This article is still widely quoted in research publications and appears to be a "basic" article on learning from captioned viewing. Perhaps, the qualitative and relatively informal nature of the research enabled me to draw out and discuss the very special nature of captioned viewing to an extent which would not have been possible with a more controlled intervention.

My objectives were ambitious to say the least:

1. To find out learners' changing reactions to captions over the period of the study with regard to attentiveness, motivation, attitude and engagement.
2. To find out what strategies learners were using to exploit captions and for what purposes.
3. To find out at what levels of language proficiency different captioned programmes seemed most useful.
4. To verify the comprehensibility of the language input.

5. To identify limitations and shortcomings of captions, and to assess the "quality" of the text.
6. To identify which programmes especially needed captions and why.
7. To explore the role of extensive captioned programme input in the language acquisition process.
8. To identify what learners learnt or got out of watching programmes with captions.
9. To identify how captioned programmes could fit into the present teaching-learning structure.

One of the limitations then, as now, of this type of study is that it is not easy to set up a well-controlled trial involving captions simply because of the enormous number of variables (and confounding variables). I also felt that I needed to gain a lot more information from my learner-viewers on the value and effects of captioned programmes before testing hypotheses that I might have. Then, as now, I was not really interested in simply showing that learners might acquire more vocabulary or understand a programme better with captions than without—it seemed obvious to me. The important question for me has always been the longer term one: whether learners with reasonable reading ability (about B1/B2/intermediate/upper intermediate) in the foreign language could enhance their listening skills, especially in terms of tuning in to different accents and increasing speed of processing, improve their knowledge of foreign language structure and lexis and gain confidence through watching TV programmes and films with captions. The difference between my objectives and those of most other researchers in the field was, and is, that I have always been primarily interested in the contribution of captions to language development, while most others appear to be interested in whether the presence of captions increases the listening comprehension of short clips or single episodes of a programme and improves vocabulary recognition and later recall, in other words, short-term classroom task performance.

I showed a variety of entire programmes up to one hour a week over a nine-week period and asked the students to carry out tasks that might be as simple as noting new or striking words and phrases, or more elaborate such as describing relationships between characters. I also wanted feed-

3 The Value of Closed Captions and Teletext Subtitles

back on their reactions to the captions and how much or little they felt they depended on the captions to follow and understand the programmes.

Among the findings were:

1. All the European exchange students found captions useful and beneficial to their language development, while some Arabic-speaking students (included for comparison with the first programme and with lower levels [especially slower] of reading skill) had negative reactions to the presence of the captions and complained that the text changed too rapidly (I shall discuss my reflections on this in Chap. 5).
2. Initial disturbance and distraction tended to disappear over the period of the study.
3. Two students reported that they still had feelings of guilt and laziness at needing or wanting to use caption text even after nine sessions. They felt that they would have listened harder without the text, and would have tried and improved their listening ability if the text had not been present.
4. All the exchange students developed techniques and strategies for minimising distraction and maximising the usefulness of the captions; some had become used to switching from sound to text, and vice versa, flexibly and according to need, whereas others stated that they could follow text, sound and pictures simultaneously. Some reported that they felt able to process longer stretches of sound and text after a few hours of watching captioned programmes, that is, they appeared to be developing a "chunking" ability.
5. Students reported that they were conscious of learning a great deal of language from the programmes watched. They talked of "finding" new words and phrases, which they would be able to use themselves, and of learning the spelling of many proper and place names. The students also reported that they felt that they were unconsciously picking up a great deal of language that they would use at some later time.
6. Captions made fast, authentic speech and unfamiliar accents (regional and American) much easier to tune in to and to follow. Some mentioned that they had never been able to follow some of the programmes watched (such as *Eastenders*, a daily soap opera set in London with strong London accents) because of the accents. All

found comedy programmes, plots, relationships and characterisation were much easier to understand and appreciate with captions.
7. Even with captions, programmes with large amounts of information could be difficult to follow, while a police thriller with a strong plot caused little difficulty with the caption text. American programmes and soap operas often presented additional problems of culture and assumed knowledge of plot and characters. With regard to documentaries, while the students really did not need the captions very much to follow and understand natural history/wildlife programmes, they nonetheless found the caption text of documentaries very useful for "finding" large numbers of new and unfamiliar words and phrases (more than for any other programme).
8. There was a high level of retention and recall of language used in programmes, and of specific words and phrases, as shown by feedback sessions and by their performance in exercises and activities. In particular, students were able to ask detailed questions about the language used in programmes, and especially about the language that they had followed in the text but had not understood.
9. The students reported few cases of caption dependency (i.e., being tied to the text) or of overloaded channel capacity caused by the addition of the text. This was a paradoxical finding, since it might have been expected that if watching television programmes without captions already took all their concentration and effort, then adding another channel would overload their processing capacity. By the end of the term-long study, students reported that they could use the captions so flexibly and manage such larger chunks of text and sound (which, of course, had the same semantic content) that, in fact, they had spare processing capacity, which could be used for maximising the potential usefulness of the language in the programme, in both speech and text.
10. The more familiar the students were with watching programmes with subtitles in their mother tongue, as in the case of a Danish subject, the more rapidly they adapted to English captions and developed strategies for using them to best effect.
11. The quality of the text in some programmes was, at times, rather poor and there were inconsistencies, omissions, errors and misleading inaccuracies. Differences between text and speech were seen as a hindrance

at first, but were used as a useful and productive self-monitoring device later, and, of course, could be a very useful teaching technique.

In the original article, I discussed the findings at considerable length under the headings of acquisition and learning, listening comprehension and language teaching, speech perception and language processing, levels of learner proficiency and accent and dialect. Many of the themes and ideas have stood the test of time and have found support from Maribel Montero Perez and her colleagues (2013) in the discussion of their meta-analysis of research into captioned material and language learning (see also Chap. 4 of this volume). I have summarised some of these ideas and themes below:

3.3.1.1 Acquisition and Learning

I attempted to fit captioned viewing into Krashen's (1981) acquisition model, arguing that watching television fitted into the informal acquisition context, with low affective filter, positive attitudinal and motivational factors, plenty of challenging comprehensible input, which the learners had clearly attended to, especially new and striking phrases, and the "monitor" largely ruled out by the pace of programmes. The findings suggested strongly that captions, far from being a dangerous and disturbing distraction in language learning, could bring benefits to those who were "hard-of-listening."

However, the presence of text with sound, at times, did lead to a conscious focusing on the form (especially on correct form), particularly when new or striking expressions, unfamiliar technical words or proper names were used. For many learners, the text of the captions provided a conscious monitoring of the speech, by which words and phrases could be "found" in what would otherwise be a constant stream of speech. The findings also suggested that learners made progress in being able to cope with larger stretches of text at a time, and from this to processing the message in longer stretches of speech. In other words, the presence of the captions helped them to develop a "chunking" ability in both reading and listening, which, in turn, released spare capacity for conscious learning.

As far as motivation and attitude were concerned, for most of the students, negative attitudes and feelings of guilt regarding reading the captions while viewing disappeared over time. I was not surprised that many of them felt like this. Indeed, as I shall report in the chapter on the current EURECAP project (Chap. 7), such feelings of guilt and that reading captions or subtitles is somehow cheating are still widespread. Yet, my observations of subjects then and now confirm that many were and are very anxious about watching films and programmes without captions or subtitles, as they could never be sure of not mis-hearing or missing something important.

In this first study, the practical use and value of captions found by subjects largely changed negative attitudes and associations over the period of the study. They felt no anxiety and could relax when watching, secure in the knowledge that they could check what they heard in the text. This appeared, in turn, to produce growing confidence in their own listening ability and greater enjoyment as they began to feel that they could manage without the text in some programmes, as shown when they looked away or closed their eyes. The captions text seemed to contribute to security, greater self-efficacy and a low affective filter—all factors encouraging intake.

As I said earlier, I was fortunate in having an ideal group of subjects in well-motivated European exchange students. My pre-study observations of the students watching uncaptioned programmes indicated a high level of insecurity and anxiety before and during viewing, and defensiveness after viewing, while in other respects, their knowledge of English varied from intermediate to advanced level. In psychological terms, it might be argued that the caption text provided instant feedback, and therefore positive reinforcement for learning. It seems highly plausible this constant positive reinforcement was an important factor in building up the subjects' confidence, and in allowing them the spare capacity to develop sophisticated and flexible strategies for using captions.

3.3.1.2 Listening Comprehension and Language Teaching

In this section, I attempted to deal with the argument that providing captions is a distraction for learners, who will come to rely on them and will never be good enough at listening to watch TV programmes unsupported. What learners need, it is often argued, is more graded practice in listening. I certainly agree that learners should not be deprived of training in listening, but why should we wish to deprive them of massive quantities of authentic language, of a variety and quality unattainable in the language laboratory or classroom? Text-supported viewing can increase the redundancy in the language, bring down the level of ungraded, authentic language for learners and enrich the sound and images, thereby encouraging strong associations for retention and use of language.

A key point in my discussion was that to maintain and develop strategies for maximising the benefit of captioned programmes, learners needed regular viewing of varied and well-selected programmes. Learners also needed to be able to develop their own conscious, critical faculties and their ability to draw language from programmes and build it into their own competence, a process that takes time. But, at the time, fitting extensive television watching, with or without text, into a language-learning syllabus was (as now) difficult, and in the end, the choice, time and duration of viewing had to be left to the individual learner in self-access and independent forms of learning.

At the time of the study, I was quite sceptical about the proposition that a learner with reasonable knowledge of English might come to Britain, hire or buy a television with captions available, watch it for an extended period three or four hours a day (or even more frequently) and end up understanding and speaking English proficiently. Now, I must say, having heard many anecdotes over the years about autonomous learners making huge progress from doing just that, I am much less sceptical.

An important claim, which I developed later in my article, "A Very Verbal Medium" (1993), was that most programmes consist of spoken language supported by visual images, rather than vice versa, and intensive language practice, whether independent or teacher-guided, is needed to identify and activate that language, but first it must be made accessible and comprehensible.

One key point missing from my discussion was the question of whether providing captions helps to develop learners' listening comprehension ability over the longer term. The Price and Dow study (Price, 1983), and many studies since then, have demonstrated that learner-viewers can understand a foreign language film or programme better with captions than without, but this was never really going to be in much doubt if they have a level of reading ability high enough to read the captions as they appear. But to my mind, the real question, then, as now, is whether watching captioned programmes and films over the longer period helps develop the knowledge and skills required to follow and understand a wide variety of speech in the foreign language without captions.

3.3.1.3 Speech Perception and Processing

I also offered an explanation for how the caption text provides for phonetic matching of the sound, which is strikingly close to that offered by Mitterer and McQueen (2009) and Chap. 4 of this book in their groundbreaking article comparing subtitled and captioned viewing (see Chap. 4 for a full account).

I suggest that speech is processed by the listener in an active matching way, as proposed by Sanders (1977:153). We might say that native speakers know or recognise what they hear and make an approximate active match at a sort of linguistic interface. To make an analogy with television watching, it is as if native speakers have the script in their heads, or at least something very close to a script. This is not to say that it is a template on to which the received speech fits neatly, but it is a much more active process. Learners, evidently, do not have the full script, or indeed anything like it, and with their faulty listening, they usually generate only fragments at the interface of sound and perception, often based only on rough phonetic matching. The text of captions may provide the learner/viewer with a recognisable and intelligible script, which can be used to fill in missing parts of the speech, and thereby provide an accurate match at the proposed interface and a tuning in to the new speech. As I suggest in the article, feelings of guilt on the part of the learner may, in some cases, come from having the script on the screen, rather than in the head.

However, the presence of a script naturally makes considerable demands on reading skills, and it was not surprising that, in this study, it was the highly literate learners, familiar with Roman script and used to learning through text, who appeared to benefit most from the textual support. However, the presence of text did not reduce television watching to text reading + pictures, as learners continued to try and match sound and text, and indeed tried to monitor the correctness of their own matching of sound and language via the text. In this sense, then, captions can be regarded for many learners as a potentially valuable mediating device. An alternative and less charitable view, I suggest, is that my perspective is too optimistic and that what is going on is not really listening, but hearing sounds while reading text and watching pictures, with consequent lack of attention to meaning in the sound. However, since I take a long view of language development taking place through watching captioned programmes on a very regular basis, I think it is reasonable to claim that there could be a degree of unconscious integration of the senses, with long-term benefits in retention and recall from the richer environment created by the different channels.

3.3.1.4 Levels of Learner Proficiency

The study certainly threw up issues, with level of reading proficiency as a key variable in the value of captioned programmes for language learning. Learners who were below intermediate level or were slow readers found captioned viewing difficult, and even threatening, as their poor reading skills were exposed. All the programmes shown were the daily diet of broadcast programmes, and it was probably unfortunate that more attention was not paid to selection and grading issues at the time, since the issue of reading speed is shared by many deaf viewers, young and old (Independent Television Commission, 1999; Ofcom, 2005); there are many programmes with far fewer words per minute than a fast-paced comedy, news programme or soap opera, and relatively straightforward delivery in standard, clear English.

3.3.1.5 Subtitles, Accents and Dialects

One insight that I gained from this study was that even native speakers are little different from non-native speakers when it comes to tuning in to unfamiliar accents and dialects. I well recall that it took me sometime to tune in to Scottish accents when I moved to Edinburgh (I am sure my butcher thought there was something wrong with me in the first few weeks as I struggled to follow his Borders accent and the different names for cuts of meat). We all take time to adjust. How have Glaswegians got used to understanding programmes set in London or Londoners to understanding programmes set in Glasgow, or how indeed in the 1930s did British people tune in to American accents other than by regular and extensive watching of popular films with such accents and dialectal features? We all need a large amount of comprehensible input in order to tune into unfamiliar accents and dialects, and with learners, I would argue, captions, together with the images on the screen, provide the comprehensible part of the multichannelled input. Simple exposure alone will probably not be sufficient to enable a learner to tune in to what is perceived as a difficult and normally incomprehensible accent. As Mitterer and McQueen ((2009), and Chap. 4 in this book) found in their study comparing captioned and subtitled viewing, it helps to know what people are saying in order to make the approximate match with one's own or with a way of speaking previously encountered. The important aspect regarding captions in programmes with strong regional or American accents is not that the subjects in the study were able to understand what the actors were saying, but that they were hearing the accent and knew what was being said. Thus, they were not simply exposed to accent, but they could also use the comprehension of the speech to facilitate tuning in to the value of the sounds of a particular accent.

3.3.2 Study 2 ("Paying Attention to the Words," *System*, 1990)

3.3.2.1 Finding Differences

In a follow-up study with a larger and more heterogeneous set of exchange students, I attempted not only to replicate my first study but also to develop a model which would capture the factors that appeared to be at work in language learning from watching captioned TV programmes. While most of the findings of the first study were confirmed, it was evident that in order to gain much in language terms from a captioned programme, students needed to pay a great deal of attention to the language of the programme, perhaps with tasks set, note-taking or some other activity, rather than sitting back and watching a programme purely as

3 The Value of Closed Captions and Teletext Subtitles

entertainment, since the pace of a programme meant that much was lost in the stream of speech and caption text.

In this study, about four hours of programmes were shown each week, and the group, whose proficiency varied again from about B1 to C2, watched the programmes with the minimum of interruptions. In some sessions, students were asked to note striking, unfamiliar and useful words and phrases. In other sessions, they were told that they would have to carry out oral or written tasks, which were sometimes specified beforehand, sometimes only after viewing. For example, for a documentary on how breakdowns in routines can lead to catastrophic consequences, students were asked to talk in groups about breakdowns in routines they had experienced. For an episode of *Yes, Prime Minister*, a very popular comedy series at the time, they were asked to start a conversation with someone who had not seen the programme, beginning "I saw a really good *Yes Prime Minister* yesterday," and explain what went on, what some of the jokes were and so on. For a documentary on *The Greenhouse Effect*, they were asked to write a letter to an English friend back home, describing the Greenhouse Effect and saying what they thought should be done.

I felt strongly at the time that setting up highly constrained experiments or interventions would lose the essential affective and individual dimension of television watching and would be overly restrictive of what might be key variables, such as the attitude of viewers to particular commentators, the cultural perspective of viewers or even variables such as viewers' current state of knowledge and awareness of a particular topic. In the circumstances, I thought it was most important to continue collecting data on the informal basis until clear patterns of factors and variables emerged, which could be subsequently tested under rigorous conditions. What I was concerned with investigating was not whether one method of captioning was better than another, or whether one approach to using video was better than another; rather, I was concerned whether, in terms of language learning, generally available television programmes were made more useful and accessible with captions, and what the factors and variables appeared to be if we wished to exploit captioned programmes as a valuable language learning resource.

My findings were mostly the same as in the first study regarding the students picking up words and phrases. In the earlier report, I was happy to claim benefits for learners in conscious and unconscious development of language ability through watching captioned television programmes, with few conditions apart from a certain "literateness" and a roughly intermediate level of proficiency in English. However, in the larger and longer follow-up study, with a more heterogeneous group of subjects and with some subjects who attended only occasionally, I found that the students were able to collect and ask about words and expressions they had never seen before, such as "Bounce an idea off you," "I'm entitled to the occasional fling," "These errors are not random or bizarre." They were also able to appreciate dialectal and accentual features present in the speech of characters in programmes, features which are usually a barrier to following, let alone understanding (even among native speakers of English), but with the aid of captions, subjects could enjoy programmes such as *Auf Wiedersehen, Pet* (Newcastle/Geordie); *Bread* (Liverpool/Scouse); *Eastenders* (London/Cockney); *Cagney and Lacey* (New York/American), and could even begin to mimic accents successfully. Subjects were able to follow and understand complex information and ideas, and verbal humour. Subjects were also able to compare their own lexical and grammatical knowledge with that presented in the programmes and update if necessary. That is to say, questions that followed programmes always involved a great deal of comparison with subjects' current knowledge of vocabulary and grammar. For example, "Is 'peep' the same as 'look'?" and "Why does he say 'I is their age'? What's wrong with 'I wish I were their age'?"

A crucial factor in learners benefiting from captioned programmes in terms of measurable language and skill development was the degree of conscious attention paid to the language used in programmes, which is why, of course, the article was titled, "Paying Attention to the Words." That is, there was evidence, in the form of written tasks and tape-recorded discussions, that paying close attention to the language used in programmes through note-taking or other aids to retention helped subjects produced an altogether higher level of English in terms of accuracy and specificity of language (i.e., both correct structure and terminology), and a richer and more varied command of the language of social interaction than their general level of ability in English would have suggested. And, of course, as both the pilot and the follow-up study showed, subjects needed captions in order to extract the language used in programmes in any systematic way.

In contrast, in the case of those subjects who chose to sit back and enjoy programmes as programmes rather than as language learning resources (i.e., they said they followed and understood programmes, but took no notes or other aids to memory), I found the following:

- There was little or no recall of language used in programmes. Subjects claimed that they had been able to follow and understand everything in programmes such as *The Greenhouse Effect*, but could produce no precise or accurate terminology. It appeared that no language had gone beyond short-term memory.
- Language produced in tasks showed a gross level of generalisation and/or frequent use of translation with few specific references and little specific terminology, or in a sort of "translationese," which indicated that the subjects were familiar with the subject matter in the mother tongue, but had not attended to the English equivalents of specific terminology. Not surprisingly, this was particularly marked in tasks set for some of the documentaries. One student, who had written a letter of educated, informed native-speaker quality on *The Greenhouse Effect* after attending and taking notes, tried to rely on memory for holding language and information when watching the next documentary, and found that the "push-down" effect had come into play and there was simply nothing for him to recall, much to his surprise.
- Frequent mixing of characters, events and information.

This finding is, of course, predictable after viewing a densely packed programme, and, as with the first two findings, not in the least surprising, as all three are what one might expect to find with native-speaker viewers who sit back and enjoy the programmes without paying any particular attention to what was being said. How often has one watched a programme and taken little or nothing out of it? If one is asked to recall a programme, how much of the language of the programme would one use? How much would be one's own favoured words and expressions? With regard to these findings, it should be emphasised that I was not seeking to criticise those learners who did not consciously attend in such a manner as to be able to recall and use the language of the programmes. There may have been some unconscious learning going on, but, if so, I failed to capture it. Either way, with or without notes, it was clear that attending to the language was essential to fully understanding and appreciating many programmes such as comedies, crime dramas and documentaries. However, this was the one skill that most learners of a foreign language are not good at undertaking with any confidence in watching general, broadcast programmes until they have reached at least a high level listening proficiency in the foreign language. Captions enabled my students to attend to, and follow, what was being said.

3.3.2.2 Building a Model for Language Learning from Captioned Viewing

In this article, I proposed two models, which, in some respects, identified only too well the challenges for both learners and teachers of making use of programmes and films for language learning and teaching. In the models, I attempted to capture the factors that I had observed in the students who had gained from watching captioned programmes. I began with the entirely simplistic model of Fig. 3.2 in which I tried to define "attention" in terms of the factors that would most likely produce attentive viewing.

The attention factors are clearly not far removed from those that might determine whether a learner-viewer would put the essential effort into watching a programme to gain in language learning terms and are certainly related to the perceived self-efficacy that a learner-viewer is likely to bring to watching. For this model to work, it is clearly vital for learners to be able to have some control over what they give their attention to, and as I have indicated earlier, the students who watched captioned programmes needed to take out language in order to derive any measurable benefit.

Thus, according to this model, we are concerned with conscious language learning rather than absorption or taking in language, and I further refined the model, especially the attention part, to try and capture what was found in the study and to account for what learners do with extensive

3 The Value of Closed Captions and Teletext Subtitles

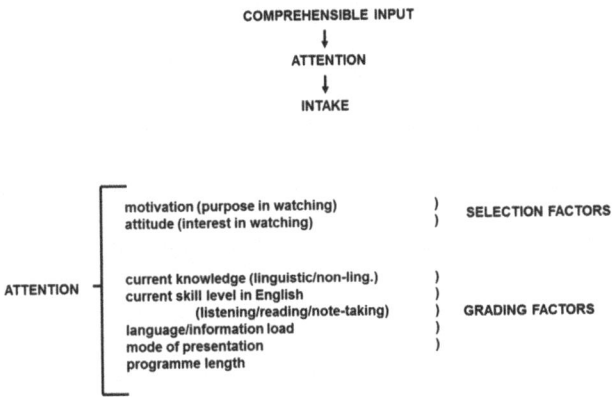

Fig. 3.2 The central role of attention

comprehensible input. Figure 3.3 was offered as a somewhat speculative model, which, it was hoped, would capture most, if not all, the observations and findings made in the two studies.

In the model in Fig. 3.3, learners attend to the extensive comprehensible input consciously, systematically and reflectively—all three being components of watching attentively. Both ATTENTION and ADAPTATION are included in TAKING OUT. The learner may then adopt what has been adapted by producing appropriate spoken or written language. I was not trying to suggest in the model that ADOPTION corresponded to TAKING IN. Adopting (or "taking on") someone else's language does not mean that it is taken in, in the sense of being absorbed or assimilated into one's linguistic competence. It seemed to me then, as now, that real and genuine regular use is the only guarantee of "taking in."

As I tried to validate the models with my students' experiences over the following years, I increasingly felt that I had correctly set a very high hurdle for learning from captioned TV and films, and that in the pre-Internet and multi-media circumstances prevailing in the 1990s, it was unlikely that language learners, in general, would be able to sustain the effort and motivation needed to gain substantially from captioned viewing. There were also two issues that kept coming up in my attempt to exploit TV programmes such as informative and topical documentaries.

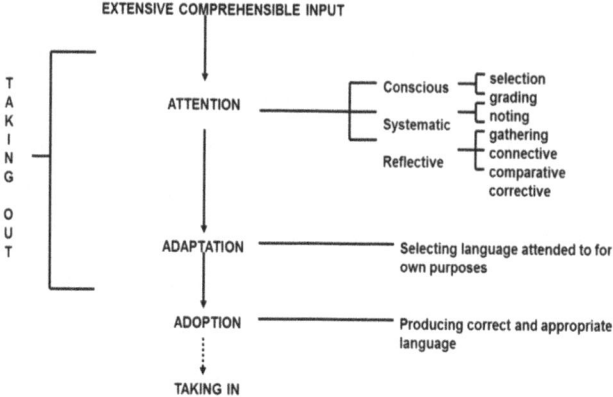

Fig. 3.3 "Paying attention to the words" model

1. The mental sets that the students brought to viewing.
2. The very structure of the programmes themselves, with their arguments or messages often being obscured by the narrative structure or by engaging case studies.

It seemed to me that I was finding exactly the types of problems that had been found at the OU (see Chap. 2), and outlined so well by Salomon (1984) and Laurillard (1991). While the captions increased the students' perceived self-efficacy in watching the documentaries, their leisure-orientated mental sets towards the programmes were very strong, so that even (perhaps especially) high-quality documentaries tended to be watched with limited attention to the language, and only general understanding and appreciation of the content remained.

3.3.3 The Third Study (Paper Given at the AILA Congress in Jyväskylä, Finland, 1996)

3.3.3.1 Applying the "Adaptation" and "Adoption" Parts of the Model

I decided to carry out a third study examining these issues (Vanderplank, 1996b). Would advanced-level learners of English, who had been in the

UK for some time and were familiar with British TV, respond positively to the presence of captions when called upon to carry out a series of simple recall and discussion tasks following viewing programmes with and without captions? I also wished to see whether the presence or absence of captions would make a difference in terms of speaking turn, detail of recall, language of programme used on recall and discussion. Finally, following the viewings and tasks, I wished to investigate whether the learners themselves made any distinction between programmes with and without captions and the purposes to which programmes were put. In other words, did they make a distinction between viewing for entertainment, viewing for the simple class-based tasks of the study and viewing for assessed academic work.

Again, my subjects were exchange students, fifteen in number, who had been in Edinburgh for between 3 and 8 months. They were all between B2 and C2 levels in the CEFR in their proficiency in English, and were from a wide variety of European countries and from Mexico. They completed a short questionnaire on their current viewing behaviour, their confidence in watching different programme types and the difficulties they found in watching TV programmes.

They were then shown a series of sequences from a variety of programme types (two consumer affairs programmes, two documentaries and two plays), with and without captions, and were give a task sheet for each sequence on which they could write notes. These sheets were collected afterwards. Each video sequence was about ten minutes long. The questions in the task were designed to elicit responses, which would reveal the different discourses present in each sequence and to see what personal associations each student would bring to the discussions. For example, the sequence involving a body found in a glacier was for the most part a narrative (who found the body, where, what happened then and so on). Also mentioned was the issue of ownership of the body and the dispute that arose between Italy and Austria over ownership. I felt it was important to let students talk about their associations with each sequence. Viewers engage with programmes at an affective level (bringing personal associations to the viewing, comparing the values and messages with one's own, re-evaluating one's prior knowledge and attitudes) and I was interested in seeing what "interested" each student about the different sequences. Following their viewing of each sequence, they were asked to respond to a series of written questions, and their responses were recorded.

Although the setting was far removed from home/leisure viewing and was quite stressful at times for some students, sequences had been carefully chosen (on the basis of past experience) to interest and engage students and thus retain an element of informal viewing. They were also used to taking long turns in discussions, and as the recordings of their discussions indicated, many just loved to talk in English.

The results of the questionnaire showed that all watched TV, both in Edinburgh and back home, and they were "experienced" viewers with a wide range of interests and motives for watching TV. Watching TV was a normal part of post-work and evening life, carried on without much thought or effort. Watching TV in English was no longer a novelty as it was when they first arrived in the UK, and they had become accustomed to watching British TV. Time spent watching TV in Edinburgh varied from 1 hour per week to 25 hours per week, though most watched more than 10 hours per week. Back home, most watched more than 15 hours per week. Favourite programmes included quiz shows, news, detective thrillers, documentaries, comedies and films. Main reasons for watching were entertainment and "distraction," as well as keeping up with news and current affairs, improving listening and learning more English. None had access to a TV with Teletext subtitles (captions) in Edinburgh. One student mentioned that she and her flatmates tended to switch the TV on and then chat with the programmes running. The mean confidence level of ability to follow programmes was around 75 %, though there were considerable difference between programmes and individual students with regard to confidence levels. Comedy programmes were rated between 25% and 75 %, with a mean of approximately 50 %. News and current affairs were watched most confidently and were rated between 75% and 100 %. Major barriers to less than full understanding were accent/dialect, pace/speed of speech and unfamiliar words and usage. Different value, beliefs, ways of seeing things and ways of thinking were not considered barriers.

Given the students' level of proficiency in English and their familiarity with watching English language TV, it was not surprising that they demonstrated high confidence ratings for most types of programmes. Thus, while less than fully confident in the native-speaker sense when turning on a TV programme, they were, as a group, sure of following a great deal and "at home" while watching British TV.

Almost all students were very responsive to all the sequences shown. Many talked at some length (5 minutes or more) about what they had watched, the issues involved and the impressions the sequences had made on them. The key factors in accuracy and detail of recall and understanding, as well as the length of their turn, appeared to be not so much whether they found a programme interesting and informative or the presence/absence of captions, but whether a programme had some personal meaning, provided new insights on prior knowledge or was, in some sense, arresting (e.g., the "shock" report on skin cancer). A number of students remembered the case of the pre-historic body found in the glacier on the Austro–Italian border and spoke at length about it. On the value of the captions, while opinions differed if programmes were to be watched for general interest or entertainment, all stated that they preferred to have captions if programmes were to be watched for study purpose. They were divided as to whether the captions made any difference for the sequences shown, apart from a sequence from *Hamlet*, for which students considered the captions essential for following and appreciating the scene. The main difference between watching for leisure and watching as part of a course of study for them was that for the latter, they would want a complete understanding and would want to know all the words, or at least be able to check them later. Some mentioned that they would like to treat each programme as a text through the captions: language could be checked and then paused to freeze the captions.

3.3.3.2 The Importance of the Mindset and Attitude

Overall, the findings were not surprising—TV watching was something they were familiar with as a leisure activity, they felt confident as viewers and even had a "take them or leave them" attitude to the captions in some cases. A key finding was the understanding by the students that their subjective "viewer" responses to programmes were less important when the understanding of a programme and its intended messages were to be checked or assessed. The context of the study itself was perceived by the students as being between home viewing and watching programmes as part of a formal course of study. Again, thinking of print media, this is altogether unsurprising. We bring different mindsets to our reading according to the manner or context in which a book is to be read. A person reading a novel for pleasure or leisure almost certainly has a rather different mindset and attitude to the task from when they are required to read a novel for an assessed course.

It seemed that for at least some members of this group, there were two major changes which occurred in watching programmes as part of a formal programme of study compared to familiar, informal viewing behaviour. The first and most obvious change was the degree of attention to be paid to the language, content aims and intentions of a programme in terms of the producer. That is, the messages that the producer intended the viewer to receive became more important. Secondly, and following on from the first change, the cognitive response in terms of critical understanding and analysis became more important than simple recall of what a programme was about and the viewer's affective, impressionistic response.

What also emerged from the findings, though, was that the students were not confident about making the change to viewing for study purposes unless captions were present. While much of the stimulation and subjective response to a programme may lie in the illustrations, examples and an easily followed narrative, students indicated their awareness that any focus on the verbal messages and content of the programme required the additional support of the caption text. They could not be sure they had got words and messages right without the text. In this respect, it would seem that captions were the key to opening up the educational potential of TV programmes for these non-native speaker viewers.

The findings also suggested that for some of this group at least, familiar with watching English-language TV and reasonably confident when they turned on the television, the presence of the captions altered the viewing experience in both negative and positive ways: negatively, when programmes were being watched for leisure or pleasure; positively, when programmes were being watched for educational purposes. However, effort and attention (and there was clearly effort and attention in contrast to the "couch-potato" characterisations of some video English Language Teaching (ELT) writers) tended not to be fully focused on the verbal messages but on the visual images and on rich subjective associations and connections. Meaning and understanding were seen in affective and personal terms rather than in cognitive and analytical terms.

3.3.3.3 *Au revoir* to Captions Research

This study was my swansong for research on captioned viewing at the time. In the paper I gave on this research at the AILA Congress in Jyväskylä, Finland, in 1996, I described this study and also indicated that the model I had proposed in my 1990 article was simply too difficult to be feasible for most learners and in most class-based learning situations. The model, I suggested, could only be fully realised by independent learners outside the classroom. Yet, what I had found in my own students over the years was that they, too, were unlikely to give the attention and effort required to benefit greatly from watching with captions if only owing to the perceptions they brought to TV and film watching and the difficulty of exercising true choice and control, factors I had already identified as essential to my model operating successfully. Certainly, there would be some autonomous learners who might be so motivated and so strategic in their learning that they would exploit the opportunities offered by captioned viewing, but my experience over almost ten years was such that I had not found them in anything other than in very small numbers.

While it was, therefore, with some disillusionment that I stopped actively working on captioned viewing in 1996, changes in the very nature of language learning as far as new social and media technologies, together with the empowerment of independent learners, mean that it is time to revisit my model in the new world of language learning. I shall discuss the revised model in Chap. 8.

3.4 Capturing Caption Use in Informal Settings

As I shall report in Chaps. 4 and 5, the majority of research into the value of captions has been in formal settings, with carefully constructed intervention and tests. While the findings of these studies have certainly been useful in demonstrating the value of viewing captioned programmes in specific respects, such as increased comprehension of programmes and vocabulary learning, there have been very few studies that attempt to capture what happens with captioned viewing in informal or naturalistic settings.

As we have seen in this chapter, my own attempts to capture this with diaries during the *Teletext 888 Project* were not altogether successful and indicated, by the end of the project, that without altering the context and task demands from leisure-orientated viewing to learning-orientated viewing, watching captioned programmes in itself was not going to produce significant enhancement in language skills, even if it did "open the box" in terms of providing the potential for massive and extensive comprehensible input. Writing this book has provided me with a stimulus for uncovering research I had not found earlier, which has reported on captioned viewing in informal settings.

A very thorough, but unpublished (as far as I can tell), Masters dissertation, which investigated captioned television as a means of self-help among second language learners in the USA, was carried out by Sarah Rose Zamoon (1996). Zamoon conducted a survey among international students of varying levels of English language proficiency at the University of Iowa. Of the 210 respondents, 51 were taking English courses, as they had not yet reached the level to be accepted and 159 respondents had already been accepted and were taking in-sessional English classes. They were 29 nationalities, with the majority from eastern Asia. About one-third had been in the USA for 3–6 months, a little less than half longer than 7 months and the remainder only 1–2 months. Zamoon wished to know who watched captioned television at home, how often, what they watched and how much use they made of it (i.e., the strategies they used). Ninety-seven responded that they watched with captions; 22 of these were of the intensive English group and the remainder were a mixture of undergraduate and graduate students.

She found that most of the proficient students continued to watch with captions (six stated that they had used them initially but no longer did so, as they wished to concentrate on listening), while at the other end of the proficiency scale, students at intermediate level found it hard to make use of captions, and the lower the proficiency, the less use was made of them.

Some of those who did not make use of captions did not have access to the technology, but the largest group of non-users, 29 in total, was made up of those who preferred to listen so that they could improve this skill. Of these, some felt that they became caught up in reading the captions to the detriment of listening. The majority (87.5 %) who did watch with captions did so for at least ½ hour per day and up to 5 hours or more, though more than half watched for between ½ and 1½ hours per day. News programmes and films were most frequently watched. There were some interesting similarities and differences between programmes watched with and without captions. Both news and films were largely watched by both users and non-users of captions; however, sports programmes were rarely watched with captions, while largely watched without captions. Sitcoms did not figure greatly, which Zamoon attributes to respondents not being familiar with the term, since her own experiences of talking to students was that they watched a great deal of sitcoms. Documentaries were also not popular, though, as Zamoon says, they were recommended by teachers and were used in class.

Areas they felt captions were most helpful with were (in order of ranking) new words, idioms/slang, pronunciation, listening to Americans speaking with American friends, reading and other skills. When asked about their function, helping understand what is said and helping understand the main idea were the main ones mentioned. Students also identified familiar issues with the format of captions: errors, speed (too fast, too slow), not being detailed enough, not being easy to read/confusing and variation in quality from programme to programme.

One of the most novel and interesting sections of this study deals with strategies. A minority reported using social strategies (interacting with co-viewers while viewing a programme, during a commercial break or after a programme) and most watched alone. Zamoon also gathered data on cognitive strategies: (1) videotaping, (2) replaying the captioned programme, (3) replaying the captioned programme with no sound, (4) resourcing by using various books and (5) writing down something significant. Use of any strategy was limited, with the lower-level groups tending to use more strategies than the higher-level groups. Zamoon makes the insightful comment that "It would seem that if strategy employment is an indication of effort to learn on one's own through use of closed captioning, the IEOP students (those who have not yet been accepted in the University) are making a greater effort to improve their English skills than the other groups (who have already achieved academic acceptance)" (p. 65). She also makes the point that it would be very helpful to learners if teachers could guide students in useful strategies to use in watching captioned programmes and films at home.

What Zamoon's findings bring out so clearly is that while lower-level students may make little use of captioned viewing initially, since they cannot really take advantage of them, they make steadily more use as their English improves and that, for the most part, even proficient students continue to watch with captions. Quite rightly, Zamoon considers that "comprehensibility" is the key (p. 66).

3.5 Moving On

Over the years of the *Teletext 888 Project* (and indeed until recently), I came to increasingly doubt whether, for the ordinary classroom-based language learner, learning a foreign language from watching captioned programmes was realistic, as I had set the hurdles so high in my model, even if the captions made a programme or film comprehensible and some new words and phrases were learnt. Yet, perhaps, in this, I was doing no more than making explicit the hurdles that all language learners face, particularly at higher levels, in trying to cross the threshold of proficiency to where one can confidently watch films and TV programmes with a high level (95 % or more) of understanding. As mentioned earlier, after 1996 and after my move to Oxford University, I ceased to work actively on language learning from captioned TV until the events described in the Introduction drew me back. As I shall report in Chap. 8, it is only recently, and in a very different context, that my original model has finally received a degree of validation through new research findings.

4

The State of the Art I: Selected Research on Listening Comprehension and Vocabulary Acquisition

4.1 Montero Perez, Van Den Noortgate and Desmet (2013): The Case for Captions

One of the pleasures of being a journal reviewer is that you may occasionally receive an article that really does move the field on. In my case, it was the meta-analysis of eighteen empirical studies on captioning and language learning by Maribel Montero Perez, Wim Van den Noordgate and Piet Desmet (2013), which is another recent "watershed" for studies of captioned video, films and TV. I have always considered that the case for captions is self-evident from the fact that while second language viewers and learners may not be hard-of-hearing, they are "hard-of-listening" and find the speech of foreign language TV, films and videos difficult to follow and understand. However, Montero Perez et al. suggest that a rationale for using captioned video can be found in research on multimedia materials, research on listening comprehension and the dual-coding theory.

With regard to the first rationale, they highlight the fact that adding video to audio, especially within a multimedia environment, while enriching and offering the benefit of visual support, has also presented opportunities for adding a variety of textual support, including captions intended for deaf and hard-of-hearing people.

As developing listening comprehension skills is difficult, especially in foreign language contexts, this is certainly the most obvious rationale, given the dynamic and fast-paced nature of much of the speech on TV and in films. Among the many issues they identify, speech stream chunking, word recognition and having sufficient vocabulary knowledge are highlighted as areas in which captions have been found to be useful in overcoming problems of limited foreign language listening skills.

I shall leave my discussion of various theories, such as the dual-coding theory, as frameworks for informing studies on captioned video until the end of Chap. 5, after my review of research on captioned viewing.

4.2 The Meta-Analysis of Listening Comprehension and Vocabulary Acquisition Research

In their key article, Montero Perez et al. identify two main areas in which the bulk of research has been carried out over the past thirty years or so: first, learners' listening comprehension, second, fostering vocabulary learning. I have always found it slightly odd that so much time has been devoted to finding out whether learners understand video clips better with or without captions, as the Price and Dow study was so conclusive, and, in my view, it is not really the central issue. The question, I would argue, is not so much whether a learner understands better watching a video clip or TV programme with captions rather than without, but whether watching captioned audiovisual material can help to make a learner a better listener.

As Montero Perez et al. report, while some studies failed to find differences between captioning and other conditions used in the interventions (Hernandez, 2004; Taylor, 2005), most studies show better comprehension test scores for the group(s) watching with captions than for those watching without (Baltova, 1999a, Chung, 1999, Garza, 1991, Guichon and McLornan, 2008, Huang and Eskey, 1999–2000, Markham, 1989 and Markham, 2001). Similarly, studies such as those by Bird and Williams, 2002, Chai and Erlam, 2008, Markham, 1999, Sydorenko, 2010 and Winke, Gass, & Sydorenko, 2010, show support for claims that captioned viewing may enhance vocabulary learning.

As I mentioned in my review (2010) of ten years of research, which included studies involving captioned viewing, there are often two main issues that arise in reported research which make claims problematic. The first is that the relative effectiveness of captioned viewing varies according to language level. Some studies suggest that certain types of captioning can be beneficial even at low levels (Guillory, 1998; Markham, 1989; Neuman and Koskinen 1992), while others, such as the rather poorly designed study by Taylor (2005), found little benefit for low-level learners. In reporting my own studies (1988a, 1990), I suggest that captions may not only be unhelpful to learners with poor comprehension, limited vocabulary and low reading speeds, but may also be threatening. However, I used only mainstream popular broadcast programmes intended for normal hearing adult native speakers and did not consider that I should have put more effort into selecting more appropriately graded material for the lower-level learners. Secondly, the research on both listening comprehension and vocabulary learning has used a wide variety of test designs and measures, both productive and receptive, making it hard to compare results.

A meta-analysis takes data from multiple studies and combines them to estimate the effect of a particular independent variable on these studies and whether the effects vary over studies. In this case, the researchers wanted to see the overall effects of captioning for L2 listening comprehension and vocabulary acquisition, the relationship between the test type and the effect of captioning on listening comprehension and vocabulary acquisition and the relationship between proficiency level and the effect of captioning on listening comprehension and vocabulary acquisition.

From a search that revealed 150 studies, eighteen were identified, which met the criteria for inclusion in the meta-analysis regarding quantitative and statistical data, L2 learning and L2 on-screen text, listening comprehension and/or vocabulary learning and a control condition and a treatment condition.

Inevitably, many qualitative and descriptive studies, which have figured heavily in the literature, were omitted, including my studies and the Price and Dow (Price, 1983) study. They were left with thirteen published journal articles and five unpublished doctoral dissertations (Danan, 1992; Chung, 1999; Hayati & Mohmedi, 2011; Hernandez, 2004; Huang & Eskey, 1999–2000; Hwang, 2003; Markham, 1989; Markham, 1999; Markham, 2001; Markham, Peter & McCarthy, 2001; Markham & Peter, 2003, Park, 2004; Winke, Gass & Sydorenko, 2010; Neuman & Koskinen, 1992; Taylor, 2005; Baltova, 1999a; Sydorenko, 2010; Liversidge, 2000). Only two of the studies, which met the criteria for inclusion, contained delayed post-tests (Baltova, 1999b and Neuman & Koskinen, 1992). Obviously, this is not a large number considering they were carried over a long period, and is an inevitable limitation, especially as there were few studies in particular areas such as advanced levels of proficiency.

Montero Perez et al. set out three research questions:

RQ1: What is the overall effectiveness of captioning for L2 listening comprehension and vocabulary acquisition?

RQ2. What is the relationship between the test type used and the effect of captioning on L2 listening comprehension and vocabulary acquisition?

RQ3. What is the relationship between proficiency level and the effect of captioning on L2 listening comprehension and vocabulary acquisition?

Separate meta-analyses were carried out for the fifteen studies involving listening comprehension as a dependent variable and the ten studies involving vocabulary learning. Seven studies measured both. In the listening comprehension studies, participants were mainly Asian (seven studies) or English (eight studies). Eight studies used university-level students, eight involved beginning-level learners, eleven intermediate-level learners and four advanced-level learners. Several studies involved multiple levels. English was the target language in ten studies, Spanish in four and French in one. Eight used a receptive test, four reported using a productive test and three used a combination of both.

It would be difficult to overestimate the value of the authors' meta-analysis to the field. Of particular importance to me was the fact that much of what I had asserted in my earlier studies on the basis of my observations and student feedback was confirmed empirically by their findings. In general terms, the effect of captioning on listening comprehension demonstrated the overall superiority of the captioning condition over the control group. The analysis of test types showed that captioning had a significantly larger effect when comprehension was measured with a receptive comprehension test. Interestingly enough, when the authors looked at the relationship between captioning effectiveness and proficiency level, they found a medium effect for both beginners and advanced-level learners, and a large effect for intermediate-level learners.

For vocabulary acquisition, there was a large effect size of captioning on the immediate vocabulary post-test, showing that learners who watched captioned videos significantly outperformed learners in the control group. Results for both recognition and recall test were similar and showed large effects for all proficiency levels.

As the authors suggest, captioning can be considered a powerful tool for reinforcing learners' comprehension of video materials (p. 731). More than that, they feel able to state the following:

> the presence of captioning may ensure 'conscious monitoring of the speech' (Vanderplank, 1988a:277), and 'bridge the often sizable gap between the development of skills in reading comprehension and listening comprehension' (Garza, 1991:246). By doing so, it may deal with word recognition and speech stream chunking problems (Graham, 2006) and reduce listeners' decoding effort, which would otherwise produce comprehension breakdowns related to the 'real-time nature' of the aural input (Buck, 2001:6). The use of captioning can also be considered a means to encourage sound-script automatization and therefore deals with typical problems of the L2 listener (Goh, 2000).

Likewise, for vocabulary learning, there was a large effect for captioning, and the analysis confirmed the claim that bimodal input fosters vocabulary learning. Montero Perez et al ask why captioning should foster more vocabulary learning than single modality input and consider that the reasons may lie, firstly, in the presence of captions contributing to "a conscious focusing on the form (especially on correct form), particularly when new or striking expressions are used" (Vanderplank, 1988a:276), and, secondly, in captioning encouraging attention, which is crucial to "taking out" language (Vanderplank, 1990) and, thirdly, in captions also supporting learners in constructing an initial form–meaning link (Winke et al., 2010). In addition, they suggest that captions seem to help learners isolate words better (Winke et al., 2010:79) and reinforce contextual clues for inferring word meaning.

The differences made by different test types are striking, especially in listening comprehension. Receptive tests showed the greatest effect of captions, whereas productive tests (e.g., written recall) such as that used by Liversidge (2000) appear to interfere with listening skills and reduce the benefits of captions. The authors found large effects for vocabulary recognition, but as the analysis was based on only two studies, it needs to be treated with caution; they are able to express greater confidence in the large and significant effect found for vocabulary recall.

With regard to the proficiency levels, their analysis throws up some fascinating and very valuable findings, some of which certainly run counter to much of what has been written in the literature. While the authors found no significant effect of captions for beginners for listening comprehension, they found a large and significant effect for intermediate-level learners with (authentic) video materials. As they point out, authentic video can indeed be "unlocked" for those intermediate-level learners by using captions (Vanderplank, 1988a:278). Unfortunately, only one study involved advanced-level participants. Overall, they found no difference in the effect of captioning between the proficiency levels for listening comprehension and suggest that this finding may possibly be explained by the difficulty level of the video materials used (Vanderplank, 1988a, 1988b; Winke et al., 2010), since, in order for captions to be of value to learners, the material needs to be selected or developed with the learners' actual proficiency level in mind. It could, they add, also be that, in line with the findings of Pujolà's (2002) study, higher-level learners use captions more as a backup, whereas lower-level learners find them essential for understanding.

For vocabulary learning, the analysis found the biggest effect of captions on beginners. They sensibly suggest that this may be because beginners need more help at the decoding level and the captions show where the word boundaries occur, giving learners more time to pay attention to the words. They also mention the "rich get richer principle" (Neuman and Koskinen, 1992:164), where those who are more fluent can use this skill to gain more vocabulary. Again, there was only one study using advanced-level learners. So, in the end, proficiency level does not seem to be a crucial fact in whether captions are effective for listening comprehension and vocabulary learning. All levels seem to benefit, provided the material is at the appropriate level for the learners.

Montero Perez and colleagues conclude with a simple, yet groundbreaking, statement:

> The overall results of our meta-analysis revealed a large superiority of captioning in that captioning groups significantly outperformed the control group on both listening and vocabulary posttests. Results thus support the claim that captioning helps learners to improve comprehension and fosters vocabulary learning. (p. 733).

Certainly, as they admit, there is a need for more research with advanced learners as well as research that focuses on the different types of vocabulary knowledge. More importantly, we also now need to move on to more research with delayed post-tests and longitudinal studies to assess the long-term effects on listening development in particular.

In the end, though, while a meta-analysis is an impressive statistical instrument, we also need to put some flesh on the bones of research studies to assess their contributions to research on captioned viewing. In the following sections, I review some of the studies highlighted in the meta-analysis, along with more recent studies and others, which are particularly relevant to the themes of the meta-analysis.

4.3 With or Without Captions

Several studies in the Montero Perez et al. meta-analysis have included the issue of captions or no captions in their research questions. While it might be argued that little new has been learnt since the Price and Dow (Price, 1983) study, which found that learners understood more when watching a video with captions than without, the quality and findings of these studies have added to our understanding of how and when to use captions to best effect.

Garza's (1991) study on Russian and ESL learners compared their comprehension of video segments with second language captions to that of video segments without captions. Five segments of authentic American and Russian video, each between two and four minutes in length, were selected. Each segment depicted a particular genre of video (drama, comedy, news, animation and music). A ten-item (multiple choice) comprehension test was used to measure students' comprehension of the video segments. A total of 140 students, with varying levels of proficiency in Russian, viewed the Russian video segments with or without captions. Comparison of the comprehension test scores of the two groups of students revealed "a mean gain of 75.2 % of correct answers, a mean decrease of 61.16 % of incorrect answers, and a mean decrease of 83.76 % in unanswered questions for students who viewed the video segments with captions over those who viewed the same segment without captions" (p. 244).

A much-cited study by Huang and Eskey (1999–2000) investigated the effects of captions on the listening comprehension of thirty intermediate English language students who watched the programme, *Family Album, USA*, a series designed for ESL students. Students were randomly placed into two groups, one with captions and the other without. The group that viewed the programme with captions scored significantly higher on a post-programme assessment involving vocabulary/phrase acquisition and comprehension.

In another well-designed and insightful study, also using *Family Album, USA*, Chung (1999) compared listening comprehension rates for video texts using advance organisers, closed captions, a combination of both and none of them, with 183 randomly selected low-level learners. Four different treatments were used for four video segments in a "Latin Square" arrangement. The advance organisers consisted of the teacher reading aloud in Chinese six to eight sentences about the segment the learners were about to watch.

Learners in the combined treatment of advance organiser and captions scored significantly higher than the advance organiser only treatment and no support treatment. The treatment with captions only scored higher than that with advance organiser only. There was no significant different between the captions only treatment and the combined treatment, or between the advance organiser treatment and no treatments. Simply playing videos as a means of developing language skills was not enough, and some form of help was needed to enhance access for students to benefit. The majority thought that L2 (English) captions would be more useful than L1 (Chinese) subtitles, and that one form of support would be enough for higher-level proficiency students while both might be needed for lower levels.

Although included in the meta-analysis, Taylor's (2005) study of low-level learners to assess whether they could understand a video in Spanish better with or without captions, what processing strategies they used and whether these varied according to the length of time they had been studying Spanish is less convincing. Students in the captions group with 3 years of Spanish study significantly outscored those in their first year of study on free recall. However, there was no difference in the no-captions group. When the two groups of first-year students were compared, the no-captions group had significantly outscored the captions group, suggesting that the captions may have had a detrimental effect. Captions neither helped nor hindered the third-year students. Regarding strategy use, six of the seventeen first-year students found captions distracting or confusing or that they could not use the three channels simultaneously. Not surprisingly, half of the third-year students reported that they did not find this a problem, several stated that they would have understood nothing without the captions and many found them helpful. The research, perhaps unwittingly, appears to confirm that unless video material is carefully selected and graded, together with judicious editing of captions, attempting to use captioned videos with low-level learners is likely to be a waste of time and may well produce a negative response from students.

Another study that compared a captions group with a no-captions group is by Yuksel and Tanriverdi (2009) on incidental vocabulary learning from watching a video clip with and without captions, using Wesche and Paribakht's (1996) five-level VKS as a measure of development. One hundred and twenty intermediate-level EFL students were tested using the VKS two weeks before the treatment. They were randomly assigned to the captions or no-captions group and shown a 9-minute clip of a single episode of *Seinfeld*. Ten target words were chosen, validated by pilot tests. Both groups made significant gains from pre-test to post-test.

While the captions group improved a little more than the no-captions group, the difference was not significant. The authors question the validity of the self-report scale in capturing differences between groups. In addition, the subjects had been primed for these words in the pre-test, making it difficult to assess to what extent the video clip was the source of knowledge of the meaning of these words. Furthermore, the number of words was so small that differences were less likely to be significant.

In contrast, the study by Paula Winke, Susan Gass and Tatiana Sydorenko, "The effects of captioning videos used for foreign language listening activities" (2010), included in the meta-analysis, is a high-quality piece of research.

In this rigorously conducted study, 150 students at an American university, learning different languages (Arabic, Chinese, Russian and Spanish), watched short clips, 3–5 minutes in length, from a documentary that had been translated from English into each language and then dubbed with captions inserted. Groups watched with or without captions; they took tests of reading and listening, in addition to stimulated recall tests and interviews. As far as the overall effects of captioning were concerned, the authors only looked at Spanish second-year learners who watched twice, with or without captions. Not surprisingly, those who watched with captions both times scored significantly higher on tests of vocabulary, listening and comprehension than the no captions group.

They also looked at the effects of the order of caption presentation in Arabic, Chinese, Russian and Spanish. In general, those who watched with captions first did better on the tests than those who watched first without and then with captions. This was a wholly unsurprising finding and it could be argued that watching first without captions was probably a marginal exercise in terms of what we know about viewing with and without captions. Evidence that orthography made a difference was also found: Spanish and Russian captions seen first seemed to be better than Arabic and Chinese, which seemed more beneficial being seen second, though the results were mixed for Chinese and Arabic.

In addition, the authors considered the effect of proficiency but found nothing to report, as they had little data on proficiency level apart from the subjects being second- and fourth-year and non-beginners to start with. This was something of a lost opportunity, as there were clearly a number of key variables regarding language proficiency, which needed to be taken into account. For example, general reading comprehension and listening comprehension ability probably matter less than the ability to follow (i.e., decode) what is being said, and this is the problem for L2 viewing. When you add captions as a supposed support, which assumes the ability to read and understand at reasonable speed, you introduce a reading speed variable. The authors are clearly correct in asserting that an important factor is the appropriate selection of captioned material for lower-level learners.

A study missed by Montero Perez et al. was carried out by Eric Smith and Chung-wei Shen (1992), using a videodisc player (a technology now largely forgotten). They are frequently cited in literature reviews in the usual "black-boxing" manner, but few details of the research are given as a rule. I mention this study as an example of how captions have been used for different functions, in this case, mainly as a feedback tool—a role which it is well suited to. They investigated the effects of English captioning on content knowledge and recall during English listening comprehension practice for Taiwanese students. Seventy-two students at National Taiwan Normal University, thirty-six with "above average" and 36 with "below average" English reading proficiency according to their scores on the Joint College Entrance Examination participated in the study, using an interactive videodisc programme, which provided 1 hour of material every 2 weeks over a period of 10 weeks. This consisted of the film, *The Last Emperor*, along with tasks and tests. Two versions of the programme, one with captioning and one without, were used. The effects on listening comprehension were measured by a treatment content-specific listening comprehension test and by the listening comprehension subtest of the Test of English as a Foreign Language (TOEFL). The results indicated that subjects in the captioning treatment had a significantly higher score on the treatment content-specific listening comprehension test. However, there was no significant difference between the groups on the TOEFL listening comprehension test, which measured general comprehension skills. So, while they found that using captioning for specific content improved the comprehension of learners within that context, they were unable to show that the improvement transferred to other listening situations. In addition, English reading ability had a significant impact on listening comprehension performance, with the subjects in the "above average" group performing better than those in the "below average group."

The finding that improved content-specific listening comprehension did not transfer to general listening skills could be because of several factors. Firstly, the design of the study involved a very restricted use of captions, very different from their use in other studies. The caption treatment group watched a complete 'chapter' of the film then watched clips answering embedded multiple-choice questions about each clip which students were encouraged to answer using contextual cues. As far as I can judge from the report, it was only if they answered correctly that the clip was played again with captioning as a 'knowledge of results feedback' to confirm every correct response. If they answered incorrectly, they reviewed the clip one more time, and if they answered correctly or incorrectly, the captioned clip was shown with the correct answer. This brings to mind the strategies used by some participants in the EURECAP Project described in Chap. 7, as the captions on the films in DVD format could be switched on or off by the participants. In the case of the videodisc, as used in the Smith and Chen study, branching programmes automatically took the students in different directions according to their responses. Secondly, the function of the captions appears to have had more to do with reading and feedback than with training in listening.

4.4 Captions and the Development of Listening Comprehension

One of the arguments frequently raised against the use of captioned programmes and films is that even if captioning allows for language gains and improved comprehension, students are not being truly trained to develop their listening skills without written support. The two studies reported in this section attempted to tease out this issue. Markham (1999) looked at the effects of captioned video on advanced-level ESL students' aural word recognition, attempting to establish a link between using captions to improve learners' listening word recognition skills and subsequently presented audio material without textual or pictorial support. In other words, does the dual input of reading and listening contribute to subsequent improved listening performance on related tasks?

One hundred and eighteen university-level students, grouped according to their ability range in terms of TOEFL scores, were shown two 12–13-minute excerpts from educational television programmes, one about whales, and the other about the civil rights movement in the USA. The main difference between the two videos was that the "whales" video had a high correlation of audio track and video, with pictures corresponding closely to the soundtrack, whereas the opposite was the case for the "civil rights" video, as pictures accompanying the latter provided little support for the sound or text.

Markham attempted to isolate the listening variable by relying solely on a 50-item multiple-choice listening test without printed material for each video. Each class saw each video once only, with or without captions, in alternating order, and then completed the relevant multiple-choice test. Roughly equal numbers watched captioned or non-captioned videos (so forming treatment and control conditions) by alternating the presence or absence of captions in each of the five classroom groups. Classes that watched captioned versions recognised more words from the passages in the listening test than those that watched un-captioned versions. Effects of captioning were consistent for both passages, a finding which was unexpected, as it had been predicted that the students would score higher on the "whales" passage, with or without captions, than they would on the "civil rights" passage. Markham contends that the findings extend the value of captioned video material beyond improvement of L2 reading and listening comprehension to L2 listening word recognition. Exposure to captions can improve ESL students' listening-based recognition of words that are also present in subsequent listening material without captions.

To test how captioning affected listening ability regardless of semantic information, so as to assess recognition memory in relation to sound alone, Bird & Williams (2002), in a much-quoted study, focused on the implicit and explicit learning of spoken words and non-words. They used auditory word recognition to measure implicit learning, whereas explicit learning was operationalised as the intentional recollection and conscious retention of aural stimuli. A first experiment with sixteen English native-speakers and sixteen advanced-level non-native speakers demonstrated that subjects in the captioned condition were better able to retain the phonological information they had just processed implicitly. When asked to aurally identify words that had been presented in a previous phase, they also showed better explicit recognition memory. A second experiment with twenty-four advanced EFL students found that captioning had a beneficial effect on word recognition and implicit learning of non-word targets paired with two rhyming and two non-rhyming aural cues, especially in the rhyme condition. For example, the subject might first be presented with a non-word cue such as *glemp*, followed by the target *fremp*, and would have to decide as quickly as possible whether the target rhymed with the cue. In both experiments, prior bimodal presentation improved recognition memory for spoken words and non-words compared to single modality presentation. Bird and Williams conclude from their tests that the captions of video materials may have a significant facilitative impact on the long-term implicit and explicit learning of spoken word forms. Perhaps, more importantly, for captioning/subtitling research and practical questions about teaching listening comprehension, the key outcome of their study is, as the authors say, that the bimodal condition created no apparent interference with auditory processing and learning. Any fears that dividing attention between sound and text might interfere with listening comprehension were not borne out in their study.

4.5 Learning and Understanding Using Different Modes of Subtitling and Captioning

What combination of subtitles/captions and sound is most beneficial to learners? A strand of closed caption/subtitle research has followed up work by Holobow, Lambert and Sayegh (1984), which looked at learners' comprehension using a combination of dialogues in learners' L1 with printed scripts, which they referred to as reversed subtitling, and L2 audio input with L2 printed scripts (bimodal input). Studies by Danan

(1992) and D'Ydewalle & Pavakanun (1996) suggested that at different levels of proficiency, different effects of learning and understanding may be found according to the mode of subtitling.

Martine Danan's (1992) study examined how subtitled video programmes could enhance foreign language learning by comparing three viewing methods in a pilot study: French audio only, standard subtitling (English subtitles) and reversed subtitling (English dialogue with French titles). Following the findings, in two subsequent experiments, standard subtitling was replaced with bimodal input (French audio with French captions). The beginning and intermediate French college students selected for the study were tested on vocabulary recall after watching a five-minute video excerpt of *French in Action*. Reversed subtitling proved to be most successful condition, and Danan suggests that its success may be explained by the way translation facilitates foreign language encoding. Retrieval is also enhanced by the multiple memory paths created by the visual and bilingual input, drawing on Paivio's bilingual dual coding model (Paivio, 1986). Dual processing in the bimodal input condition (French audio and French captions) also gave positive results.

Iva Baltova (1999b) also explored whether authentic L2 video with L2 captions or with L2 captions and L1 audio could enhance the understanding and learning of French by low-level school learners who watched a short scientific documentary designed for native-speaker viewers. L2 captions were edited, leaving in important content and "key words" in complete sentences so that approximately one-half of the script was captioned.

Students watched in several conditions:

1. Reversed condition: English audio and French captions first (reversed format), then with French audio and French captions (bimodal/caption format) and finally with French audio and no captions (traditional format).
2. Bimodal condition: the same video in bimodal format twice followed by a traditional format.
3. Traditional format: the same video three times in traditional format.

Students were given a short-answer comprehension post-test to measure learning and retention of the video context, while vocabulary learning and retention were checked with a C-test. The tests were given again two weeks later. Students' learning of the video context under the reversed and bimodal captioned conditions was significantly superior to that in the traditional condition, but there was no significant difference between students' performance under the two captioned conditions. French vocabulary learning in the bimodal group was found to be significantly higher than in the other two groups, which had similar outcomes. After two weeks, retention was higher in the two captioned conditions, with no significant difference between them. Vocabulary retention was significantly higher in the bimodal group than in the reversed group, and there was no significant difference between the reversed and the traditional groups. Students in the first two conditions commented that captions enhanced their ability to notice, comprehend, spell and recall new L2 material. Baltova suggests that under similar circumstances, students who are learning both vocabulary and content in an L2 will benefit more from watching French videos subtitled in French (i.e., captions) than from watching English videos subtitled in French. This might not be an altogether surprising outcome were it not for the fact that Baltova is working with lower-level learners here, though we are given no details of precisely how low their level is in international terms.

Markham, Peter and McCarthy (2001) and Markham and Peter (2003) also take advantage of the multilingual flexibility of DVDs in their studies comparing Spanish captions, English subtitles and no captions with a Spanish-speaking soundtrack on the comprehension of intermediate-level students of Spanish. In both studies, students watched a short clip about the Apollo 13 mission to the moon and viewed in one of the three treatment conditions. After taking a Spanish pre-test in reading, writing, listening, vocabulary and grammar, they viewed the clip only once in their normal class time. In the 2001 study, immediately after viewing, students had 10 minutes to write a summary of their viewing in English followed by a ten-item English multiple choice test with words taken from the DVD. In the second (2003) study, the Spanish language-dependent measure consisted of a twenty-item multiple-choice listening comprehension test. Students who watched the video without captions did significantly worse than the other groups in both tests. The English language subtitle group significantly outperformed the Spanish captions group in both studies. Number of years of previous Spanish study was shown to be an advantage in all groups. Based on their findings, the authors suggest that it might be reasonable with lower-level learners to begin with L1 subtitles on a challenging L2 video, then progress to L2 captions and then finally to no captions.

Stewart and Pertusa (2004) obtained different findings when they compared vocabulary recognition gains of intermediate-level students watching a Spanish film with English subtitles or Spanish captions. Unfortunately, this study lacked rigour, so its findings must be viewed with some caution. Seven intact classes watched two full-length Spanish films, fifty-three students with Spanish captions and forty-two with English subtitles. Pre-testing was rather haphazard and produced varied results. The students viewed the film in three segments, and a short multiple-choice vocabulary test in Spanish was given to all seven classes before and after each segment. Differences in improvement were found to be slight, and no statistics on the significance of differences are given. In general, the classes that watched with Spanish captions tended to do better. The length of the segments shown appeared to have an effect, as the shorter the segment, the greater the improvement, suggesting a short-term memory effect. Students liked the Spanish captions and felt they would benefit in future from watching with these. Those watching with English subtitles were much less positive.

In the study by Bianchi and Ciabattoni (2008), not only the subtitle/caption form but also the interaction of variables such as video type, topic familiarity, complexity of language, language level of viewer and familiarity with subtitling were considered, with very mixed results. English learners at different levels of proficiency at an Italian university watched clips from two films (*Harry Potter and the Philosopher's Stone* and *Fantasia*), either with English captions, Italian subtitles or no captions/subtitles. The eighty-five students were randomly divided into three treatment groups on the basis of their language ability, and they watched the clips on a computer. At the end of each clip, they answered questions on content, vocabulary and use of lexico-grammatical phrases, as used in the film clips. They could replay each clip and review the questions twice. A further delayed post-test was given one week after viewing.

The findings varied according to question type, level, film clip and treatment condition. For example, in content comprehension tasks, the subtitle and caption treatment groups obtained the best results regardless of level and type of film. Captions, rather than no subtitles, proved more useful for beginners and advanced students. This was not the case for intermediate students, where the no-subtitles group outperformed the captions group. Where there was a semantic match between the audio and video input content, comprehension was constantly higher regardless of proficiency level and type of support, and differences between experimental and control groups were less marked. The small number of students in each group and the lack of incremental development in such a short study make the findings of limited value, although this is partly compensated for by the presence of a delayed post-test. With such varied findings, participant feedback on strategies and the use of subtitles would have been particularly valuable.

Another study attempting to capture the interplay of subtitles, captions and other variables, in this case, background knowledge, is reported by Chang (undated) who investigated the effects of schemata/background knowledge and captions/subtitles on second language listening comprehension of two 13-minute-long video films, one with familiar content, *Valentine's Day*, and the other with unfamiliar content, *Business Bargain*.

Chang works within the framework of my 1990 model (see Chap. 3, p. 64), which inserts attention, adaptation and adoption as three essential factors between input and intake. Ninety-seven university students at intermediate level, divided into three treatment groups, watched the programmes in one of three modes: Chinese translation subtitling (Class 1), captions (English sound and captions) (Class 2) and dual subtitling/captioning (Chinese translation + English) (Class 3). Comprehension tests consisted of three sets of ten-item multiple-choice tests to check word recognition, factual understanding and inductive inference. Levels of background knowledge were checked with a background questionnaire prior to viewing.

Class 3, using the dual captions/subtitles, outperformed Class 1, with translation subtitles, and Class 2, with captions. Class 2 outperformed Class 1. This was the case for both films. Dual captioning/subtitling appeared to provide more contextual support than the other two treatments. Chang suggests that the combined subtitling/captioning complement one another, the one bridging difficult concepts and meaning, the other compensating for poor listening and aural word recognition. Students did not feel overwhelmed by the trimodal input. Only a weak relationship between the subjects' background knowledge scores and their listening comprehension tests was found. In contrast to what both Markham (2001) and Herron, Corrie, Cole, and Henderson (2002) had found, schemata did not appear to demonstrate a strong facilitating effect on student understanding, though, in their questionnaires, students indicated that they had used their background knowledge more when watching the familiar film than when watching the unfamiliar film.

The very complexity of this issue has been reinforced recently through the findings of a study in Norway by Mila Vulchanova, Lisa Aurstad, Ingrid Kvitnes and Hendrik Eshuis (2015), which looked at the effect of captions and subtitles using authentic material on English comprehension and acquisition in a group of 114 Norwegian High School students aged 16 and 17 years old. The findings of the study indicated that both English captions and Norwegian subtitles had a significant facilitative effect on comprehension of a single episode (approximately 20 minutes) of an American animated cartoon series, *Family Guy*, watched in one of three conditions, with captions, with subtitles and without either. The participants completed baseline language tests and a background questionnaire that asked them to assess their skills and provide information on the frequency of watching films in English, watching *Family Guy* and playing computer games in English. They also took a comprehension test immediately after viewing the episode of *Family Guy* and delayed word definition (choosing between four definitions) and word recall (identifying whether a word had been in the episode) tests four weeks later. Both the 16- and the 17-year-old participants who watched with captions or subtitles performed significantly better than the group that watched without either on the comprehension test. For the 17-year olds, the language of the subtitles did not appear to matter, but for the 16-year olds, perhaps surprisingly, the English captions were more facilitative than the Norwegian subtitles. While higher grammar competence and vocabulary knowledge predicted performance in the comprehension task, the most significant predictor was the amount of time participants spent playing computer games in English. In addition, to their surprise, neither captions nor subtitles were predictive of performance on the word definition or word recall tasks. There appeared, from their results, to be no long-term effects of viewing with or without captions or subtitles. Is this surprising? As they say, four weeks is a long time, and the episode was only watched once. While the participants could well have paid attention to the captions and subtitles during the viewing of the episode, as I have suggested earlier in reviewing my own studies in 1988 and 1990, paying attention to the words does not in any way guarantee retention, as long-term non-native speaker residents of the UK who have watched programmes with captions for many years will confirm.

One of the best designed studies of subtitle or caption use was conducted by Koolstra and Beentjes (1999), who investigated whether children in two primary school grades in The Netherlands would learn English words through watching a television programme with an English soundtrack and Dutch subtitles. A total of 246 Dutch children in Grades 4 and 6 (aged 9+ and 11+ years) watched a 15-minute documentary, having been assigned to one of three experimental conditions: (a) programme about grizzly bears with an English soundtrack with Dutch subtitles, (b) the same programme with an English soundtrack but without subtitles and (c) a Dutch language television programme about prairie dogs (a control condition to establish a baseline of English vocabulary knowledge).

Vocabulary scores for those watching with subtitles were higher than for those watching without subtitles, and scores in the latter group were higher than those in the control group. Grade 6 children performed better than those in Grade 4. More words were recognised after watching the subtitled documentary than the non-subtitled version, and, again, children of Grade 6 outperformed those of Grade 4. Children with a high frequency of watching subtitled programmes at home had significantly higher English vocabulary scores than those with a low frequency and medium frequency of watching subtitled programmes. The findings confirm the many anecdotal accounts that children can acquire elements of a foreign language through watching subtitled television programmes. The children were able to switch easily from one mode to another, and word recognition was better in the subtitled condition, suggesting that word recognition on the basis of two-channel processing (reading and listening) may be easier than through one channel (listening).

Koolstra and Beentjes suggest that the absence of any interaction effect between condition and age is explained by the fact that both age groups were above the threshold of English competence at which subtitled television constituted comprehensible input through which new vocabulary could be acquired. The Dutch Grade 4 children appeared to have picked up English knowledge before they began to study English formally in school, perhaps through regular watching of subtitled English TV programmes at home. The authors rightly caution that the experimental conditions may have encouraged the children to pay more attention to the language of the programmes than they might otherwise have done. In contrast, the authors argue, since children may select programmes at home themselves, they may pay even more attention. Most tellingly, the authors confirm Vanderplank's (1988a, 1990) contention that the effect of watching captioned television programmes regularly over long periods may be strong and cumulative.

4.6 The "Bombshell" of the Mitterer and McQueen (2009) Study

In contrast to some of the positive findings of the aforementioned studies and also contrary to the experiences of many independent learners (including myself), it could be said that arguments about the relative benefits of subtitles and captions have now been put to rest with the findings of Holger Mitterer and James McQueen ground-breaking research (2009). It is such a key article in captions research that I am reporting it in detail. They asked whether watching video programmes without captions or subtitles and with L1 subtitles or L2 captions can help or hinder the adaptation (i.e., "tuning in") to an unfamiliar regional accent in the foreign language. Their key point, as far as captions are concerned, is that lexically-guided retuning of speech-sound categories benefits comprehension. Lexical knowledge helps listeners adapt to the unusual speech of a speaker in, for example, a television programme, thus allowing them to understand that speaker better. Native speakers are able to match what other native speakers say against their lexical knowledge all the time (which we can test by asking native speakers to shadow speech), even if, at times, they may not fully understand the content.

In their study, they asked two questions. Firstly, can watching videos help listeners to adapt to an unfamiliar foreign accent? Secondly, can captions or subtitles influence this process? Their results showed that this kind of adaptation is possible, even after watching a relatively small amount of video material (2 × 25-minute clips), and that subtitles that match the foreign spoken language help adaptation, whereas subtitles in the listener's native language hinder adaptation.

If lexically-guided retuning operates in second-language listening and is open to any influence from subtitles, they suggest, then the influence should depend on the language of the subtitles. English subtitles should give viewers most of the words in the speech stream (though not all, as subtitles are not usually literal transcriptions). Like many researchers before them, they posit that the printed English words can provide an additional source of information about the words being spoken, and hence about the sounds being heard; therefore, they ought to reinforce lexically-guided learning. In contrast, they suggest, native Dutch subtitles may be easier for the observers to read, but provide misleading information about the phonological forms being spoken. In this respect, they say, Dutch subtitles would interfere with perceptual learning.

Six groups of Dutch native speakers, who were unfamiliar with regional accents, 121 subjects in total, watched a 25-minute video, either the one with strong Scottish accents (a clip from the film *Trainspotting*) or the one with strong Australian accents (the sitcom *Kath and Kim*). Each group watched a different version, one with English captions, one with Dutch captions, or one with no captions/subtitles. For *Trainspotting*, the captions or subtitles available on DVD were used. For *Kath and Kim*, the available captions were used but Dutch subtitles had to be specially made.

They were then required to repeat back 160 audio excerpts. These excerpts were phrases from the videos that were bounded by pauses. Half of these came from the material viewed (old items), and the other half were completely new items, taken either from unused parts of *Trainspotting* or from another *Kath and Kim* episode. Every participant had to repeat back all 160 utterances, so that all participants were exposed to Australian accents as a no-exposure control for the Scottish participants, and vice versa. Participants heard either the Scottish and then the Australian excerpts, or the reverse. Old and new items were randomly mixed within these accent blocks.

Each excerpt was presented twice, and participants were instructed to respond to the first presentation of the excerpt as fast as possible, but only if they were certain about what they heard. After the second presentation, they were encouraged to repeat back any words they might have heard. They were told there was no need for them to imitate the accent of the speaker.

The authors found that after only this short exposure, participants who watched with English captions had quickly adapted their ears to regional accents and, strikingly, even new words were spoken better with captions. However, while native-language subtitles helped the recognition of previously heard words, they actually harmed recognition of new words. In contrast, the captions improved repetition of previously heard and new words, the latter finding, they suggest, demonstrating lexically-guided retuning of perception. This was a particularly gratifying finding for me, as in my 1988 article, I had suggested that in helping learner-viewers to "tune in," there were parallels to be drawn with the rapid adaptation of British filmgoers in the 1930s to American films and unfamiliar American accents.

It is worth quoting at length from their discussion section:

The effects (of watching with captions) on the new items, however, are the key results. The adaptation effect shows that listeners were able to retune their perceptual categories to characteristics of the exposure speakers, leading to long-term changes in speech perception. The enhancement of this adaptation by English subtitles suggests in turn that the retuning benefited from listeners knowing what words they were hearing. This indicates that the listeners were using lexical knowledge to retune phonetic perception. Although it is possible that some of the adaptation and enhancement effects reflect word-specific learning (many of the words in the new items had been heard and seen before, in other exposure phrases), the lack of an effect of exposure-test repetition in the correlational analyses is inconsistent with the hypothesis that the effect of the English subtitles is due to word-specific learning. Instead, it appears that the enhancement caused by the English subtitles reflects, at least in part, retuning of pre-lexical perceptual categories. Retuning at the pre-lexical level benefits the recognition both of words that have been heard before and of completely novel words containing the retuned sounds (2009, retrieved at http://journals.plos.org/plosone/article?id=10.1371/journal.pone.0007785 on 09/09.2015).

For the dramatic finding that while the Dutch subtitles enhanced performance on old items, they led to worse performance on new materials, the authors suggest that the semantic crutch provided by the Dutch subtitles did not allow participants to retune their phonetic categories so as to improve their understanding of new utterances from the same speaker. In other words, "the orthographic information in subtitles can influence learning in speech perception either in a facilitatory manner (as when the English subtitles indicated which words, and hence phonemes, were being spoken) or in an inhibitory manner (as when the Dutch subtitles specified the wrong phonological information)."

As Mitterer and McQueen say, their research design is naturalistic so their findings that lexically-guided retuning of perceptual categories and learning can occur with real speech has significant implications in our view of how native listeners adapt not only to foreign-accepted speech but also to second language listening. In theoretical terms, they suggest, the same perceptual-learning mechanism appears to apply in first and second language processing, just as there are learning effects across colour categories and letters.

In short, both native and foreign listeners can use their knowledge about how words normally sound to adjust the way they perceive speech that is spoken in an unfamiliar way. For foreign listeners, captions help this process. If an English word is spoken with an unfamiliar accent, English captions usually tell the perceiver what that word is, and hence what its sounds are. In the study, this made it easier for the students to tune in to the Scottish accent. In contrast, the Dutch subtitles did not provide this function, and, because they told the viewer what the characters were saying in Dutch, may have drawn the students' attention away from the unfamiliar speech.

I have one major reservation about the findings and claims made by this research. At several points, the authors state that listeners are able to retune their perceptual categories to those of the characteristics of the speaker. This suggests that listeners are somehow active and consciously do this retuning. Yet, anyone who has been in a similar situation of needing to adapt to unfamiliar speech will know that such adaptation usually happens at a psychomotor level and is largely subconscious. We do not "retune our perceptual categories" in the way we actively re-tune radio frequencies. Such passive retuning seems to happen (or not) more or less rapidly, depending on a number of variables such as how different the speech is from what we are used to, how "tuned-in" we are and our need or desire to fully comprehend. For example, a participant in the EURECAP Project (see Chap. 7) described how, while watching a series of short films in Spanish-Argentinian accent, it took him just about the length of a film to tune in to the unfamiliar accent of a speaker. Unfortunately, by then, it was the end of the film, and when the following one started, he had to tune in to yet another unfamiliar Argentinian accent.

One way of understanding the retuning process is to consider that it is a development of a psychomotor skill. During the last thirty years or so, we seem to have put aside the discussion of psychomotor skills (perhaps because they usually involve intensive practice, which might be regarded as drilling, as well as knowledge on the part of the teacher, which may no longer be available, such as tongue placement in pronunciation). A useful description of the psychomotor domain is given by Elizabeth Simpson (1966). She identifies the objectives of psychomotor development as being linked to physical functions and reflex activities. Our skill in a specific area progresses from a guided response (consciousness of what we are or are not doing correctly) to a reflex or habitual response. So, in music, for example, we need to practice the movement of our fingers intensively to the point that we can do this without conscious thought about finger placement. In speaking, an example would be placing the tongue correctly to make dental sounds rather than alveolar ones. It may be wholly unnatural for me as an English native speaker to pronounce a /t/ dentally as I should do in pronouncing a Finnish or Spanish word with a /t/, but with intensive practice, it should "come naturally." Similarly in perception, we can be trained or train ourselves to hear sounds that may not be perceptually different to our ears initially, as they do not occur in our first language, such as singleton and geminate consonants, but again, with practice, we can retune our hearing to perceive these consonants in a language such as Finnish or Italian in which this difference is phonemically important. I should stress that the key point of such training or subconscious psychomotor development is not only to be skilled in pronunciation or perception in a foreign language (and this, of course, is what comes out of the Mitterer and McQueen study) but also to support the development of cognitive and affective objectives in learning a foreign language, which I shall discuss in detail in Chap. 6 and again in Chap. 8. In other words, retuning our perception of foreign sounds and rhythmic patterns is one of the essential changes in our listening behaviour if we are to fully understand a film or programme in a foreign language, and captioned viewing is an effective way of developing this retuning.

As I have stated at several points, researchers should use standard captions as produced for deaf and hard-of-hearing people in their research, and again this is what makes this study so remarkable, since their results are generalisable and have practical implications. As the greatest benefit from this kind of exposure comes from the use of captions, the authors suggest, with the advent of digital television broadcasting and multiple language DVDs, it is time broadcasters and producers exploited current technical possibilities and used multiple audio channels and multiple types of subtitles/captions.

While this is certainly an immensely valuable piece of research, the findings have already been disseminated in a way that, perhaps, exaggerates the claims and even goes counter to the experiences of the many who have used translation subtitles successfully to support their foreign language learning. For example, the press release on the website of the Max-Planck-Gessellschaft for November 2009, tells us:

> Do you speak English as a second language well, but still have trouble understanding movies with unfamiliar accents, such as Brad Pitt's southern accent in Quentin Tarantino's *Inglorious Bastards*? In a new study, published in PLoS ONE on November 11, 2009, Holger Mitterer (Max Planck Institute for Psycholinguistics) and James McQueen (MPI and Radboud

University Nijmegen) show how you can improve your second-language listening ability by watching the movie with subtitles. That is, if these subtitles are in the film's language! Subtitles in one's native language, the default in some European countries, are harmful to learning to understand foreign speech.

While I myself in the past might have wished to claim, without reservation, that learners can improve their second language listening ability by watching films with captions, it is quite shocking that a responsible institution such as this one would choose to use the word "harmful," as it is certain to be picked up and recirculated, soon forming part of the mythology of learning language from television and films. Not everyone has easy access to captioned programmes and DVDs (as Chap. 7 on the EURECAP Project will confirm), and there is a wealth of anecdotal evidence to support the view that having translation subtitles in the L1 can help learners who seriously want to gain from watching programmes and films in the foreign language (see Vanderplank, 2010).

Nonetheless, this research has recently found a degree of corroboration from the findings of the study by Vulchanova, Aurstad, Kvitnes, and Eshuis (2015) (reported on p. 93). While they found that both English captions and Norwegian subtitles had a facilitative effect on the comprehension of a single episode of *Family Guy*, the data from the background questionnaire which asked, among other things, the daily practice of watching English films with either Norwegian subtitles or English captions, indicated that watching with Norwegian subtitles had a negative impact on comprehension and lexical skills such as assessing word definition. Indirectly, at least, their findings confirm the importance of captions in the target language compared to having no captions or subtitles.

Rather than treating L1 subtitles as "harmful," it would be better to characterise them as second best compared to L2 captions, as potentially useful where L2 captions are not available (as is the case throughout much of the world) and where learners are below the threshold of reading speed and knowledge. I have no intention of suggesting to learners who ask my opinion that they should avoid watching foreign language films with English subtitles on the grounds that this might be harmful to them.

4.7 Captions and Incidental Vocabulary Language Learning from Television

In addition to comprehension, the meta-analysis confirmed that captions can help with word recognition and vocabulary building. A number of the studies described earlier in the text used vocabulary recall or recognition instruments to measure gains from watching with or without captions or subtitles (Danan, 1992; Baltova, 1999a, 1999b, Markham,1999), but there are several studies that have focused explicitly on vocabulary acquisition. An early and much cited study was reported by Susan Neuman and Patricia Koskinen (1992), who conducted a nine-week experiment with 129 Grades 7 and 8 ESL students (mostly at an advanced level) watching nine 5- to 8-minute-long segments of an American children-orientated science production. The researchers found that captioning was more beneficial to vocabulary recognition and acquisition than traditional television watching, or reading while listening. A series of increasingly complex tests demonstrated the beneficial effects of captions. These tests ranged from weekly word-recognition exercises, which entailed distinguishing written target words from non-word distractors, to sentence-anomaly exercises testing word comprehension in context, and, on the most difficult level, meaning identification of words presented in isolation (Neuman & Koskinen, 1992:101).

Tetyana Sydorenko (2010) also investigated which modality, video with captions but without audio, video with audio and captions or video with audio but without captions, would have the largest impact on overall vocabulary gains, with twenty-six student learners of Russian at an American university, divided into three roughly equal groups. All groups watched three video clips, each 2–3 minutes long, from a popular Russian comedy series for native Russian speakers. The clips contained target words that were highly unlikely to be known, as they were not part of the syllabus and were not in the students' textbook, but which could, it was considered, be understood from the visual support offered in the video clip.

Groups watching with captions scored higher on written than on aural recognition of word forms, while the reverse (perhaps not surprisingly) applied to the video + audio group. The video + audio + captions group learnt more word meanings than the video + audio group. The students also completed questionnaires on their strategies following the viewings. Sydorenko found that learners paid most attention to captions, followed by video and audio, and acquired most words by associating them with visual images.

In feedback, which was a far cry from my own early research (1988a, 1990) in which students reported so positively on watching with captions, Sydorenko's students reported significant difficulties with watching the videos, such as the speed of the dialogues, lack of time to read all the caption text and the burden of reading captions while watching the videos at the same time. One learner, for example, reported reading captions and scanning the images, but having no time to listen to audio.

Many participants mentioned that they could not work out the meanings of new words or that there was too much new vocabulary. Perhaps most tellingly, bearing in mind that these were relatively short clips of only 2–3 minutes, the learners also mentioned not remembering which specific words were used in the videos, especially their aural forms, and some reported that they could guess the meanings of the words while watching the videos, but forgot the actual words by the time they had to take a vocabulary test. It is perhaps, quite unrealistic to expect learners to retain much, if any, vocabulary given the constant, dynamic flow of speech. Perhaps all we can hope for is that learners can follow and understand as they are watching unless they have control over their viewing.

Sydorenko's study is useful in confirming, yet again, the value of captions for making popular programmes more accessible to learners. However, the limitations of the study, especially in terms of the selection and grading of the clips, underline again the need, firstly, to offer more authentic settings for research with captions in which learners can have a measure of control over their viewing as they might in informal contexts for viewing popular programmes, and secondly, the need for teachers to pay close attention to the selection of programmes for both language and content so as not to alienate learners.

Longer and more elaborate studies of incidental vocabulary acquisition have been conducted by Bravo (2008, 2010), Rodgers (2013) and Frumuselu, De Maeyerb, Doncheb, and María del Mar Gutiérrez Colon

Plana (2015). These studies are described in detail in the next chapter, which deals with issues not covered by the meta-analysis.

4.8 Making the Case

I hope that this chapter has served to illustrate how research into captioned viewing and language learning is still a live and a dynamic field, justifying my claim that it deserves a research and practice space which is distinct from both research and practice involving translation subtitles and also language teaching using TV and video. In the next chapter, I further develop the case for the research space, reviewing studies in areas such as keyword captioning, speech segmentation, literacy development and the thorny issue of caption dependency.

5

The State of the Art II: Selected Research on Other Issues in Watching Captioned TV, Films and Video

Montero Perez et al.'s review of research on captioned viewing, published in 2013, identified 150 relevant studies. At the time of writing this book, the pace of research has been quickening, and we appear to be generating ever more research, most of it replicating what we already know but in different contexts; there have been approximately 130 published studies or unpublished dissertations on captioned viewing and language learning since the cut-off time of my state-of-the-art review in 2009. As going back to original sources is really an obligation on all serious researchers, we are very fortunate in having an up-to-date database of research on captions and second/foreign language acquisition maintained by Günter Burger at http://www.fremdsprache-und-spielfilm.de/Captions.htm

In this chapter, I continue reviewing some key areas of research into captions and language learning and highlight the insights that have been gained from this work. I end by considering the different theories and notions put forward for how captions work, to enhance comprehension without overwhelming learner-viewers' senses.

5.1 Keyword Captioning

The interesting thing about the published research by Montero Perez et al. (2013), following the meta-analysis, is that instead of going for longitudinal studies testing the effects of captioned broadcasts over a long period, they go for further tests on the value of the reduced form of captions known as "keyword" captions. It is rather ironic that they should be testing these so extensively and thoroughly when, firstly, using keyword captions on regular programmes and films would necessitate them being introduced specially by teachers or other material developers, therefore adding time-consuming work to an otherwise free add-on, and, secondly, reduced-form captions were rejected (as being patronising, among other weaknesses), by the deaf community back in the 1970s when they were tried out. The authors justify the use of variations in captioning in terms of their interest in the effect of the salience of keywords or highlighted keywords and having more or less textual density in captions. Their research, which I report later in the chapter, published in several highly respected journals, also contributes to aspects of our understanding of captions in language learning, and their findings will almost certainly serve to keep alive the debate about the value of keyword captions.

Research on keyword captioning has produced studies with mixed results. The motive usually given for using keywords in captions rather than verbatim or near-verbatim captions is to lower the (cognitive) load on learners, especially lower-level learners and those with slower reading speeds, without reducing greatly the comprehension of what is being viewed.

5.1.1 Guillory (1998)

A much-cited study on the value of keyword captions was reported by Helen Gant Guillory (1998), who compared full verbatim captions, keyword captions and no captions to try and ascertain the optimum amount of French text in captions. In her video clips, taken from a French video accompanying a textbook, there were three levels of captioning: full verbatim, partial (approximately 14 % of the script established by a preliminary study) and no captions. In addition to the usual question about whether captioning enhanced comprehension, another was regarding evaluating keyword captioning.

Two video clips for all input conditions—full text captions, keyword captions and no captions—were chosen from the videotape accompanying the textbook, *Parallèles*, and were shown to 202 first-year French students at the University of Texas, Austin, who were randomly distributed among the three conditions and watched the clips in a computer laboratory. Students had no control on the pace of viewing and watched in linear fashion. Immediately after the treatment, they completed a short-answer comprehension test and a questionnaire.

The results showed that the keyword captions group outperformed the no-text group, and that the full text captions group outperformed the keyword captions group on the comprehension tests, though there was no significant difference between the means of the full text captions group and the keyword captions group. Guillory was interested in analysing differences in scores on recall and inferencing questions and also investigating the effect of cognates in understanding the clips in view of the large number of questions that were unanswered, about half for the full and keyword captions groups, suggesting that a full pilot study should have been held first to establish an appropriate level. The students were better at inferencing questions than recall, which might suggest some guessing strategies were at work, though Guillory dismisses this idea. Only the keyword captions group appeared to benefit from cognates, especially those that had been highlighted in text. In Guillory's terms, the absence of a significant difference between the keyword and full caption groups indicated that keyword captions could be just as effective as full text captions for understanding the content of a video; so, as she says, "Learners no longer need to be subjected to volumes of text to read." This, perhaps, misses the point about the value of captions in helping learners who use them to acquire linguistic knowledge.

The feedback from questionnaires reinforced the fact that the clips were just too difficult for the students: the keyword group was positive about the keywords but the full captions group felt, on the whole, that while they were useful, the speech and text went too fast. As she herself says: "The difficulties posed by authentic video material to beginning second language learners cannot be overemphasized." (p. 103).

This research has been frequently cited as supporting the use of keyword captions, especially with lower-level learners, but, in fact, its main finding was that video clips, whether captioned or not, need to be carefully selected and graded by the teacher before being used, especially in testing situations.

5.1.2 Montero Perez et al.'s Research into Keyword Captioning

Montero Perez and colleagues published a series of articles on the value of keyword captions, which may prove to be the "last word" on it. In the first of these (though appearing second in publication order), Montero Perez, Peters, Clarebout, and Desmet (2014) examine how three captioning types can assist L2 learners in the incidental acquisition of target vocabulary words and in the comprehension of L2 video. One hundred and thirty-three Flemish undergraduate students watched three French video clips twice. These were short clips of news broadcasts including interviews on three topics: the production and export strategy of a French brewery (first clip), the marketing strategy (second clip) and history of the Lego factory (third clip). The clips were between 2.5 minutes and 4.5 minutes long. The control group (n = 32) watched the clips without captioning, the second group (n = 30) watched fully captioned clips, the third group (n = 34) watched keyword captioned clips and the fourth group (n = 37) watched fully captioned clips with highlighted keywords. Before the learning session, participants completed a vocabulary size test that helped in selecting seventeen target words, which were unfamiliar to the participants and which appeared as keywords alongside other keywords (which totalled 295 words out of 1724 words in all three videos).

Participants completed three comprehension tests, four vocabulary tests measuring (1) form recognition (whether they could recognise the target words), (2) meaning recognition (a Dutch multiple-choice translation test on the seventeen target words), (3) meaning recall (modelled on the vocabulary) and (4) clip association (checking which clip they thought a target word appeared in) and a final questionnaire. Participants were not allowed to take notes, so that the incidental aspect of vocabulary learning was not undermined. Each clip was played twice and was followed by the relevant comprehension questions. The vocabulary tests were given after all three clips had been seen.

Contrary to their hypothesis that those watching captioned videos would outperform the no-captions group on comprehension tests, there were no significant differences between groups. Salience does not seem to have helped the keyword and highlighted keyword groups outperform the no-captions and full captions groups. The authors offer a range of explanations for this, such as the concrete, factual nature of the information and the lack of focus on target words in the comprehension question. Perhaps, the overall content was not that challenging for these participants, with captions falling into the "backup" category rather than "essential," as identified by Pujolà (2002).

For the vocabulary tests, the captioned groups outperformed the no-captions group, and they suggest that as far as form recognition is concerned, the results are consistent with my 1990 model in which the role of captions is considered crucial to taking out words from captioned input. Again, it was the availability of captions, rather than salience, which seemed to have an overall positive effect on these tests.

For meaning recognition of the target words, the keyword captioning and full captioning with highlighted keywords groups outperformed the control group but not the full captioning group. No differences were found on meaning recall between the groups, and all achieved low scores, perhaps, unsurprisingly, as the simple presence of a word in captions is no guarantee that its meaning will be understood in a fleeting news interview context. Participants' vocabulary size correlated significantly with their comprehension and vocabulary test scores. The results of the questionnaire indicated that participants in the two groups with full captions found them more useful than the keyword group, though all caption groups were positive about the usefulness of captions for recognising and learning new words. I am not altogether surprised that the keyword group provided the highest mean score for the captions being distracting.

Although published online before the *Language Learning and Technology* article, the research reported in *ReCALL*, "Is less more? Effectiveness and perceived usefulness of keyword and full captioned video for L2 listening comprehension," was originally intended as a follow-up to this article and was built on the findings of the previous study. In this study, Montero Perez, Peters, and Desmet (2014) investigated the effect of two types of captioned video on listening comprehension and learners' perception of the usefulness of captions while watching a foreign language video. A total of 226 university-level students from a Flemish university who were taking an intermediate-level French course were randomly assigned to one of the three conditions; they were made to watch three short French news and interview clips. Of these, seventy students in a control group watched the clips without captions, eighty-one students in the second group watched with fully captioned clips and seventy-five in the third group watched with keyword captioned clips. The clips used appear to have been the same ones used in the aforementioned study, which was rated at being about B1(+) level in Common European Framework of Reference (CEFR) terms. Full verbatim captions (2704 words) were specially prepared along with keyword captions (377 or 14 %) for each clip.

After each clip, all participants took a listening comprehension test. To answer detailed questions, participants were given access to the corresponding audio clip, which they could listen to once while they wrote down their answer. The full captions group outperformed both the no-captions and the keyword captions groups on the global comprehension questions, whereas there was no difference between scores of the keyword captions and the no-captions groups. They found no differences between the three conditions for the detailed comprehension questions (with the audio support), though there was a large effect for vocabulary size, suggesting that participants had to rely on their stock of vocabulary knowledge, as there was no text or visual support while listening to the audio only.

The authors take time to discuss why the keyword captions group did not (as they expected) outperform the other groups, since, in their terms and in terms of earlier reported research by Garza (1991) and Winke, Gass, and Sydorenko (2010), having only keywords should have provided aural cues while also reducing their decoding load, giving them more time to allocate attention to aspects such as meaning-making processes. As they suggest, any link between decreased decoding effort and better interpretation is far from clear in this type of context. It could also be, as in the Montero Perez, Peters, Clarebout and Desmet study (2014) study, that while the news clips were not that difficult to follow (so the captions were not strictly essential for any group), the full captions provided that group with the words they needed to better grasp both the language and content of the clips.

Participants also completed a questionnaire and survey questions about their perception of captions and their usefulness: learners' perceived need for full captions was strong, and they thought they were useful for both speech decoding and meaning-making processes. Several of them mentioned that they found the bimodal input was easier to understand than video only. Issues of perceptual processing such as speech segmentation (cf. Charles & Trenkic, 2015, and Chap. 5, Sect. 5.3 in this book), managing the fast speech rate and disambiguating unclear pronunciation were also mentioned frequently, and participants also reported that they found watching with captions was more relaxing than without—something I mentioned back in 1988 when my students reported a similar reduction in anxiety. Surprising for the authors (though not for me!) was that keyword captions were considered highly distracting, rather than helpful, and hampered listening activity. More particularly, as the authors report, the very salience and irregular appearance of the keywords hindered the participants from following the rest of the video. They conclude by suggesting that full, rather than keyword, captioning should be considered when proposing video-based listening comprehension activities to language learners, and that future research should focus on full-length programmes and films rather than short clips.

These very well-conducted studies should put to rest the question of whether keyword captions are more useful than full captions. For me, they have always been a distraction in several ways (time-consuming to prepare, as well as distracting rather than supportive for learner-viewers) and have diverted research effort away from the more important questions. If this is the case, then Montero Perez and colleagues will have performed a valuable service to both the research and the teaching communities.

In a third study, focussing on vocabulary learning, Montero Perez, Peters and Desmet (2015) investigated whether the following factors would enhance vocabulary learning: (1) full or keyword captions and

(2) announcing or not announcing to students a vocabulary test that would be followed. They also wanted to assess how these enhancements affect learners' allocation of attention to the target vocabulary items in the captions through using eye-tracking technology to capture fixations. Announcing the test or not was used as an operational device to differentiate between incidental and intentional vocabulary learning. The presence of the two independent variables (full captions/keyword captions, test announcement/no test announcement) produced four experimental groups.

A total of fifty-one Dutch-speaking undergraduate students taking an intermediate-level French course took part in the study. Owing to problems with sample quality, only thirty-four participants could be analysed for eye-tracking.

The participants watched two clips in French from a Swiss and Belgian current affairs programme, one about a Lego factory, the other about a brewery, which appear to have been the same or similar to those in the earlier studies. Both clips had a single narrator who described the scenes and included short interviews in which the interviewee was shown.

The researchers added full captions and keyword captions to the clips, and accompanied these with a comprehension task, including short open-ended questions and multiple-choice questions in Dutch. Participants were randomly assigned to one of the four conditions and were tested individually. All students were informed of the comprehension task; only the intentional groups were also informed of the vocabulary test that would follow. After the two clips were viewed once, the eye-movement recording was stopped, and participants were given the short comprehension task followed by the vocabulary post-tests and the questionnaire. They also completed a questionnaire on their linguistic background at the end of the session.

As in the earlier (2014) study, the researchers used three vocabulary tests, which measured, respectively, form recognition, clip association and meaning recall of eighteen target words (which had previously been selected as being unfamiliar to participants on the basis of the earlier vocabulary size test), nine keywords that were not target words and six distractors. The clip association test was designed to control for guessing by asking learners to indicate whether they could associate the words that they thought had appeared in the clips with the corresponding clip (Brewery or Lego). The form recognition and clip association tests were combined with a meaning recall test, which checked whether learners could translate the target words into their L1. The fourth test measured meaning recognition of the eighteen target words and asked learners to choose the translation of each target word from four Dutch translation options.

For the vocabulary tests, they found a significant main effect for the type of captions and for test announcement and a significant main effect of test announcement, but no significant interaction effect for test announcement and caption type. So, while announcing or not announcing the post-viewing test appeared to make a difference on test scores, as the test announcement groups did a little better than those who had no prior announcement (though both conditions achieved low scores), the type of captioning did not.

For learning the eighteen target words, type of captioning did make a significant difference to the form recognition test but not the clip association or the meaning recall tests. As the authors suggest, it may be that visual salience aided form recognition of the eighteen target words but did not necessarily lead to more elaborate target word processing. For the other tests, the results were very much in line with their other studies, though it is worth bearing in mind that the participants viewed clips only once in this study owing to the demands of eye-tracking, so the low test scores are not really surprising given that it is hard to learn a word on a single occurrence.

Perhaps more interestingly, again the results of the ANCOVA analyses on meaning recall supported the view that vocabulary size is important for recall. The larger the size of a learner's vocabulary, the more likely a learner is to make successful word inferences (Nation, 2001).

The idea behind the eye-tracking part of the study was to assess whether the type of captioning and/or test announcement would lead to increased focal attention on the target words. Three eye-tracking measures were used: early (gaze duration), late (second pass reading time) and total fixation duration. Not surprisingly, given that participants did not have to divide their attention across a longer span of words, it was found that the keyword captions group spent longer looking at the target words than the full captions group. For the second pass, the test announcement groups spent significantly longer looking at the target word area than the no announcement groups and the keyword group test announcement group spent longer on the second pass than the full captions group, suggesting that visual salience played a role in stimulating them to fixate longer.

The analysis of total fixation duration also indicated that the test announcement groups attended to the target words longer than the no announcement groups, though the keyword captions group again differed significantly from the captions groups on total duration of fixation on target words. These are important findings as they suggest that captioned viewing can be enhanced and learners' attention heightened by devices such as announcing tests or tasks beforehand (as I suggested in my 1990 article) and by increasing the visual salience of keywords. Since doing this with prepared captions may be difficult and certainly time-consuming, it might be worthwhile simply preparing a glossary of keywords and phrases with translations beforehand.

In terms of my earlier research, the analysis of the data exploring the relationship between eye-fixation and vocabulary learning confirms much of what I had observed over long periods of student viewing and reported in my 1990 article. Firstly, while "gaze duration" was insufficient to account for any significant learning gains, those in the test announcements groups spent longer on second pass and did better on the test of form recognition. The authors interpret this as indicating that the test announcement groups demonstrated a clear intention to commit a word to memory, and this resulted in greater learning gains. This finding underlines the importance of the moment-by-moment tracking, as different processing stages may have differential effects on learning.

Finally, only the eye movements of the full captions groups were found to predict learning. Why wasn't this the case for the keyword caption groups? They suggest it may be because longer fixation does not necessarily lead to elaborate processing. The eye is drawn to a word, and one may fixate on it rather than processing it deeply or giving it conscious attention.

The last intervention in the series (Montero Perez, 2013) has a very interesting addition compared to that by Montero Perez, Peters and

Desmet (2014) and Montero Perez, Peters, Clarebout and Desmet (2014), namely, that glossed keyword captions were added as a variable to try and find out whether access to meaning enhances the acquisition of form-meaning connections. The test announcement variable was still present, along with the tests and procedures used in the earlier studies. Glossed keyword captions in this case were keyword captions with access to meaning: each keyword was linked to its corresponding L1 context-bound translation. Participants tapped the space bar to access the gloss. This action paused the video and simultaneously showed the translation of the keyword in a box centred on the screen. Tapping the bar again restarted the video.

A total of 227 undergraduate, Dutch-speaking students (122 males, 105 females) taking a compulsory course in legal or economic French at a university in Belgium participated in the study. They were considered intermediate to high intermediate learners of French, based on their scores on a self-designed vocabulary size test.

Participants were randomly assigned in whole-class groups to one of eight conditions:

- Full captions and incidental vocabulary learning (i.e., no vocab test announcement)
- Keyword captions and incidental
- Glossed keyword captions and incidental
- No captions and incidental
- Full captions and intentional (i.e., vocab test announcement)
- Keyword captions and intentional
- Glossed keyword captions and intentional
- No captioning and intentional

The material for the video clips and tests appears to have been the same as in previous studies or very similar. Those belonging to the glossed keyword captions groups had their look-up strategies tracked and logged (though they were not informed of this). As they watched the clips, the number of activated glossed keywords (i.e., the total number of look-ups), the unique target word look-ups and, lastly, the frequency of target word look-ups (i.e., the sum of learners' subsequent clicks on the target words during both viewings) were logged, in order to find out how many of the eighteen target words had been looked up.

The findings of the vocabulary tests showed that on most measures, the glossed captions groups outperformed the other groups, with the largest effect for the meaning recall test. For the glossed captions groups, test announcement did not significantly affect look-up behaviour, though look-up behaviour was significantly linked to vocabulary size—the larger the participants' vocabulary size, the fewer their look-ups.

As in the earlier studies (apart from the eye-tracking study), participants watched the clips twice. As one might have expected, target words were looked up more in the first viewing than in the second viewing. Test announcement, unique target word look-up and vocabulary size were all predictors of success on both the meaning recall and word recognitions tests for glossed captions groups.

Comparing the glossed captions group with the other groups, the glossed captions group was also most successful on the meaning recall test, recalling the meaning of approximately seven target words, whereas the other groups averaged two or three. They also looked up a lot of words—an average of over fourteen of the eighteen target words. Are these findings surprising? Certainly, the difference is so convincing that glossed captions seems like an excellent technique for enhancing the power of captions. It is all very well to have the captions, but being able to instantly see the translation of an unknown word is obviously a great advantage and one that will be discussed further in the EURECAP chapter (Chapter 7). Of course, instant translation of words has existed some time in apps for e-books and will probably come in time for captions, too, though the time and cost of producing such devices accurately will certainly be an inhibiting factor.

Finally, there is the question of whether keyword captions or glossed captions are practical? As I discussed earlier in the chapter, selection and preparation of keyword captions is time-consuming compared to the ready availability of full captions. As this series of studies shows, full captions come out very well against keyword captions, and, on the whole, learners prefer them to keyword captions.

5.2 Longitudinal Studies of Caption Use

Despite the need for such research, there are few substantial studies that have involved watching captioned videos or films over a period of a few weeks in order to asses changes of behaviour and gains over time. In this section, I describe three studies that adopt a longitudinal approach and identify some of the changes in learner-viewers' behaviour that occur as they develop their skills and strategies while watching over weeks or months. The findings of these three studies confirm that learners tend to experience changes in their viewing behaviour over time which are beneficial to their language learning.

Maria da Conceição Condinho Bravo (2008) carried out two longitudinal studies as part of her doctoral research, on the value of watching programmes with or without captions, covering both English and Portuguese learning, attempting to apply and test many of the principles that had appeared in my published articles, such as the model I had presented in my 1990 publication (see Chap. 3, p. 64) and my 1994a chapter on using a variety of genres of captioned programmes (see Chap. 6 of this book). In her studies, she compared the relative value of subtitled, captioned and/or uncaptioned or unsubtitled programmes for learning unknown words and lexical phrases in a classroom situation.

In the first study, thirty-two adult learners of Portuguese (of mixed L1s) attending a one-month summer school in Portugal and with Portuguese proficiency levels ranging from A2 to C1 watched six clips of programmes or films of different genres (musical, feature film, soap opera, animated comedy with plants and animals, satirical news cartoon, documentary) with and without captions. It was important for the author that the programmes were authentic, broadcast programmes, had conventional captions for the deaf and hard-of-hearing and were the types of programmes that the participants might watch back home in their L1s. Viewing took place in class time; participants were briefed about the content and given content comprehension questions to complete as they watched. They also completed questionnaires on their viewing and attitudes to watching with captions before the start of the first viewing and after twelve viewings, and took two vocabulary recall tests, one after six viewings and the other after twelve viewings. Bravo's findings were complex and fascinating. Initially, approximately one-third of the participants said that they found captions distracting or disturbing rather than useful, but this had dwindled to one out of the thirty-two by the end of the twelfth viewing (cf. very similar findings for the EURECAP project in Chap. 7). The ten who had found captions initially disturbing or distracting were all from Italy or Spain, countries with a tradition of dubbing rather than subtitling. It should be said that some of those who found captions useful felt that, at times, they distracted from the listening.

Their performance on comprehension questions differed according to genres, though not to any great extent. All three levels scored better on captioned versions of programmes than on uncaptioned, apart from the animated cartoon feature film where the intermediate (B1) and elementary levels (A2) scored higher on the uncaptioned than on the captioned version. This was a children's film, and it seemed that some of the participants preferred to concentrate on the pictures and sound. Again, there are interesting parallels with my experience of captioned natural history programmes where my learners found captions distracted from the images. Overall, uncaptioned programmes produced low scores, and listening comprehension was poor for these clips. Scores were relatively low (approximately 50 % and lower) for both the intermediate and elementary groups on the recognition and recall tests after sessions 6 and 12. Feedback from a small number of participants (primarily advanced level) indicated that they would have preferred to watch the clips out of class and under their control. Bravo also mentions that the participants tended to have the attitude that audiovisual activities were purely recreational, though, certainly, attitudes did change over time and many made notes on new words and phrases as they watched.

In the second study (also reported in Bravo, 2010), which was designed to compare the "usefulness" of subtitles and captions for acquiring new words and phrases, seventy-five 13- and 14-year-old (Grade 9) Portuguese teenagers were divided into two groups of thirty-eight and thirty-seven, and were made to watch ten 15-minute-long episodes of the American sitcom, *The Fresh Prince of Bel-Air*, in one of two conditions, English + Portuguese subtitles and English + English captions, during their normal class time. Participants are reported as being at "intermediate" or A2/B1 level on the basis of their final grades in English the previous year. The episodes selected were chosen for their key themes, such as the generation gap, ethical values, family relations, racial discrimination and environmental issues, which, it was hoped, would engage the learners.

For each episode, Bravo identified a list of ten target words or phrases, which were tested after each viewing. For example, in the second episode watched, *Mixed Identities*, the list was:

For crying out loud, straighten things out, take care of someone, punch it man, to be heading for, to be glum, take chances, every other weekend, trade something, when in Rome do as the Romans do

Each test consisted of twenty words and phrases from the programme tested by multiple-choice options randomly given in English or Portuguese. The viewing was paused twice for learners to answer seven questions each time, with the six remaining questions given at the end. There were three "consolidation" tests, one after week 5 on the first five episodes, second test on episodes 6–10 after the tenth episode and a third test, which could be counted as a delayed post-test, consisting of 50 items (5 from each episode) on all ten episodes, three weeks after the last viewing and after a two-week holiday. Both groups steadily improved their test scores over the 10-week period, from a mean of over 8/20 for both conditions in the first week to a mean of 16 for the subtitles condition and 15½ for the captions condition, with occasional rises or dips in between, when, for example, an episode proved more difficult or learners were distracted. Overall, those in the subtitles condition had higher scores and improved more. In the final consolidation test, scores were very similar, though those in the subtitles condition scored higher than the captions group. For example, in the delayed post-test, the subtitles group's mean score was just over 34/50, whereas the captions group's mean score was just over 33/50.

A further multiple-choice post-test was given three months after the viewing, with twenty-five items in English and twenty-five in Portuguese, in order to assess whether learners' good performance on recall was the result of exposure to the lexical phrases accompanied by Portuguese translations. The scores for the Portuguese items were always higher than for the English items, though the difference in scores was never higher than 5.8 %. Scores averaged around 69 % for the Portuguese items and 65 % for the English items.

While this is a valuable study, there are certainly many problematic features, such as the absence of an accurate pre-test, the shortness of the sequences before each part-test each week, the absence of any data on the reliability of the test items and the mixing of test items in Portuguese and English "randomly." As the author herself notes, when reading the Portuguese translations, the learners might have profited from information in the translations, even if they did not fully understand the lexical item or content in English. Is it surprising, then, that that those in the subtitled conditions generally scored higher on the test than those in the captioned conditions? Probably not, given that the learners had relatively low level in CEFR terms at A2/B1, and, as their feedback indicated, they found it hard to keep up with the captions. Yet, as Bravo stresses, the most telling findings were, firstly, how much groups in both conditions improved in their test scores over the ten weeks and how close those in the captions condition were to the subtitles condition group in their scores, and, secondly, how the active viewing and student participation reflected on their performance in different vocabulary tests.

The study provides convincing evidence of how learners become accustomed to using the captions over time and develop strategies for using them flexibly, together with the sound and the images, to gain a variety of words and phrases. They reported that they learnt new expressions, enriched their vocabulary and learnt to speak better; in addition (among other things), the captions helped improve their concentration while watching the episode/film, helped them understand what they sometimes missed out on in the spoken text and helped them pick up the pronunciation.

The third study describes a course in captioning taken by undergraduate students at the University of the Algarve using the *Learning via Subtitling* (*LeVis*) package (http://levis.cti.gr/index.php?option=com_content&task=blogsection&id=19). This study is described in Chap. 5, Sect. 5.6, Learner training and strategies with captioned viewing.

Michael Rodgers' name will be familiar to those in the field, as co-author with Stuart Webb, of articles on vocabulary in films and programmes (Webb & Rodgers, 2009a, 2009b). His doctoral research (Rodgers, 2013) on measuring incidental learning of vocabulary from watching captioned TV programmes that formed a series (in this case, an American comedy series, *Chuck*) provides some evidence as to whether there are changes in learners' viewing behaviour and vocabulary gains over time. As he says, much of the previous research on video and incidental vocabulary learning has found positive results, but, in general, the studies have not been a representative sample of what a language learner might choose to learn English from over a prolonged period.

The study involving captioned programmes was the fifth of five studies. The first four studies involving more than 200 Japanese university undergraduate student participants with reported English language levels of pre-intermediate to intermediate levels had produced quite mixed findings on aspects such as vocabulary gains over the series; gains linked to specific episodes; incidental vocabulary gains and lexical coverage and lexical coverage and comprehension. Participants became more positive about learning from watching television over the course of the series, and, by the end, they held generally favourable attitudes towards language learning through watching television. Looking at the overall results and the survey attitudes, it is easy to believe that while the volunteer students found watching the programmes enjoyable and believed they had gained some benefit in terms of their English language, the studies, on the whole, contribute little new to our knowledge and understanding of language learning from watching TV programmes.

One issue, in particular, was that the very manner of data gathering undermined the validity of the research: each episode was divided into six sections, and participants looked at the listening comprehension questions which would follow each section before viewing that section; they then watched the section and did those comprehension questions before starting the process for the next section. Advert breaks in programmes can be disruptive and annoying, but the sort of priming on the one hand and disruption on the other does raise questions about the validity of the design and procedures, and the generalisations that might be made from the findings.

The fifth study, which involved four "experiments" in total, investigated how the presence of captions affected the aspects of language learning examined in the first four studies. In this study, forty first-year students in the same Japanese university and at about the same level watched the same series, but with captions. These were captions provided on the DVD for the deaf and hard-of-hearing and followed the standard format for such captions, including naming speakers when several speakers spoke together. The participants followed the same procedures that were in place for the earlier ones and took the same tests with the aim of assessing the benefits of captioned viewing in terms of comprehension, incidental vocabulary acquisition, lexical coverage and attitudes of participants. The results of the tests and attitudes survey were then compared with those of the groups that had watched the same series with no captions.

Participants increased their comprehension scores significantly between the initial episode shown and the final episode shown, and also improved their comprehension scores for successive episodes steadily over the course of watching the series. However, there was a considerable difference between comprehension test results for individual episodes.

Comparing these results with those of the no-captions group, while both groups made significant gains from initial to final episodes, the no-captions group made significantly greater gains. However, the no-captions group started off with a considerably lower mean comprehension score, suggesting that the captions already helped the comprehension of the captions group in the initial episode. A similar pattern emerged for all episodes, with the captions group scoring consistently higher than the no-captions group, though both groups steadily improved their scores. The differences were also consistent across episodes, where scores suggested they were more challenging, and in three episodes, the differences in scores were significantly higher for the captions group.

With regard to vocabulary knowledge (as manifested by the Vocabulary Levels Test (Nation, 1990), which all participants had been given initially), the comparison of the captions and no-captions groups showed that while vocabulary knowledge was related to increased comprehension of certain episodes of television viewed with captions, vocabulary knowledge was more consistently correlated with comprehension when episodes of television were viewed without captions. This needs some explaining. Rodgers puts it like this:

These findings suggest that vocabulary knowledge may be more important for comprehension when language learners encounter the spoken dialogue of television only aurally, and the added support of captions appears to reduce the effect of increased vocabulary knowledge on comprehension. (2016:187)

For the captions group, there were significant correlations between vocabulary knowledge and relative vocabulary gains on both tests, whereas no significant correlations were found for the no-captions group for either test. In other words, those with greater vocabulary knowledge in the captions group were able to use both the aural and written input in captioned television to learn vocabulary more effectively than those with less vocabulary knowledge. Or, perhaps, those with higher vocabulary knowledge had less need of the captions than those with lower vocabulary knowledge. Again, Pujolà's (2002) conclusion that those with greater knowledge use captions for backup while those with lower levels find them an essential support helps to clarify Rodgers' somewhat opaque gloss. Rodgers goes on to suggest that the reason no significant difference was found for the no-captions group may be due to the way vocabulary knowledge was measured in this study, using the combined results of the 2000-, 3000-, and 5000-word levels of the Vocabulary Levels Test (VLT) (Nation, 1990). This was done for both the captions group and the no-captions group.

How did lexical coverage or levels of vocabulary knowledge affect comprehension? The comparison of the results from the captions and no-captions groups showed that there were a number of episodes where there was a significant difference in comprehension between participants with different levels of lexical coverage. In the captions group, there were three episodes of *Chuck* where the participants with mastery of the 2000-word level of the VLT had significantly higher comprehension scores than participants without mastery of the 2000-word level compared with the six episodes for the no-captions group. As might be expected, the greater the vocabulary knowledge, the better it is for comprehension when captions are not present. As Rodgers notes, it is possible that the participants had more knowledge of the written form of vocabulary than the aural form, so when captions were present, participants with less vocabulary knowledge could still make better use of what they knew.

There are obvious limitations to showing learners films or programmes in teacher-controlled conditions and then testing them or asking them what they have learnt or understood. These approaches are far too restricted and restrictive in the current technological, social and media context, and, in the end, over-elaborate designs such as Rodgers', with so many precautions taken to guard against confounding variables, undermine the validity of the research and any generalisations from the findings that might be made. The reality is that watching episodes of programmes such as *Chuck* each week in the classroom, with or without captions, has always been, in Frances McKnight's (1983) terms, "a Friday afternoon treat," unless it is handled carefully as part of a strategy to develop learners' knowledge and use of colloquial phrases and idioms as Bravo's (2008) studies were. However, if we want to seriously research the long-term benefit of learners' watching these programmes, it has to be in contexts in which they are in control.

The most salient finding from this study was that the presence of captions improved comprehension for episodes early in the viewing process and for difficult episodes. In other respects, the contribution is quite limited, except to show that there may be changes in viewing behaviour over time, watching TV series with or without captions, but that watching with captions is likely to bring greater gains.

A far more nuanced approach to the value of subtitles or captions over a substantial period is given by Frumuselu, De Maeyerb, Doncheb, and Gutiérrez-Colon Plana (2015) study in Spain in which forty Spanish/Catalan, Dutch, German, Russian, Romanian and Moldavian second-year university English language undergraduates with A2 to C1 (CEFR) proficiency level in English were randomly assigned either to interlingual mode (English sound + Spanish subtitles) or to intralingual mode (English sound + English captions). They watched thirteen episodes of the American comedy series *Friends*, two each week, apart from the first week, for seven weeks. Each episode was 25 minutes long, so this amounted to quite a substantial amount of total viewing time (325 minutes).

The researchers wished to investigate the learners' acquisition of informal and conversational speech, such as slang, phrasal verbs and colloquial expressions and their understanding of the programmes. The students took a multiple-choice and open questions pre-test and a post-test; there were 15 multiple-choice and 15 open questions drawn from expressions and words used in the programmes. The multiple-choice questions were intended to see if students recognised and identified the correct item present in a specific scene and context in the episode; for example, for the items "to have a blast" the alternatives were (a) to be busy, (b) to have a great time and (c) to have memories about someone. There is no information about the reliability of test items. The open questions had the form: Explain the meaning "pick on" in the context "You're picking on every detail":_____.

They found that learners performed significantly better on the post-tests (a medium-size effect) watching with captions than with subtitles. In the authors' words, students were able to rely on the visual, audio and written elements from the videos in order to identify the correct meaning of the informal expressions and words in the provided context, leading the authors to conclude that students who were exposed to captioned programmes for seven weeks benefited more in terms of their lexical learning than those who watched the episodes with subtitles. Of particular interest and in contrast to some other studies mentioned in Chap. 4, the difference in scores between the two conditions, captions or subtitles, did not appear to be dependent on students' prior proficiency level. So, independently of their low, intermediate or high proficiency level, students benefited in terms of lexical learning from watching the captioned programmes and to a greater extent than watching with subtitles. This finding is in line with studies that claim that "viewers regardless of educational level or language background benefited significantly from captioning, even with only one viewing" (Price, 1983:8), and the authors are certainly correct in suggesting that a plausible reason for this lies in the educational context of viewing. Their students, they argue, are more likely to be interested in viewing with captions, as they were all studying for an English degree and wished to maximise their exposure to English in all its forms. They sum up as follows:

> Accordingly, by being able to see the written form of the spoken language, especially the informal and colloquial expressions that are so challenging to

acquire and to remember, they felt confident and reassured that the item they were listening to was the correct one and in this way they could easily identify its meaning by connecting the visual, the oral and the written form. (Frumuselu et al., 2015:9)

In my terms, the students appear to have behaved as learners rather than as recreational viewers, despite the genre and nature of the programme. The findings suggest that they did "pay attention to the words," rather than sitting back and just enjoying the programmes.

The aims of the research are certainly laudable in trying to increase students' exposure to colloquial speech, since, for those in foreign language context, this can be one of the most difficult areas for achieving high levels of proficiency. Yet, at the same time, one has to question whether spending 325 minutes of class time in watching *Friends* is time well spent given what the students appear to have learnt. We can hope that students became fully "tuned in" to the speech of the characters in *Friends* and could follow without difficulty, but this was not tested with a no-captions episode at the end. As the post-test was limited to a relatively small number of items, we also have no real idea as to how much more the students had picked up actively or could recognise passively. In a future study, I would hope that the classroom would be flipped and students would watch these episodes of *Friends* in their own time and under their control as work set with tasks so that they could pause and rewind, consciously and systematically working through an episode. This might reduce the comedic quality of the programme somewhat (though in the case of *Friends*, the language and humour is so engaging that people watch episodes repeatedly) but would ensure full value in language learning terms. As I say in my 1994a article:

> The autonomous learner needs not only conscious and reflective control over the dynamic stream of speech which closed captions/teletext subtitles help to provide, but also a specifically educational orientation to viewing which may be assisted by active tutoring, task setting and an integration of activities using different media. (Vanderplank, 1994a:119)

5.3 Captioned Viewing and Speech Segmentation

Charles and Trenkic (2015) report an all-too-rare study on how learners may improve their segmentation skills in English through watching captioned programmes. They report that English language learners often find it difficult to identify which words are present in the continuous stream of speech, even when the words are familiar, and they hypothesised that simultaneous presentation of aural and written form of a word, as takes place in the bimodal input of captioned programmes, could boost learners' ability to segment English speech (cf. Mitterer and McQueen's (2009) conclusions discussed on pages 95–100 of this book). The authors rightly highlight some of the methodological issues in much of the research regarding the benefits of captions, in particular, that often the tests used to check comprehension are tests of reading comprehensions or memory tests. While the results may show that general comprehension is improved by the presence of captions, it is far from clear whether the presence of captions leads to better listening comprehension.

Their study involved twelve Chinese female graduate students at a UK university with a mean IELTS score of 7 (so about lower C1 level in CEFR terms) They were randomly assigned to three treatment groups, bimodal, no subtitles and no sound. They completed a shadowing test as a pre-test (consisting of hundred short excerpts from five documentaries) and then watched 30 minutes of two of these documentaries (a travel/cookery programme by a celebrity chef and a popular science programme presented by a celebrity science professor) in their assigned conditions. The treatment for each documentary was spread over two weeks to explore the cumulative effects on listening of watching captioned programmes. In each week, an immediate post-test (120 excerpts) was carried out. Post-test materials also consisted of multiple excerpts drawn from the five documentaries and three new ones. Immediate post-tests mixed some pre-test excerpts and new excerpts to check on whether learning was becoming generalised to new utterances produced by the same speaker (or the "tuning in" phenomenon, as I have called it). The authors also carried out a delayed post-test consisting of 160 excerpts, again mixing old and new items, and this time final, unrelated items from the fifth documentary (*How We Built Britain*).

The number of correctly repeated scores for each excerpt for each participant was counted and calculated as a proportion of the total. Averages for each test and for old, new and unrelated items were also calculated. One participant had scored 8.5 on IELTS, and her scores were much higher than those of the others (lending support to the notion I have proposed elsewhere (Vanderplank, 1988b) that accurate shadowing is a skill, which all adult native speakers of a language may be assumed to have).

The overall mean scores of the participants on the four tests indicated that while the bimodal group scored lower than the other two groups on the pre-test, it consistently and significantly outperformed the controls on all the post-tests, showing that bimodal presentation of input can help the foreign language segmentation of continuous speech. There were also trends for the bimodal group to perform more strongly than the control groups on the old items, and also to outperform the control groups on previously unheard utterances from the documentaries they watched, suggesting that they had indeed been able to "tune in" to certain speakers.

But, for me, the key finding was that after starting from a lower listening base, the bimodal input group, after watching the two documentaries and taking the immediate post-tests, was able to follow the unrelated items in the delayed post-test significantly better than the other two control groups, thereby offering strong evidence to support the notion that bimodal input may lead to the generalisation of learning to previously unheard utterances by different speakers with broadly similar accents. In other words, after having watched captioned TV programmes, foreign language listeners may be able to follow (if not fully understand, according to my 1988b definition) new non-subtitled programmes and speakers. For Charles and Trenkic, this finding suggests that watching with captions may not just be helpful for speech segmentation but may have more far-reaching effects as far as the development of segmentation abilities in the foreign language is concerned.

Sadly, the research was carried out on a very small group of learners, making it difficult to make generalisations about their findings. For me, the study offers some validation for much of what I said about the potential of captions to assist in the development of listening skills (of which, to my mind, accurate speech segmentation is a, if not **the**, core skill) in my 1988a article.

5.4 Captioned Video as a Cultural and Educational Resource

As I shall discuss at some length in the next chapter, captioned audiovisual material offers almost limitless cultural and education resources. Yet, in these areas, while there are any number of articles, presentations and workshops on how to exploit video for these purposes in the language classroom, only very limited research has been carried out on the value that providing captions may bring. Paul Markham (2000–2001) investigated background cultural knowledge in a study involving advanced ESL students with mixed religious backgrounds watching two ten-minute excerpts, one on Islam and the other on Buddhism, from a series of public television broadcasts. Students watched each excerpt once, either in a captions or no-captions group, and wrote summaries after viewing. Both religious background knowledge and captions contributed substantially to their comprehension. The Muslim and Buddhist students performed at a higher level after viewing videotapes concerning their respective religions. However, the smaller sample of Buddhist students (only nine) performed somewhat more erratically than the Muslim group (sixteen). Conversely, the religion-neutral students (fifty-four) performed at a higher level with the captioned versions of the videos concerning either religion.

Using video to broaden learners' perspectives and their language skills is also the theme of Chapple and Curtis's (2000) informative study of how they used films in an ESL environment in Hong Kong for developing language and other transferable skills such as analytical and critical thinking. Thirty-one Cantonese tertiary-level students were asked to rate their own English language skills development in relation to six specific areas after watching eight films in English or with English captions. The films were followed up in discussion and analysis sessions. The students reported that their English language skills had improved in all areas, particularly their speaking and listening skills, and that their confidence in using English had increased together with improved analytical and critical thinking, content and technical knowledge and a broader perspective.

5.5 Captions and Literacy Development

Several studies in the past have highlighted the possible benefits in the development of reading skills in both the L1 and the L2 that the presence of captions may bring (Bean & Wilson, 1989; Neuman & Koskinen, 1990). To my mind, the most interesting and innovative studies are certainly those undertaken by Kothari and colleagues in the context of Indian illiteracy and subliteracy.

After the positive results of a small-scale study (Kothari, Takeda, Joshi, & Pandey, 2002) in a Indian school setting, which showed that captioned songs improved the decoding ability of elementary school students, Kothari, Pandey, and Chudgar (2004) reported a fascinating study on the incremental effect of viewing programmes with captions in a context far removed from the classrooms of Europe and North America. The authors describe the implementation of what they call SLS, same-language subtitles (captions), on a programme of film songs, specifically for first language literacy. *Chitrageet*, a weekly 30-minute TV programme of Gujarati film songs, was broadcast across Gujarat state in India, with the song words captioned in Gujarati, over a 10-month period. Kothari (1999) had already made a well-argued case for the captioning of songs in the context for group and family viewing in India, arguing that the passion for film songs and the enormous interest in knowing and memorising song lyrics would provide strong instrumental motivation for viewers to "take out" some lyrics from the captions.

Two groups were formed, an experimental group, who watched the programme regularly and who could just about manage to read the text, and a control group, unfamiliar with the programme, who were "early literates." Twenty five episodes were shown with 20 minutes of captions per 30-minute broadcast. Both groups took pre- and post-reading tests. Subjects were selected from villages and slums in the state of Gujarat and the city of Ahmedabad; 358 people in the Experimental Group (EG), and 121 in the Control Group (CG), which was formed from people in a different district who could receive the programme but who reported very low or practically no viewing of it. The EG significantly improved more than the CG on two of the three post-tests. Those who had a higher education level appeared to improve more than those who had little or no education. Those with some skills in reading the captions benefited more than those who did not.

To gauge reactions, viewers were offered a copy of the printed lyrics of the most recent programme if they sent in a postcard or letter. A total of 2060 postcards were received, mostly from rural areas. Many wrote with their opinions of the subtitles, and indirect and direct expressions of support for the educational perspective totalled about one-third of responses. Many of the comments on subtitling made the link with literacy, though this was never expressly stated during the programmes.

As the authors state, while the study showed an improvement in decoding ability, far more integration of captions with popular entertainment programmes would be needed to see any really meaningful improvement, such as being able to read a newspaper. Nonetheless, the study is important as a rare example of incremental effects over a reasonably long period in experimental terms, and the testimonies provide a useful measure of evidence that captions provide benefits in literacy development.

5.6 Learner Training and Strategies with Captioned Viewing

Insights into procedures for class use of captions, training in their autonomous use by learners and also the need to select videos with captions are offered by Annamaria Caimi's (2006) informal study in Italy, in which fifteen pre-intermediate university students of English attended captioned video sessions. Students were tested on lexical, semantic and visual recognition memory after viewing these videos. Positive results were achieved only if the subtitles were faithful to the source dialogue and appropriately tailored to the semantic and pragmatic markedness of the plot, speed of images and scenes. Students confirmed that their concentration on listening comprehension was second to reading comprehension. Some students were disturbed during the screening of the video because they were unable to combine viewing, listening and reading at the same time. In order to follow the storyline, they had to give priority to the skill they felt more familiar with.

Marianne Herbert's (2004) small-scale investigation of the strategies used by language learners when using a target-language DVD to complete meaning-focused and form-focused tasks is a Masters dissertation, which deserves to be widely known. Herbert hypothesised that her subjects, seven proficient French students who had recently spent nine months in French university, would show a greater propensity to use subtitles when faced with meaning-focused tasks and would use both captions and subtitles when using form-focused tasks such as remembering specific words and phrases. They watched two, three-minute-long segments from a French film, *Le Dîner de Cons*, followed by meaning- or form-focused tasks. The students were also interviewed about their strategies. Students were able to view each segment three times, pausing and replaying as they went through.

In summary, Herbert's findings, both qualitative and quantitative, suggested that learners use systematic caption-/subtitle-viewing strategies and that they are influenced in their patterns of use by the purpose in viewing. There were clear differences in caption/subtitle use between the two groups. For example, the form-focused group rewound four times more than the other group. They also used captions much more and subtitles much less. Those in the form-focused group found the captions helpful in associating written words with speech, and this helped their understanding of the rapid speech. One of the subjects made the useful comment that she found the subtitles helped her understand what was said and she then used French captions to discover the actual words used. Students also varied subtitles/captions, pause and rewind when confronted with an unfamiliar phrase. This was common to both groups, but more so in the form-focused group. Herbert suggests that in terms of teaching, for meaning-focused tasks, learners with reasonably good proficiency should only use subtitles as a last resort, as captions appear to produce much better recall and use of the language of the DVD. In contrast, for beginners, an opposite strategy might be appropriate, using subtitles to gain an understanding of what is going on followed by captions, as Danan (1992) had earlier suggested.

In Chap. 2, Sect. 2.3, I described the guidelines for captioning for deaf and hard-of-hearing people and mentioned "fansubbing" and the availability of sites such as www.*amara.org* to help amateur captioning. Those who are involved in training students in translation noticed some years ago that there were benefits to be gained for language learners in practising not only subtitling but also captioning. One of the best articles in training in subtitling is by Williams and Thorne (2000), who describe a course at St David's University College, Lampeter, in Wales, in training high-level students in subtitling in Welsh.

As Williams and Thorne say,

> Subtitling can be either interlingual, where the language of the television programme appears translated into the target language on the screen, or it can be intralingual, where it is usually targeted at a deaf audience, where the source language production is also used for the subtitles. …Both, however, can be used successfully for language learning. … (and) make different demands on the students' linguistic skills and are equally as valuable. (2000:219)

They go on to list the benefits for language skills of training in subtitling. I have adapted these for captioning in this case:

1. Listening attentively, recognising and fully absorbing the content of the programme or film in the foreign language.
2. Reading and viewing the screen for visual clues, which place the language into a meaningful context, such as the age, social background, appearance and gestures or expressions of the characters.
3. Appreciating the different linguistic styles of different characters and elements in different genres.
4. Editing the content so that the original meaning remains intact while allowing for comfortable reading by the deaf or hard-of-hearing viewer or second/foreign language viewer. The amount of editing will depend on the type of programme, and for some programme, such as news, the captioner should try to aim at verbatim captions, whereas in some Natural History programmes, there will be a minimum of caption text.

5. Taking into account the register of the programme. Short forms may be acceptable in soap operas and situation comedies, but may be less acceptable in formal documentaries. How are swearing, taboo forms, dialect forms, jokes and puns to be handled?
6. Creating easy-to-read captions, which enable the viewer to absorb the programme's meaning as effortlessly as possible whilst ensuring complete understanding.
7. Displaying the language in a smooth, pleasing and consistent way on screen, keeping the syntactic units intact, if possible, along with punctuation.
8. Reviewing the captions with a teacher, being self-critical about one's editing, proof reading and checking skills.
9. Respecting technical conventions, such as not allowing captions to over-run cuts in the film (as also mentioned in Chap. 2, Sect. 2.3). (Adapted from Williams & Thorne, 2000:220–221)

Evidence for these benefits is provided by Bravo (2008) in the third of her studies. In this study, Bravo evaluates production skills through a screen captioning activity. The audiovisual materials were the same as in the previous study with captions used, and the participants were a group of twenty university undergraduates, enrolled in English language classes, with lower intermediate/intermediate English language skills (A2/B1).

Students watched an episode of *The Fresh Prince of Bel-Air* without captions, and then captioned the episode using the special subtitling simulator software *LeViS (Learning via Subtitling)*, specially designed for language learning through training in subtitling and part of a collaborative programme of eight European universities in using subtitling for language learning. The project ended in 2008, but the software is still available to download at http://levis.cti.gr/index.php?option=com_docman&task=cat_view&gid=100&Itemid=27

Before watching the episode, they were asked to write down the meanings of ten idiomatic phrases from the episode. These were expressions that had caused particular difficulty in the second study with Portuguese high-school students:

1. To take a shot at someone (figurative meaning)

2. To pass away (phrasal verb)
3. To say grace (transitive verb + object)
4. To clear the table
5. To hurt someone's feelings
6. Spoiled kids
7. To mow the lawn (transitive verb + object)
8. To miss someone/something (transitive verb + object)
9. To take after someone
10. A free ride in a fancy car

Students then watched the episode as a group with captions and took a post-viewing test of ten items contained in the episode with multiple-choice options in English or Portuguese (five in English, five in Portuguese). This test showed a marked improvement in their understanding of the expressions. In the initial test, most of the students had known or understood few of the expressions (between 0 % and 50 % of the students for each of the items), whereas after viewing, no item scored less than 50 %, and one item, "to say grace" reached 100 % understanding by students. "To take after someone," which no students had known before viewing, was understood by fourteen of the students (70 %) after viewing.

One week later, students were asked to caption selected sections of the same episode, which contained the colloquial and formulaic expressions that they had been tested on. After viewing, correct answers ranged from 75 % to 100 %.

Three weeks later, to check for retention and students' ability to produce the expressions correctly and appropriately, Bravo introduced a written task in which they were required to write a text in English, selecting seven of ten Portuguese expressions that were paraphrases of the original ten English expressions. Again, the results were very positive, with fifteen of the twenty students constructing coherent and cohesive texts, with all seven expressions used correctly. Three students got the meaning of one expression wrong, and two wrote two of the expressions incorrectly.

What I find so interesting about this study is that Bravo has actively tried and succeeded in implementing the later stages in my model of language learning with captioned viewing (see Chaps. 3 and 8) by taking the learning beyond the "Attention" stage to "Adaptation" and then "Adoption" through written tasks set.

Although not a research project, it is worth mentioning *ClipFlair* (www.clipflair.net), a project which came out of *LeVis* and which sought to develop activities for learners including captioning, subtitling, dubbing and voice-over using film clips in a range of languages. The project ended in 2014, but is still available online. Benson and Chan's (2010) descriptions and analyses of the exchanges online of fansubbers' subtitles and captions of the Beijing Olympic Games song, *Beijing Welcomes You*, on *YouTube*, are also worth highlighting. These exchanges produced a great deal of useful, language-focused comment and informal language learning. As they say, activities such as fansubbing are opening up new opportunities for young people to interact in globalised online spaces.

5.7 Sound or Text: Where Are Learners Focusing Their Attention? Teasing Out and Testing Reliance on Captions

Over the years, many teachers and others have expressed concerns that learners watching captioned films and programmes may become over-reliant on the captions to the detriment of developing their listening skills. This is certainly a concern expressed by some learners watching captioned material, as will be shown in the findings of the EURECAP project in Chap. 7. There are several issues that come into play when considering reliance or becoming dependent. Certainly, there may be selection and grading issues: if the audio material is too far above a learner's level, then, of course, they will focus on the caption text and will resist the removal of captions. They may also become stressful and overburdened by the bimodal input, instead of being helped by it. If the material is at an appropriate level, as Pujolà (2002) has reported, learners are likely to use the captions for reassurance and back-up. However, this reassurance or back-up may, as some fear, turn into a dependency or near-dependency even at very high levels of listening ability; non-native viewers may prefer to have the support of captions in case there are difficult accents, very fast, unclear speech or just the occasional unfamiliar word.

Leveridge and Yang (2013:202) go as far as to suggest that providing captions for too long may prevent these learners from being able to listen confidently in real-life, interactive situations. They also consider that captions may be distracting for higher-level learners who have developed a good level of listening ability and then find that the captions directly interfere with their comprehension. Using these and other arguments, they build their case for a testing instrument, which will indicate the degree to which learners are reliant on captioning support, the Caption Reliance Test (CRT). Such an instrument, they suggest, will assist teachers in providing instruction support that matches individual learner needs. With such an instrument, instructors may assess the degree to which learners are reliant on captions and gradually remove them, thereby reducing learners' reliance on the support that the captions provide.

The authors based their approach to reliance testing on the notion that if foreign language learners are challenged by the listening content, they may choose to attend to the captions, as it may be more easily understood than the speech. Thus, learners who rely heavily on the captions will tend to answer questions based on what they read, rather than what they hear. In addition, as captions may be distracting for higher-level learners who have a reasonable level of listening ability, they may find that the captions directly interfere with their listening and will try to ignore or even block the captions provided, so as to answer questions according to what they hear.

As learners develop their listening ability, they will come to rely on the captions less and less. In this way, their CRT test is intended to provide information on the point at which the learner has progressed towards the place at which captions are no longer necessary and may be removed. This, of course, begs many questions, particularly with regard to the nature of individual programmes and films, which may vary in the demands of listening, from sequence to sequence or character to character. Nonetheless, we know that higher-level learners often express a wish not to become reliant on captions as they themselves fear that it will inhibit their progress to confident listening in interactions as well as in watching TV and films in the foreign language.

The authors' CRT consisted of an auditory track, accompanied by congruent textual captions and particular incongruent textual words, and was used with 141 Grade 12 Taiwanese students who had studied English for a minimum of five years. Before taking the CRT, they were divided into three groups according to matched listening comprehension and general English proficiency ability.

The audio was broadcast over a portable public address system connected to a laptop computer audio port, and the text was presented as black text captions on a white screen using a digital projector connected to the same laptop. The captions appeared with the audio track simultaneously, exactly like captions on a DVD movie or CD. Before test commencement, participants were instructed, in both their native language (Mandarin) and the target language (English), to listen to the audio and then choose the correct answer.

Participants were told that if they noticed any discrepancies between the audio and the visual text, only the audio was to be considered as correct. After three sample questions, they were given multiple-choice CRT questions, which were divided into two types, congruent and incongruent, with the incongruent questions randomly placed throughout.

The researchers found a correlation between academic achievement and reliance on captions. In other words, the more a learner progresses, the less they are reliant on captions as a learning support and the more the captions may interfere with listening comprehension. There was a high degree of individual variation in the degree of reliance and a negative correlation between caption reliance and L2 achievement; that is, lower-level students relied on captions for listening comprehension more than their high-level students. The authors argue that by using the CRT, instructors can evaluate the degree to which learners rely on the caption supports and thus make informed decisions about what learners need as caption support. This is an interesting area, which would probably merit further investigation. Certainly, as I found in the EURECAP Project (Chap. 7), there was considerable variation in reliance on captions, both within individual participants and within films, as well as between participants and films. Will it be possible to design delicate-enough instruments that really tap into reliance across so many variables, or will the need to control factors mean that valid and reliable studies are always going to lack face validity and authenticity?

Winke, Gass, and Sydorenko (2013) also concentrate on time spent focusing on captions in their investigation of English-speaking Arabic, Chinese, Russian and Spanish learners' viewing behaviour when watching two videos, each dubbed and captioned in the target language. Using eye-tracking, they wanted to find out how the relationship between the English and the target language affected the caption-reading behaviour as well as the effect of content familiarity on the attention given to captions.

The study was relatively small scale. Thirty-two (10 men, 22 women) second-year foreign language learners at Michigan State University took part in the study. There were seven learners of Arabic, seven of Chinese, eight of Russian and 10 of Spanish. They are described as being at "intermediate" level, but no baseline data on varying levels or skills are provided.

Students watched two videos, each approximately 3–5 minutes in length, which had been dubbed from English into the four languages. One version of each was provided with captions in the target language, the other without. The soundtrack consisted of a narrator (female in all cases), who described the scene and told the story, together with the original sounds and music. Both clips were natural history documentaries, one about salmon, the other about bears. The choice of genre is significant in my terms, as this tended to be the least successful of genres for viewing with captions in the *Teletext 888 Project* and one of the least likely to be viewed with captions given free choice.

Participants watched each video twice, the first time with captions, the second time without. They then took a multiple-choice comprehension test with questions about the main points of each study. The authors tell us that these tests were used only to make sure that the participants paid attention to the videos!

They analysed the data from fixations in the area in which the captions appeared in the first viewing (no captions in the second viewing) and found that, on average, the participants fixated on the captioned area 68 % of the time that the captions were on screen and that this average was very similar regardless of the video (66 % on average when the video contained familiar content, and 69 % on average when it did not). The smallest variation (SD = 6 %) was within the Spanish-language learning group compared to 7 % and 8 % for the Arabic and Russian groups, respectively, but 18 % for the Chinese group. In effect, their participants tended to read the captions most of the time that they were on the screen, with some individual variations, and the variation also depended, to some extent, on the language being learnt.

They then analysed whether familiarity with the content had an effect on watching the captions more or less and whether this varied according to the language of the video. While participants watching in Arabic, Russian and Spanish spent similar amounts of time looking at the captions in the videos with familiar and unfamiliar content, those learning Chinese spent a significantly smaller percentage of time looking at captions in the video with familiar content compared to the one with unfamiliar content. They then ran the analysis again without the Chinese data and found that learners of Arabic spent a higher percentage of time looking at the captions than learners of Spanish and Russian. Learners of Spanish spent the least amount of time looking at captions, followed by learners of Russian and then learners of Arabic.

They also interviewed participants after the viewings to discuss their use of the captions and to provide more detail to the quantitative data gained from the eye-tracking. In particular, they wanted to find out why the learners of Arabic spent more time looking at captions than learners of Spanish and Russian, and why the learners of Chinese spent more time reading captions when the video contained unfamiliar content. They found that caption-reading behaviour tended to depend on several factors, including the participant's vocabulary knowledge, the speed of the speaker's speech in relation to the listener's proficiency level and the amount of action on screen, which might vary from shot to shot, depending on changes in the plot development (cf. very similar findings in the EURECAP Project reported in Chap. 7).

The Chinese learners reported that they needed to spend more time looking at the captions, as the Chinese characters, especially more complex ones, were difficult to process, whereas they spent less time reading easy and familiar ones (perhaps, unsurprisingly). Winke et al. also report that several of the Chinese learners felt that reading Chinese captions was "tricky" and that they needed more time than was given to process and make use of the Chinese captions, especially when the video content was difficult to understand. A particularly striking comment was that

> It was stressful to try to read ... maybe in another language [captions] would have been more helpful, but in Chinese it's tricky to try to read that quickly. The captions helped me ... with the context, like the easier characters, the ones with fewer strokes. I was able to see those really quickly.

One of the research questions asked by Winke et al. was whether there was differential use of captions according to language. Reading captions at the pace of the video obviously proved to be something of a challenge for Chinese learners and suggests that not enough attention was paid to reading speed in Chinese when designing the experiment. My findings have always been that reading speed is a crucial variable in whether captions help, distract or hinder learner-viewers, as the presence of captions may even be stressful if viewers cannot read them fully before the next shot arrives. In this experiment, it seems that learners did not have control of the pace of the viewing, potentially increasing the stressfulness of the exercise even more.

The qualitative findings from interviews with the Arabic learners are particularly interesting as they throw light on the difficulties of captioning Arabic language programmes (I have been unable to find captioned Arabic films for use in a follow-up study to the EURECAP Project). The authors suggest that one reason why Arabic learners spent more time on looking at captions than Russian and Spanish learners was because of the difference between English and Arabic writing systems and the complexity of Arabic morphology. These are, perhaps, the obvious reasons, but they also highlight another issue for Arabic: participants' comments indicated that some of them relied a great deal on captions to understand the words being said, especially as there were some words in Arabic they could read but could not understand when spoken. The authors propose that some of the difficulty may be due to the diglossic nature of Arabic in that there are significant differences between the written and spoken language, with the formal written system being in Modern Standard Arabic (MSA) and a large variety of colloquial Arabic systems. The matching of sound and text, which we expect in most European languages, is much less in the case of Arabic language.

Their third research question was concerned with the effects of familiar and unfamiliar content. This difference appeared to be only really significant with the Chinese learners who spent much more time looking at the Chinese captions when the content was unfamiliar. The feedback from the Chinese learners was that reading the Chinese captions was stressful and taxing, suggesting either that they could not cope with their attention being split or that they just could not process the captions in the time available during a shot. As an explanation, Winke et al. invoke both the dual-processing theory of working memory (Baddeley, 2007; Mayer & Moreno, 1998), which suggests that people have limited amounts of cognitive resources for information processing, and the cognitive load theory (Chandler & Sweller, 1991), which would suggest that when Chinese learners split their attention between reading captions and viewing the images on screen, their limited visual working memory capacity was overburdened. Again, this finding points to the need to identify clearly the levels of proficiency in both listening and reading before embarking on this type of study, and also to consider whether participants should be given control of the pace of viewing, especially if the pace of a programme is likely to prove stressful and beyond both their listening and their reading ability.

5.8 Some Theories on How Captions Work for Second/Foreign Language Viewers and Learners

Captions are essentially a practical tool developed for the benefit of deaf and hard-of-hearing people. While I have, as yet, only come across practically orientated papers, reports and articles on their use by deaf people, in the field of applied linguistics, second language acquisition, literacy development and translation studies, researchers feel a strong need to explain how they work with second language learners and to explore possible theories.

I felt such a need in my early research and drew extensively on the work of Wallace Lambert and colleagues in Canada. I wanted to understand the processes involved in watching captioned video and why our senses were not overwhelmed by the bimodal input, which, in fact, appeared to be a support rather than a hindrance, offering multiple representations of the same information. Lambert and colleagues (Holobow, Lambert, & Sayegh, 1984; Lambert, Boehler, & Sidoti, 1981; Lambert & Holobow, 1984) carried out several experiments to assess different combinations of visual (i.e., subtitles or captions) and auditory input using subjects' L1 and L2 (usually English L1 with French L2) with young (Grades 5, 6 and 7) English-speaking learners of French in Canada. They found that reversed subtitling (a combination of dialogues in the learners' L1 and printed scripts of the dialogues in the L2) and bimodal L2 input (dialogues and scripts in the L2) were "especially promising" devices for language learning and for enhancing listening comprehension. In a conclusion, which resounds with the findings of Mitterer and McQueen's (2009) research comparing the effects of translation subtitles and same-language captions, Holobow, Lambert and Sayegh say:

> However, not all bimodal (or bilingual) inputs are effective, since normal subtitling (with dialogue in L2 and script in L1) is relatively very ineffective.
>
> With the exception of normal subtitling, bimodal inputs generally strengthen or enhance the verbal message, suggesting that the double modal input may be processed more "deeply" because attention can alternate from the auditory to the visual format or be directed along parallel visual and auditory routes simultaneously. Rather than being a distraction, the double modal input appears to enhance comprehension better than simply processing script through silent reading. Perhaps reading itself would be improved if readers were encouraged to read aloud so as to provide themselves with an auditory accompaniment. (1984:73)

Yet, we should remember that Lambert and his fellow researchers are not referring to subtitled or captioned audiovisual material, but to dialogues and scripts, and end up recommending dictation as a good method for developing L2 skills. At the time when I first read and cited their articles, I was, of course, rather searching around for respectable support from acknowledged researchers, and Wallace Lambert certainly fitted this requirement. Since then, my references to Lambert and colleagues have been regularly repeated, with, I suspect, little checking on their work and its relevance to captioned viewing. For those interested, the most comprehensive account of these studies is provided by Danan (1992) in her insightful article on both bimodal and reversed subtitling (where the audio is in the L1 and the subtitle text in the L2).

In the face of a great deal of scepticism from many teachers and researchers at the time, who felt that the caption text hindered the development of listening skills or that providing the captions was somehow "cheating," it was also reassuring to find support for the potential of captions to unlock hitherto inaccessible material for language learners from Michael Halliday (perhaps an unlikely source), who appeared to be saying much the same as I was, with his suggestion that the text might function by supplying a synopsis of dynamic speech (Halliday, 1989; Vanderplank, 1993).

As Halliday (1989) puts it so well:

> Of course, there are individual differences in learning styles some learn more through the ear, others through the eye. And there are individual differences in teaching style; a teacher may be more at home in one or the other medium... the written language represents a synoptic view. It defines its universe as product rather than process.... The spoken language presents a dynamic view. It defines its universe primarily as process, encoding it not as structure but as constructing—or demolishing. (p. 96)

Halliday was right to highlight the dynamic view of spoken language. As I found (and as de Bot, Jagt, Janssen, Kessels, and Schills (1986) had found in their study of speech and text giving different information in news programmes), within the viewing of any single programme, my learners moved between the different styles, sometimes taking in more through the caption text, at other times listening carefully to the speech, sometimes using the text for support, at other times "chunking" caption text rapidly before listening. I found much the same behaviour again in the diary feedback of EURECAP participants, which I report in Chap. 7. However, it is also important to bear in mind that for those who are able to move easily between the sound and caption text, some element of redundancy may be at work. We are receiving the same linguistic (at least lexical and semantic) information through two channels (or, in fact, three, given the visual channel for contextual meaning) and, with practice, may be filling in gaps with one channel or another. However, if the caption and sound channels are not in basic synchronisation or convey dissimilar or different information, far from their being helpful redundancy, there may well be distraction and disruption for viewers.

Thomas Garza (1991:246) provides a different, but equally valid, rationale for the pedagogical use of second language audio and second language captions, when he writes,

> "By providing students with a familiar (i.e., comprehensible) graphic representation of an utterance, they are empowered to begin to assign meaning to previously unintelligible aural entities, gradually building their aural comprehension in relation to the reading comprehension." The goal of the use of second language captions, in his terms, is to help learners match written words to their phonetic realization in the language. (cf. Vanderplank, 1988a)

More recently, Mitterer and McQueen (2009) added their support for the value of captions, suggesting that, on the basis of their findings, captions provide for the lexically-guided retuning of perception. As they say, captions enable listeners to retune their perceptual categories at a prelexical level to the characteristics of the language of speakers, leading to long-term changes in speech perception, which mean that they are able to recognise both words they have heard before and novel words containing the retuned sounds. In Chap. 4, I suggested that their findings are best understood in terms of the development of key psychomotor skills, which provide the foundation for building cognitive and affective skills in the foreign language. I also build a perceptual tuning-in component into my revised model of language learning with captioned films and programmes, presented in Chap. 8.

It was Martine Danan who brought the possible relevance of Allan Paivio's "dual coding theory" to our attention, as an explanation as to why our senses are not overwhelmed by the bimodal input of sound and subtitle text and why we may benefit from the presence of both translation subtitles and same-language captions. As Danan's reports (1992:499), Paivio's dual coding theory (1986, Chap. 4) distinguishes two separate representational systems, a verbal system and an imagery system composed of non-verbal objects and events:

> According to Paivio's model, the two systems are functionally independent, yet representations in one system can also activate those in the other because dually coded items (coded verbally and nonverbally) are linked by referential connections. Visual traces are remembered better than are verbal components and also have an additive effect when items are encoded dually. Consequently, according to Paivio (1986, Chap. 11), in the case of second or foreign language learning, as more foreign words are learned in direct association with appropriate nonverbal referents (objects, but also experiential elements such as events and emotions), the richer and more meaningful are the referential interconnections, thus resulting in better language recall and appropriate use. A video program providing visual referents and an involving story line could supply some of this nonverbal support.

However, before we accept this theory as wholly supportive, we should bear in mind that over the years, Paivio's original notion of the visual and audio providing dual support appears to have switched to audio and text (e.g., Montero Perez et al., 2013, cite Paivio in their rationale for caption use), but the idea that the sound and caption text provide mutual support remains a key explanation for why captions assist, rather than overwhelm, the sensory system.

Another information processing theory, which crops up in some studies such as Frumuselu et al. (2015) and Winke et al. (2013), is Richard Mayer's cognitive theory of multimedia learning (2009), which was also based on Paivio's dual coding theory. This theory, which was developed in the context of L1 learning, is centred around a series of principles, the best known of which is probably that learners attempt to build connections between words and pictures and that they learn more deeply with both than they might have with words or picture alone. Frumuselu et al. (2015) also draw on cognitive load theory (Sweller, 2005), which is concerned with how we integrate our knowledge of human cognitive structures and instructional design principles to improve learning. They suggest that in exposing learners to several channels and modes simultaneously (audio, visual and textual in the form of captions), we ease the load of working memory, since we distribute the information among the three systems. Instead of overloading our comprehension faculties, the three systems complement each other and reinforce language meaning that may come from spoken or visual sources. Captions are not just redundant tools but offer support in understanding language in context. In cognitive load terms, learners are provided with a means of internalising new language and transforming it into long-term organised information, thereby reducing the cognitive load of the working memory (Mayer, Lee, & Peebles, 2014; Sweller, 2005). This is certainly an interesting perspective, but probably adds little in the way of useful insights to what others such as Halliday (see p. 144) and Garza (see p. 145) were saying.

Perhaps, more relevant in terms of our understanding of what engages learner-viewers in watching captioned programmes more or less attentively is relatively recent work in cognitive psychology, which enlarges the cognitive theory of learning with media to include the affective domain. Roxanna Moreno (2006, Moreno & Mayer, 2007) includes factors of self-regulation, self-efficacy and motivation in her combined model "integrating assumptions regarding the relationship between cognition, metacognition and motivation and affect" (2007:767), and these aspects of a combined cognitive-affective learning theory have clear implications for how we should treat language learning from captioned TV programmes and films. This is an exciting prospect, and I shall explore these domains and how they apply to exploiting captioned documentaries in Chap. 6, as well as using them to revise my original model of language learning through captioned viewing in Chap. 8.

5.9 Heading into Relatively Uncharted Territory

In the last two chapters, I have set out the main areas in which research has been carried out over the last thirty years. With some interesting exceptions, most of the research has been carried on around a limited number of major themes and, allowing for variation in populations, levels and programme genres, has reached similar conclusions about the limitations and benefits of captioned viewing for foreign and second language learning. In the next two chapters, I focus on two areas, which have received relatively little attention, programme genres and independent learning from captioned viewing over an extended period.

6

Focus on Genres: The Practical Uses and Limitations of Different Types of Programmes

6.1 A Lost Golden Age?

At the end of Chap. 5, I identified programme genres as an under-researched area given the volume of published research papers on captioned viewing and language learning. To repeat my "mantra," there is really nothing to compare with film and TV as resources for language learning, especially if we can make its richness and variety of language accessible through captions. In this chapter, I provide examples of different genres that I have used, mostly successfully, over the years.

Were the 1980s and 1990s a golden age of captioned programmes for the language teacher? VCRs (video recorders which recorded on VHS videotape), which could also record captions, were hardly more expensive than standard VCRs, and programmes could be recorded easily and in a simple, portable and reusable form. One drawback of VCRs was that captions were fixed in the recording and could not be switched on and off as they can on a DVD but otherwise, it was cheap and easy to make recordings and play them in the classroom on a standard VCR (though there were challenging copyright issues). Life became decidedly more complicated as the VHS format was phased out and the DVD format took over. Recording was more difficult, and even playing back DVDs did not have the ease of flexibility for teaching that the VHS videotapes had had. At the time of writing, media technology has moved to the point where recording on hard drive, online sites such as *YouTube*, streaming and boxed sets of TV programmes and films in DVD and Blu-ray formats have become the norm; now it is difficult to buy a DVD recorder in the UK.

The options are becoming limited for teachers who want to record captioned programmes and use them in their teaching, though independent learners have probably never had it so good. Of course, it is possible to capture a great deal of online material, but recording broadcast programmes and films with captions for later editing and use is less simple than it was in the days of VHS. In the UK, educational institutions can subscribe to the *Box of Broadcasts* at £5000 per year if they are members of the British Universities Video and TV Council and have a licence from the Educational Recording Agency (about £2 per student head currently). This not only gives access to an amazing resource of one million programmes covering many UK channels and ten foreign language channels but also offers members the options of requesting up to five recordings a day.

In Chap. 2, I positioned the use of captioned films and TV programmes for language learning between audiovisual language teaching and the use of translation subtitles, and argued that given the way in which captions alter the viewing experience for learners, it requires its own conceptualisations and practices in which to develop. I mentioned some of the key concepts: autonomy and self-regulation, perceived self-efficacy, value and effort as being guiding principles in successful exploitation of captioned films and programme for language learning. This may appear to have left the teacher out, but at various times over the years, I have written about the role of the teacher in using captioned programmes and films. For the teacher, the use of captions should be liberating, as programmes "speak for themselves" and learners can respond directly. On a mundane level, preparation time may be cut dramatically, programmes can be shown extensively as well as intensively and programme content and language can be studied in depth. On a professional level, the raising of learner knowledge and awareness through the caption text shifts the demands placed on the teacher from that of the "game show host" role advocated by some recipe writers on using audiovisual material in the language classroom to a more expert level.

It is difficult to believe that there has been little research on how captioning different TV and film genres may have different outcomes in terms of the responses of non-native viewers, at least, little that I have found. Paul Markham (1989) compared responses to clips about different religions with different groups of learners with and without captions, but the main focus of the study was the value of captions and the familiarity with the topics, and there was no real analysis of different genres on the subjects. Most of the research has involved short clips from educational or cultural series, documentaries (especially science) and situation comedies, but it has not dealt with the issue of genre selection, except, perhaps, in a discussion of the limitations. Rodgers (2013), for example, mentions that using a situation comedy series, intended to entertain, as his material may have created its own limitations in terms of how much learning could be expected.

Yet, just as we adjust our viewing behaviour, degree of attention and level of engagement with a programme or film according to how we regard it in terms of genre, seriousness, content, demands, usefulness, relevance and purpose in watching, so the same should be true of captioned programmes—perhaps even more so. As I found in my original work (1990), it was difficult for my students to take watching a soap opera seriously and engage with the language, no matter how much I stressed and demonstrated that there was a great deal of very useful colloquial language to be gained, along with the opportunity to tune in to local accents. As I argue elsewhere in this book, it is too limiting to talk about the effects of captions on watching audiovisual material when what we should be thinking about are the ways in which the effects **with** captions may be different not only according to our purposes in watching but also according to the genre of TV programmes and films.

6.2 Then and Now: Different Programmes, Same Genres—How Little Has Changed

It quickly became clear during the *Teletext 888 Project* that different genres evoked different responses from student-viewers. Up-to-date news and current affairs programmes were always well received, even if the live, rolling captions were annoying. Soap operas were dismissed as trivial and not worth watching (even if they watched them at home); documentaries had mixed responses, depending on the content and topic; natural history programmes proved to be problematical, as the focus is so much on the visual; what I then termed "direct-address" programmes and which might now be called "lifestyle programmes" also varied in responses, as they covered such topics as house moving, home improvement and cooking. However, comedies proved to be very popular and well received, as students could laugh in the right places and for the right reasons much of the time with the aid of the captions, and I continued to use these to focus on idioms and colloquial or metaphorical expressions.

6.2.1 Exploiting the Main Source—TV News and Current Affairs Programmes

In the early 1990s, I was approached by a publisher who wanted me to put forward a proposal for a book that they wished to publish on using TV news for language teaching and learning. A couple of years earlier, I had published a comparative review of two news programmes in terms of their value for language learners: first, *Newsbrief*, a subscription service marketed by *BBC* Enterprises, which provided a "carefully scripted and freshly produced" hour-long videotape each month, together with a study pack, index, transcripts and teachers' study guides; second, *Newsview*, a twenty-minute long weekly review of news, broadcast by the *BBC* on Saturdays, with captions for the deaf and hard-of-hearing. I showed my exchange students 30 minutes of the *Newsbrief* sample video, kindly provided by the *BBC* and the whole 20 minutes of *Newsview*. They carried out the *Newsbrief* exercises, and we discussed the items as suggested in the study pack. At the end of it all, only one of the ten student preferred *Newsbrief* (the expensive one) to *Newsview* (yours for the price of the licence fee in the UK at the time). So when it came to preparing a proposal for the publisher, I found myself in a difficult position. The publisher clearly wanted a regular recipe-type book for teachers to exploit recorded clips of news programmes, yet my review had found that the key feature of captioned news was that it was able to stand alone and did not need the support of additional printed material or extensive teacher support. Since news broadcasts were already available with captions, I argued, it was not worth the extra expense and effort to produce a magazine or glossy printed book.

My proposal was for a 50–60-minute compilation of captioned news items, grouped into topics and presented in magazine format, with an anchorperson providing continuity. The small accompanying booklet would contain a list of the news items and times, guidance for use and rationale. My proposal was not accepted, and the compilation was published without captions and with an expensive activity book.

One problem with non-captioned news and current affairs programmes is that they may be very labour-intensive for the teacher. Learners may get very little without a great deal of help and explanation from the teacher, as we have seen in some of the research reported in Chaps. 4 and 5. As already said, given the stream of sound and noise, and dynamic, fleeting images, we all tend to concentrate on the visual rather than the verbal. In contrast, news broadcasts with captions are much less teacher-centred and offer enormous potential for increasing learner autonomy. The teacher may attend to the language and content of the news alongside the learner as it were, explaining and interpreting where necessary. Learners have a sense of being in control, of taking responsibility and, most importantly, of knowing what questions to ask at the end. This is particularly helpful when there is a lack of connection between what is being reported and the visual images that accompany the report. For example, in the sequence about the war in Syria (given further in the text on p. 155), at times the images are conveying one message while the speech is telling us something completely unconnected with the scene.

A key feature of captioned news or current affairs programmes is that they can stand alone without the need for additional printed material or extensive teacher mediation, provided the material is appropriately selected and graded. Thus, we need to bear in mind that news is one of the genres with the fastest pace of speaking and often will be captioned live with rolling captions. Pre-recorded news stories with prepared captioned, rather than live reports with rolling captions, will always be the preferred option for hearing viewers.

The wonderful thing about captioned news is that it provides the language for learners to understand current news and events and then talk about them using the appropriate language. Within Europe, as I write, our news is full of stories about refugees and migrants crossing the sea and land to seek safety and asylum in European countries. One approach, which I have used successfully, is to gather stories from different news programmes, channels and presenters to create a topic based around seven or eight short (1–2-minute long) items. So, for the refugees, the topics for the clips might be:

1. The current fighting in Syria
2. Refugees in Greece landing on an island
3. Scene from Calais and attempts to get through the Channel Tunnel
4. Story of background of refugees and economic migrants
5. Interview with UK government minister
6. Speech by minister in EU country on policy towards refugees
7. Report on future options for managing refugee crises.

Depending on the size of the class, level of learners and resources available, the clips can be viewed by the whole class, in groups or, if a language laboratory is available, individually, so that learners can play clips under their own control with tasks set for each clip and for the topic as a whole. A key aim is to enable learners to identify the language (words and structures) for talking about this topic and make it their own for their own purposes. Within this topic, there is room for role plays as presenters, interviewers and interviewees, and as correspondents reporting directly. Learners could also be asked to make their own news items and stories around this or a related topic, but again drawing on the rich language provided by the captioned clips.

6 Focus on Genres 155

Following is a short extract from a current *BBC* news item (20 October 2015) on the refugee crisis, to provide an example of the richness and variety of language in a very short item.

Sophie Rayworth (Newsreader with Southern English accent): The start of winter is not slowing down the migrant crisis at all—that's the warning from the UN Refugee Agency. Around nine thousand people a day have been arriving on the Greek islands in the past four days alone. The UN says the situation is chaotic—many of those coming to Europe are from Syria—Aid agencies says that around 35,000 have fled from around the city of Aleppo after an upsurge in fighting there. Our correspondent, Quentin Sommerville, reports from the border between Turkey and Syria. You may find some of the images in his report distressing.
Quentin Somerville (Scottish accent): A mighty arsenal and mighty firepower have brought about the furious return of President Assad's forces in Syria. New fronts in the fighting bring fresh hell on the ground. An offensive in southern Syria, regime tanks taking half a dozen towns in the last five days. It's caused an exodus of tens and now today hundreds heading for the Turkish border. This man tells us that [voice over Syrian speaking in Arabic] 'we left Syria because we can't live there any more. It used to be just Bashar Al Assad. Now we have Russia and we don't know who's coming next. It's become a world war.' This was Mohamed Almawaz's house near Idlib. His father was pulled barely conscious from the rubble. Here, his mother. She died shortly afterwards. Russian jets were to blame, he says. [Voice over Syrian man speaking in Arabic] 'It's hard to describe the feeling when you flee your country and you lose your home and your family and you watch your mother dying right before you. It's indescribable', he told me. Meanwhile Russia continues to deny causing civilian casualties. Russia's intervention in Syria is beginning to make a difference, firmly in Assad's favour [continues]

And, of course, since the flow of news (especially bad news) is endless these days, there will always be stories, which fit general topics such as the sport, celebrities, music, health, lifestyle, crime, natural events and disaster, drugs and politics.

I have found that when I use news programme with captions, it is my students who ask the questions at the end of each segment or programme. They know what they need to know or what gaps need to be filled in order to achieve full understanding of a news item. Perhaps, having questions to ask is the sign that mental effort and elaboration is going on in a learner while watching; in other words, the learner is being active and independent.

Learners may benefit most from watching news programmes in the same way as native speaker viewers: they need to watch two or more broadcasts of roughly the same news or on the same topic. After all, most news for most viewers is not new at all. News stories in Britain consist mainly of updates of familiar stories: the Euro, refugees, the Royal Family, the national economy, a foreign crisis, an industrial dispute, a murder and so on. As a result, news reporting style is frequently elliptical and oblique. References are definite and known, rather than indefinite and new. Initially, learners need to be put in a position similar to native speakers. They can only achieve this through knowing the names, places, dates and usual terminology. If they do not know these basics, learners will be badly wrong-footed in their listening. Captions, on first viewing, provide exactly the lexicon that they need, together with sound/spelling/meaning correspondences. In subsequent viewings of news programmes (with or without captions), learners can then concentrate on listening and understanding programme language and content.

6.2.2 Using Captioned Films and Dramas

In Chap. 7, I shall discuss at length how the participants in the EURECAP Project made use of captioned films on DVDs. In this section, therefore, I shall restrict myself to some general comments and also draw on other sources to provide some sound advice. Obtaining DVDs with captions may not be altogether easy in some countries. In the UK, for example, while English language DVDs come with English captions, it is very difficult to obtain foreign language DVDs with anything but translation subtitles, and one needs to buy these online from suppliers in the country in which the film is made. So, for example, if one wants a French film with French captions for the deaf and hard-of-hearing, they may only be available in France, Belgium or Switzerland, and may have to be ordered through a supplier such as Amazon.fr When I was faced with this issue in setting up the EURECAP Project, the UK distributors told me that they did not think there was any market for captioned DVDs in foreign languages in the UK and they would not consider changing the policy of supplying only DVDs with translation subtitles in English. I am sure this position will change over the years as more and more people demand captioned DVDs, while in the EU and elsewhere equality legislation is already being invoked to support captioned DVDs for deaf and hard-of-hearing people.

Sound advice on using films for language learning independently is widely available, and a good example is the website, *FluentU*, which has some good, basic advice on using Chinese captions on Chinese films for learning:

> **"Best Strategies for Learning Chinese from Movies**
> Don't get the popcorn popping just yet. First, we have got to go over some strategies for how to approach Chinese language films.
>
> - **Watch actively.** Sure, some days you'll want to just sit back and relax, not worrying if you've understood every last detail. However, you will get much greater educational value out of an *active* watching experience. Pause and rewind when you miss half of a complicated dialogue. Go back and watch these tricky scenes until you understand every word. As you watch the same scene repeatedly, keep an eye on the captions below and mouth lines along with the actors if possible. Keep a notebook nearby and jot down new vocabulary or puzzling sentence structures so you can revisit what you have learned later. These steps towards actively watching movies will help you pay closer attention and become thoroughly engrossed in the language.
> - **Use Chinese captions to your advantage.** Too many language learners slip into the habit of watching Chinese movies with English subtitles and using their more comfortable language as a crutch. Alternatively, just as many Chinese students try to fly solo and play

movies without any subtitles at all, inevitably resulting in undue frustration.
- **Pick genres and topics that you genuinely enjoy.** You want to learn about Chinese history and culture, or understand more about the Cultural Revolution—that's all well and good. However, you will steadily lose interest if you keep choosing movie after movie featuring dry topics or genres you're not really into. Are you a total adrenaline junkie who needs a regular diet of action movies? Then don't force yourself to choose historical dramas because they're more educational. You can learn Chinese from all types of Chinese movies!

It is all as simple as it sounds: pick great movies, pay close attention and enjoy! Be sure to read this post for a more in-depth guide on how to learn Chinese with movies."

This is, of course, excellent advice for watching any captioned audiovisual material, especially the last point about picking genres and topics that the learners genuinely enjoy. Just as we would not waste much time on books that do not engage us, so we should select films that engage us and draw us in for their content, language, characters, plot and so on.

My own experience with films is that they are difficult to use as a class-based resource for language learning. While learners generally like to watch films with captions, they do so in order to be able to watch them as films, not as language learning objects (cf. Bird's difficulty with a "not for learning" group in his 2005 study reported in Chap. 4). The same, it must be said, has been my experience with TV dramas. As viewers, we want to be drawn into the plot and appreciate the characters, and trying to exploit films or dramas in the language classroom may produce tensions between the different purposes of watching.

One way around this is to create a space in the syllabus, which includes different film genres or types of TV dramas as objects of study and discussion. Obviously, creating the time available for learners to watch a whole film or drama may be an issue in many contexts, and it would be best if viewing of a captioned film or drama were set as preparation for the class. As I described in Chap. 3 in my third study (pp. 64–69), setting tasks around extensive viewing is likely to have the effect of (radically) changing the viewing experience for many learners and, it is hoped, will move them towards a more language learning-orientated approach to viewing, especially with the access to the language provided by the captions. There is much talk of "flipped classrooms" these days, where learners do much of the work outside and before their language classes, taking advantage of the affordances offered by audiovisual media. Viewing captioned films and dramas is one of the more obvious exploitations of such flipping.

If we want to show dramas in the class or as set work outside the class, I have found that the most productive are crime dramas. Since it is essential to be able to follow a plot closely, and plot development usually advances through key dialogues and exchanges, crime series such as *Lewis* (the successor to *Morse*, and set in Oxford) benefit greatly from being captioned. I ask my students to watch episodes of *Lewis* to prepare short reviews, sometimes asking then to compare one episode with another. If students are able to watch an episode on their own in between classes, they can be asked to pick some scenes that they think are important for the plot, and make a note of the time of the scene so that it can be watched in class. The following is an extract from a key scene in *Lewis*, which shows the importance of understanding the verbal narrative:

Hathaway: Charles James believed in a living, breathing spirituality in which we could all become Christ.
Maddox: Turn water in wine? Save me a few quid?
Hathaway: Stop it Maddox. It's about forgiveness. Because we are like Christ we can forgive the sins of the world. And interestingly, Phil Beskin claims to have direct experience of how that works.
Lewis: Interesting?
Hathaway: Well, because by implication he knew he was guilty of something that he was being forgiven for. He also had this tattoo in the middle of his chest. I want to know what it means.
Maddox: Does it have to mean anything? Maybe he just liked the image and put it where he fancied. (That's what I did with mine—*no caption text*). I'll see you later.

Hathaway: Have you ever thought about getting a tattoo?
Lewis: No, I have not.
Hathaway: One for the travels, maybe.
Lewis: I'll bear that in mind.
They enter a tattoo parlour
Lewis (to tattooist): Er, a word. DI Lewis. Do you recognize this by any chance? (shows tattoo design, tattooist shakes his head). Are you sure, because it belongs to someone you know. Phil Beskin. You were at a talk he gave last night.
Tattooist: He didn't get his tattoo out. It wasn't that kind of talk.
Hathaway: Are you a Charles Williams' fan?
Tattooist: Yeah. Not all tattooist are pagans?
Lewis: We gather you had a bit of a barney with a Wouter Eisler last night? Was Phil Beskin involved in that?
Tattooist.: Yeah. We all were. It was nothing to write home about. Why?
Lewis: Because Phil Beskin was murdered last night.

In *Lewis*, as in most crime dramas, the plot is complicated and often difficult to follow, even for native speakers. It is essential to be able to at least follow the language if one is to understand the twists and turns and the roles of different characters. As I shall report in Chap. 7, a number of the participants in the EURECAP Project noted that they had difficulty in following plots and characters in crime films and that close attention to the caption text was essential or they got "the wrong end of the stick," as one participant put it.

Now that boxed sets of series in DVD format in different languages are available, it is possible, at last, to make use of captioned DVDs in other languages. For example, the French fast-paced and exciting police and legal series, *Engrenages* (broadcast as *Spiral* in the UK with subtitles), has proved very popular with French learners who can obtain the version with French captions—even if a lot of the language one might learn from the captions is not really usable in polite company.

Asking students to watch two similar detective series and compare the approaches to solving crimes in the conversations of detectives with colleagues, suspects and other people in the story has also worked well and has provoked some good questions and lively discussion.

6.2.3 Exploiting Documentaries: The "Warm Bath" Problem

In a book chapter entitled "Resolving inherent conflicts: Autonomous language learning from popular broadcast television" (1994a), I attempted to look at the issue of engaging learner-viewers in making use of TV programmes not only for entertainment but also as language learning resources. By looking at two different genres, documentaries and situation comedies, I hoped to illustrate the potential of these programmes in language learning terms and the issues surrounding watching them for any educational purpose.

As said elsewhere in this book, one paradoxical issue is that by providing access through captions to TV programmes and films that would otherwise be largely inaccessible, we enable learners to watch in a native-speaker-like way. However, this is not an automatic benefit in terms of learning either language or content, as so ably demonstrated by Salomon and Leigh's (1984) work, and we are faced with the same issues as those faced by all who hope to exploit the educational potential of television. Firstly, viewers bring expectations of little effort to TV watching, and secondly, sophisticated programme makers understand how to make serious programme content engaging and entertaining, but in doing so, they may weaken its very educational power. In language learning terms, we want our learner-viewers to be engaged, but to also put in some effort to extract language from their viewing.

Once we solve the problems of inaccessibility caused to learners by the rich, dynamic and complex spoken language of television, we are faced with the same problems as those faced by all who hope to exploit the educational potential of television. If autonomous language learning viewers can laugh in the right places and for the right reasons, and can understand and appreciate the language of sophisticated documentary programmes, then we must ask ourselves the same questions as those educationalists who seek to use television for native speaker education and learning.

The key problem for those of us interested in the challenge of using popular television programmes for educational purposes is that TV is universal—illiterates can watch it. It can be watched and enjoyed with a very low level of mental effort, and it can appeal just to emotions and sentimentality. In this respect, it is quite unlike print, which requires a far higher level of decoding skill to begin with, that is, it requires a cognitive effort using cognitive skills (Salomon & Leigh, 1984; Salomon, 1983a, 1983b).

One way around this issue, I have found, is to treat a documentary programme as an exercise in itself for looking at the following:

(a) How TV programmes and the messages they convey are structured.
(b) What language and messages language learners are receiving.
(c) How we can watch programmes not only for information and interest but also for language development and learning.

6.2.3.1 Cognitive and Affective Objectives in Two Documentaries

I use the examples of two science documentaries to look carefully at the language and structure of the programmes and the objectives they serve.

The first is a documentary in the highly regarded and long-running *BBC Horizon* series, *The Battle of the Merozoites*. The theme of this programme is that Dr. Pataroyo, a Colombian chemist and researcher, claims to have developed a vaccine against malaria.

A fairly standard set of questions to orientate a class of language learners in the first few minutes of the programme might be the following:

"As you watch. I should like you to note words and phrases for talking about malaria, and be ready to answer these questions:

(1) What is malaria?
(2) How is it caused?
(3) Why are preventative measures ineffective?"

In fact, these questions could probably have been answered by most learners without watching the programme, even if they lacked the precise terminology, which, of course, the programme provided in the captions. The average learner in both a classroom and independent learning context would almost certainly have started watching the programme with the answers to these questions as "given knowledge," that is, the general background knowledge that the viewer brings to a programme.

Caption transcript 1

Voice-over (VO): Despite the propaganda, more soldiers are killed by malaria than by armed combat. One bite from a mosquito carrying the malarial parasite is enough to kill. The malaria parasite infects 300 million people a year, killing nearly 2 million worldwide. Now the enemy within is gaining strength with increased resistance so drugs designed to combat it.

But one scientist claims to have developed the world's only effective vaccine and to be winning the battle against malaria. Any malaria vaccine would help protect the armed forces. Over the years they've been recruited by researchers to help in the fight against malaria. An effective vaccine would also transform the lives of millions of people in the developing world. And tourists travelling to countries where drug resistant strains of the parasite are common are now more than ever in greater need of protection.

The most deadly form of malaria is caused by a parasite called *Plasmodium falciparum*. The infected mosquito injects the parasite when sucking blood.

Colonel Jerald Sadoff (Walter Reed Army Institute of Research): One of the reasons it's so hard to make a vaccine is that the parasite uses a lot of tricks to fool the immune system to prevent effective immunity from occurring. One of the tricks it does is to change from one thing to another pretty quickly. You're immune against one part of it but then it's something else. Also at certain stages, like at the first stage, there's very little of it there.

VO: (accompanying diagram): The first stage of the parasite is called the *sporozoite*. If these *sporozoites* aren't attacked by the immune system, they go on to the liver.

Col. Sadoff: Pretty soon they get inside liver cells—there is very little ability to recognise them. And when the body first starts recognising them, then they change into *merozoites* and they're bursting out of those liver cells and into the bloodstream.

VO: The next form of the parasite, the *merozoite*, is able to invade red blood cells. Once inside the cell, the *merozoites* rapidly divide and burst out to release more *merozoites* to invade more red blood cells. Every 48 hours thousands of *merozoites* are ejected from the red cells in waves causing symptoms of malaria fever interspersed with periods of shivering which can be fatal. The cycle gets repeated again and again.

Col. Sadoff: The mosquito comes in and bites the person that's infected and the cycle starts again when the mosquito bites and infects another person and then infects someone else.

Those of us who use or watch documentaries with captions know that they are a rich and powerful resource for learning both language and content in a wide range of subject areas. For the most part, I would argue, we tend to think of documentaries as being factual and informative, as the transcript of the clip shows. In using documentaries, we seek to teach and encourage our learners to learn cognitive skills and to achieve cognitive objectives at different levels, depending on levels of proficiency.

Anderson and Krathwohl's revised *Taxonomy of Cognitive Objectives* (2001) provides a well-known hierarchical structure for cognitive learning objectives:

1. Remembering: Recall or retrieve previous learned information.
2. Understanding: Comprehending the meaning, translation, interpolation, and interpretation of instructions and problems. State a problem in one's own words.
3. Applying: Use a concept in a new situation or unprompted use of an abstraction. Applies what was learned in the classroom into novel situations in the work place
4. Analysing: Separates material or concepts into component parts so that its organizational structure may be understood. Distinguishes between facts and inferences.
5. Evaluating: Make judgments about the value of ideas or materials.

6. Creating: Builds a structure or pattern from diverse elements. Put parts together to form a whole, with emphasis on creating a new meaning or structure.
(Anderson & Krathwohl, 2001)

In language learning terms, we might structure the taxonomy in the following way:

(a) Knowledge of facts and language; vocabulary building.
(b) Reading and listening comprehension; understanding how the facts and language fit together.
(c) Demonstrating knowledge and understanding, generating one's own language, transferring and adapting language to new situations and uses.
(d) Understanding the structure of language; seeing patterns in text and discourse.
(e) Using the foreign language to compare and contrast; evaluating information and positions; editing, proof-reading, checking, evaluating other people's language.
(f) Making the foreign language one's own in new and varied ways and activities.

However, as the programme progresses, its cognitive orientation becomes less evident and its focus shifts, as Caption Transcript 2 below illustrates.

Caption Transcript 2
Col. Sadoff: The main weapons that we've used in the past have been insecticides.
Unfortunately the bugs got smart or resistant and insecticides are not as useful as they were, or as with DDT, the residuals are more toxic for humans then we care to use to kill off these insects. Walter Reed have taken 10 to 15 years to develop a drug and the parasite can become resistant to it in 2 to 3 years. We're becoming quite discouraged about drugs as it takes so long to develop them and parasites are becoming resistant very rapidly. Our great fear is that we won't have any drugs for the treatment of malaria and people will be dying from malaria and

there won't be any drugs to treat them and we'll have no effective control. And just think about that. We have 300 million cases and 2 million children dying as it is -what would it be if we had no drugs? We're really almost desperate to develop a vaccine.

While we are first of all being given facts and are being expected to use our cognitive skills, the latter part of this sequence calls for other skills and serves other objectives: skills of appreciating the problem, of valuing the research done, of having one's awareness and attention raised, of having one's attitude sharpened or shaped and of asking if the programme has meaning for oneself. The skills called for generally fall into what is known as the Affective Domain, a rather neglected domain until the recent work of Roxanne Moreno (Moreno, 2006; Moreno & Mayer, 2007) mentioned briefly in Chap. 5, despite the fact that it is at least as important as the cognitive domain. Just as we cannot be all emotion and attitude, so we cannot be all reason and logic. As Moreno has shown, both domains must be addressed in any complete learning situation, and there is more to the affective domain than simply a "filter" or "attitude" and "motivation," as the taxonomy (which was originally developed to sit alongside the Cognitive Domain Taxonomy) below shows:

The Affective Domain

1. **Receiving and attending**

    1.1. Awareness
    1.2. Willingness to receive
    1.3. Controlled or selected attention

2. **Responding**

    2.1. Acquiescence in responding
    2.2. Willingness to respond
    2.3. Satisfaction in response

3. Valuing

   3.1. Acceptance of a value
   3.2. Preference for a value
   3.3. Commitment (conviction)

4. Organization

   4.1. Conceptualization of a value
   4.2. Organization of a value system

5. Characterization of a value or value complex

   5.1. Generalized set ("attitude cluster")
   5.2. Characterization

(Krathwohl, Bloom, & Masia, 1964)

Common terms used to express the affective domain are interest, appreciation, attitude, belief, value and adjustment. Under each level of the domain, we can specify learning objectives, and in language learning terms, we can think of the taxonomy in the following way:

1. Receiving and attending

- attends (carefully) when watching programme
- listens to views expressed with respect
- appreciates and tolerates cultural patterns exhibited by individuals and groups
- sensitivity to problems presented

2. Responding

- voluntarily listens to and looks at language of programme
- voluntarily seeks new language to build up own competence in both known and new areas

- engages in viewing tasks that will help develop ability
- contributes to group work and discussion on programme

3. **Valuing**

- continuing desire to develop linguistic skills and ability
- sense of responsibility for development of own performance
- appetite for good, informed native-speaker-standard English in variety of registers as means of self-expression

In language learning terms, the implications for 3 might be:

- copying up notes and vocabulary in notebook
- reading more on subject in English
- discussing topic voluntarily with others
- rewatching programme with/without closed captions
- looking up words
- reviewing specific scenes of programme

4. **Organisation/Conceptualisation**

- finding out and crystallising basic assumptions, underlying issues and attitudes expressed in programme and how expressed
- forming and expressing own judgements
- relating own attitudes to those in programme
- using programme to derive ideas and expressions about conduct and life

5. **Characterisation of value**

- "attitude cluster"/common thread
- does the programme speak directly to you? (examples of ozone depletion/skin cancer, smoking and cancer).

6.2.3.2 Putting Cognitive and Affective Objectives Together

Levels within the taxonomy are not fixed or hard and fast, but seek to capture the progression of learning and also to express the essential links between cognitive and affective development in learning (and language learning). If we progress, learn and are able to receive and process information along only one dimension, our potential for educational development and our ability to use different sources and resources are limited. The two taxonomies combine the cognitive and affective dimensions of learning in the following hierarchical pattern:

Cognitive Objectives

1. Recall and recognition of knowledge
2. Comprehension of knowledge
3. Skill in application of knowledge apprehended
4. Skill in analysis of situations involving this knowledge; skill in synthesis of this knowledge into new organisation
5. Skill in evaluation in that area of knowledge to judge value of materials and methods for given purposes.

Affective Objectives

1. Receiving and attending to stimuli
2. Responding (on request, willingly or enthusiastically)
3. Valuing what has been responded to so as to respond voluntarily and seek ways of responding
4. Conceptualisation of each value responded to
5. Organisation of these values into a system and finally organising the value complex into a single whole; a characterisation of the individual.

To summarise briefly, skills and objectives within the Cognitive Domain deal with the recall and recognition of knowledge and the development of intellectual abilities and skills. Skills and objectives within the Affective Domain describe changes in interest, attitudes and values; the development of appreciation and adequate adjustment. In other words, the

Affective Domain encompasses our ability to think through new information, which, perhaps, contradicts long-held beliefs, and arrives at a satisfactory synthesis that integrates new values into old.

One helpful aspect of such a taxonomy is that is helps us identify the levels at which we are working and expect our students to work. All too often, we find that we are not demanding enough of our learners. Take the example of attending. As we know, TV can be attended to at a very low level, barely conscious some might say. Even active attention is really not high enough to match cognitive objectives in learning from TV programmes. We really need to be aiming at least at Level 3, at valuing. Only from this level do learners begin to take control and responsibility for their performance and development.

It also shows us that much of our experimentation is at too low a level to be of real value. We insist on testing for recall and recognition, when altogether more challenging goals await learners. In terms of foreign language learning, the communicatively competent learner is the one who has achieved a certain level not only in terms of psychomotor and cognitive skills, but also in terms of affective skills.

6.2.3.3 Orientating the Learner-Viewer Through Discourse

As I have already argued, a scientific documentary such as *The Battle of the Merozoites* contains many discourses, both cognitively and affectively orientated. To put it another way, the language and images of sequences and scenes may appeal to our reason, to our values, beliefs and attitudes or to both domains at once.

In the sequence given in Caption Transcript 3, for example, we see that there are, in fact, three distinct discourse types that are being interwoven to form a rich, complex and interesting sequence:

Caption Transcript 3

VO: (the scene is Dr. Patarroyo's clinic) There were now two areas of controversy over the vaccines—the peptides chosen and the precise control over its production. In the West he would not have been able to proceed without some formal review of his vaccine and its safety. Without such regulation, Patarroyo was able to move quickly from monkeys to man.

Dr. Patarroyo: In a human being if you just by chance damage the kidneys, the lungs, the brain, that's a serious issue. Besides that there were ethical considerations. I was very scared, I hesitated and I'm not ashamed to say that. For 9 months I could not take that step. But there were several situations that forced me to do that. Having succeeded with the monkeys, also I had the other question. What if it works in humans also? Then I would have the other doubt—that I spent too long not making the decision

VO: The first human trials using the new polymer were carried out in the new military hospital in Bogota. Thirteen soldiers took part in this trial. Nine got vaccine, 3 got saline and one was deliberately infected with malaria to act as the source of the parasites. After they were infected, blood samples were taken to check the presence of the parasite. In spite of Dr. Patarroyo's doubts, the trial was a success. The vaccine partially protected the volunteers from malaria. When these results were published, the World Health Organisation in Geneva asked the malaria team at the Centers for Disease Control in Atlanta to repeat Dr. Patarroyo's work on monkeys.

Dr. Bill Collins: Dr. Patarroyo came to our laboratory to prepare the peptides as close as possible to what he was doing in Colombia for our monkeys. We challenged the animals two weeks after the last immunisation arid then followed them daily to see how the disease was progressing. After 10 to 12 days it became obvious that the vaccine as given here did not give protection. Thirty monkeys were challenged even though we didn't know which were immunized 29 became sick and needed treatment with drugs. Only one animal was protected

VO: So in Atlanta neither the polymer version of Patarroyo's vaccine nor the peptides were able so protect the monkeys as they had done ¡n Colombia. These negative results fuelled doubts and speculation about the vaccine. Back in Colombia. Paiarroyo had already started a massive series of human trials with the marines.

Dr. Pat.: The military forces of Colombia allowed us to perform the first trial which involved 63 vaccinees and 122 placebos and these people were told that we didn't know exactly who were the conditions for vaccination. And we didn't know how much and how often to give them the vaccine. We explained them every single thing and they decided to participate. We asked them to give blood samples every 13 days in order to look at clinical laboratory tests like blood chemistry, blood count and urine analysis In order to find out if the vaccine was safe in a large group of people.

VO: Other studies with the marines tested the safety of the vaccine and established that 3 doses would be needed and in what doses they would be effective. The commander of the marine base was happy to volunteer his men to take part in the trials to boost his force's effectiveness.

For the language learner, the rich mix of language and discourse types, as in Caption Transcript 3, is likely to be far too heady a concoction for conscious and reflective language learning to take place. The cognitive dimension (information, facts, understanding) is likely to be supplanted by the narrative and argument. We follow the story and are struck by the emotional appeals "millions will die if something isn't done" or shocked by the fact that the commander "volunteers" his men. Content is, as it were, wrapped up (or perhaps buried) in a framework of narrative and argument designed to engage viewers affectively. What can be done? Firstly, raising awareness of the multidimensional and multidiscoursal nature of scientific documentaries can help orientate the mental set of learner-viewers towards intentional language learning as distinct from the incidental language learning of "normal" television watching. Awareness-raising tasks for the sequence of Transcript 3 might be, as follows:

1. What facts do you learn about malaria and its treatment from watching this sequence? What expressions and language are used to present and explain these facts? Who presents and explains them? (Orientation to expository discourse)
2. What stories are told in this sequence? Who tells them? (Orientation to narrative discourse)
3. What issues and questions does the sequence try to deal with? How are these expressed? Who expresses them? (Orientation to argumentative discourse)

4. Does this sequence have any "special" and direct meaning for you. How do you respond to Dr. P's approach to testing? (Orientation to level 3 of Affective Domain).

Typical answers for Task 4 might be, as follows:

The learner-viewer is Colombian/is from a malarial area/knows someone with malaria/is a doctor/a medical researcher/has been to a malarial area and taken pills/has been to Atlanta/has been involved in trials/is shocked by the lack of ethical procedures in Dr. P's work.

In this way, the affective engagement of a learner-viewer in a programme or sequence (the special or personal meaning) can be turned to cognitive advantage in language learning terms through simple awareness-raising and orientating tasks. With my own students who watched this documentary as part of a self-study programme, it was enough to provide them with the theme of the programme: "A Colombian doctor claims to have developed a vaccine against malaria" to obtain "meaning" for them in the sense of value and attitude and to concentrate their viewing towards both cognitive and affective educational objectives. I might add that they themselves were quite shocked at their own prejudices towards claims made by doctors and researchers from Third World countries when these were made explicit.

6.2.4 Ordering Discourses: Documentary 2. "The Transplanted Brain"

Transcript 4 gives the opening sequence of this programme on Parkinson's disease, 'The Transplanted Brain' and new approaches to its treatment.

Caption Transcript 4
VO: The population is getting older as people live longer and longer. Many have active lives well into old age. In control of their faculties, they're able to enjoy their later years. But with increasing age, the chances of developing a degenerative disease get greater. A few years ago, this man was vigorous and active. He ran a clothing company very successfully. Today he can no longer recognise his wife and can

barely feed himself. He suffers from one of a number of degenerative brain diseases that afflict the elderly.

General MacArthur and Harry Truman both had one of the more common disorders, Parkinson's Disease. So did the actor Michael Redgrave. Mohammed All, the former world champion boxer, had the same symptoms. It's a disease that most often occurs in older people but not exclusively so.

At the age of 20 Don Burns was an amateur tennis champion. Today at 39, he can only sit on the side-lines and watch because Don is one of the youngest victims of Parkinson's Disease.

This disorder robs its victims of the ability to precisely coordinate their body movements. Don has come to Vanderbilt University in Nashville, Tennessee to take part in testing a new surgical technique that may offer hope to millions of victims of Parkinson's Disease. He will soon undergo an experimental operation that may help him control his involuntary tremors.

Don Burns: The symptoms really vary a lot. For me they start on the left side. There is a lot of achiness, muscle weakness, loss of small motor coordination. My face becomes like a mask, it's more frozen, I'm not as expressive. I don't blink as much. That's one of the things you really can't control. I can blink or wrinkle my face if I consciously think about it.

An analysis of the structure of the discourse of this sequence shows that the order of Information presented is as follows:

(1) Examples of symptoms and physical effects of Parkinson's disease
(2) Social effects of Parkinson's disease
(3) Clinical description and suggested treatment.

Apart from the voice-over, the order of people speaking about the disease is from those who are least expert but most affected, to those who are most expert but least affected. Case studies and stories are followed by issues and arguments, which are, in turn, followed by the facts about Parkinson's disease This may make for very good and engaging television, since it is, of course, the human dimension that most attracts us as viewers. However, the viewer, who is also a language learner and who may need a more content- and information-orientated programme in order to achieve cognitive language learning objectives, may face considerable difficulties in using such a programme for language learning, as the programme is not structured towards such objectives. Were it to have such objectives, we might expect the following order:

(1) Exposition: What is Parkinson's disease? How is it caused?
(2) Narrative: Case studies.
(3) Argument: What are the social, medical, ethical and racial issues and implications of the disease and the proposed treatments?

As with the programme on malaria, the programme makers in this case are not seeking simply to impart information on Parkinson's disease and on new methods of combating it in the way that such information might be given to medical students. They are telling human stories about the physical and social effects of Parkinson's disease, about the ethical questions surrounding its treatment and about attitudes to Third World medicine and research. They are also seeking to make controversial statements about issues on which people have strong feelings, beliefs, attitudes and responses. In other words, they are seeking to engage viewers not at a cognitive level but at an affective level. We all know something about Parkinson's disease, and the stories of its victims are frequently in the news. We, therefore, bring both knowledge and attitudes to the programme. The programme builds very little on our knowledge, but challenges or reinforces our attitudes and beliefs a great deal. Taken together with the sheer pace and dynamic construction of interwoven discourses, for language learning viewers, this must mean the strong likelihood of a mental set towards impressionistic viewing rather than conscious and reflective language learning.

6.2.5 Towards Resolving the Conflict

I found with my own students that the strong affective pull of good, engaging television documentaries is, to some extent, counterweighed by the very presence of the captions, which do provide a degree of conscious and reflective control over the dynamic stream of speech. With captions, the learner who is in control of the pace of viewing the documentary can, in effect, freeze speech, check it, analyse the language, look up words and so on. Reading and discussing related articles also helps not only in setting up a raised level of given information and vocabulary, but also in forming a critical mental set, so that ideas, values and beliefs expressed in a programme are met with an active response, on both cognitive and affective levels, rather than with passive reception—the "interesting programme" response. There are parallels with this approach in our daily lives in the way in which reading newspapers, listening to radio news and watching television and online news are all integrated activities (Pew Research Center, 2010, 2014).

What I seek, above all, in my work with learners using captioned programmes to learn language outside the classroom, at home or in self-study is to raise the effort that they put into watching and to encourage a critical and self-critical interactive approach to viewing—conscious and reflective in terms of language and content, aware and appreciative in terms of opinions and ideas. It has seemed to me that understanding how the very structure of programmes has contributed to the difficulties faced by learners in using television programmes as a language learning resource is a helpful step in resolving conflicts and improving autonomous language learning.

In summary, then, I have argued that there may be two useful ways of understanding and exploiting documentary programme language and structure.

(1) In terms of the messages received by learner-viewers and the cognitive and affective goals of a programme.
(2) In terms of the way in which expository, narrative and argumentative functions are structured within a programme to optimise the achievement of these goals.

So, in another twist to the paradox posed by Gavriel Salomon, in the case of captioned documentaries on contemporary themes that are relevant to language learners, one source of the difficulty for learners in making use of them as language learning resources may lie in them being interesting and engaging. The well-produced programme, its structure, discourses and its messages may work, paradoxically, against the cognitive and linguistic goals, which learners set for themselves.

6.2.6 Situation Comedies (Sitcoms)

In Chap. 2, I have already talked about the impact watching *Yes, Prime Minister* with captions had on my students. As I said in my much quoted line, the great thing about watching captioned situation comedies for non-native viewers is that they can laugh in the right places for the right reasons, or, perhaps, understand why they don't get a cultural reference, which is meant to be funny, or, perhaps, an ironic aside, which, again, depends on familiarity with the culture and context. I went on to show my students many more comedies and to make them available to watch in the self-access centre.

6.2.6.1 Don't Wait Up

As far as my students were concerned, one of the most successful situation comedies was a series about father and son doctors, Toby and Tom Latimer, called *Don't Wait Up* (many clips available on *YouTube*). In my article, "A Very Verbal Medium" (1993), I use the example of *Don't Wait Up* to illustrate the point that while programmes such as this one might have some visual humour, for example, facial expressions and embarrassing encounters, most of the comedic effect relies on verbal exchanges between characters. Following is a short example of an exchange:

> *Dr. Cartwright*: I can't find Mrs. Kennedy's notes anywhere … (phone rings).Hello….
> put her through…Madeleine.
> *Dr. Tom Latimer*: Hello darling. You're not still waiting, are you? Oh good.
> Everything all right?
> *Madeleine*: Yes, they're very pleased with me.
> My blood pressure's fine. I haven't put on too much weight.
> Actually, I was very lucky.
> I'd still be waiting now if I hadn't bumped into Toby.
> *Dr. L.*: How do you mean?
> *M.*: Well, he was here for a meeting so he pulled a few strings.

I was able to jump the queue (laughter).
Felicity: Your pa should be back very soon.
He's been attending a meeting at St Winifred's all morning on wastage within the NHS followed by lunch.
He's sitting on a Standing Committee (laughter).
Dr. L: Sounds like a contradiction in terms.
F: Sorry?

In just a few lines of captions, the linguistic richness of such a programme and its potential for exploiting both language and content (nothing changes with the National Health Service—queues, wastage) are evident, while at the same time, it is easy to see why it would be difficult for all but the most advanced-level listeners to follow.

To take another example from a short sequence in another episode, what is so striking about a single episode of *Don't Wait Up* is the variety of registers, styles and specific areas of vocabulary that are covered and which are revealed by the caption text.

Don't Wait Up

Topic:	Medical	House-buying	Legal	Divorce	Insurance
Example words and Phrases	You have high blood-pressure	We're exchanging contracts on Wednesday	It's your responsibility	I could have won a court order	Endowment policy
	I do a thorough examination	We'll get a bridging loan	Sue for damages	A public nuisance	The insurance would cover it
	stethoscope	They dropped out			Claim off your own insurance

Social relations: Don't poach my patient!
　　　　　　　Is she still as monstrous?
　　　　　　　But she set her heart on it
　　　　　　　Let me know how you get on
　　　　　　　Sorry, I didn't mean to shout

And this is just in a ten-minute sequence as the characters switch from topic to topic, as we do in conversations in real life. The way formal words and phrases are mixed with colloquial is also striking, and it would be worth asking learners to identify whether words and phrases are considered formal or colloquial as they watch a programme or except from it. A grid like the one above may be useful.

6.2.6.2 Big Bang Theory (Series 7, 1.)

Here are some short extracts of dialogue from one of the most popular comedy programmes globally, *Big Bang Theory*. I recommend that readers sample some episodes on *YouTube* to appreciate the fast pace with frequent scene changes and "snappy" speech and jokes. The number of characters is quite limited, and viewers can become quickly familiar with them and their traits. BBT is shown on UK TV with captions, while the auto-generated captions on *YouTube* are error-prone and largely a waste of time.

Scene opens with Penny and Sheldon together in flat

> *Penny*: I get it, I get it. You're an emotional robot
> *Sheldon*: I try
> *P*: Right. Let's just get this stupid game over with
> *S*: I'll go first. By the way. How are you with zippers?
> *P*: Why
> *S*: Well I really need to go to the bathroom and this one has gone all cattywampus

Scene changes to bar

> *Bernadette*: To the advancement of science.
> *Amy*: And to the sick and dying who make it possible.

B: This is fun. We never really get total shop with Penny around. We usually just end up talking about boys
A: Which is fine but it's nice to mix it up with a little intellectual conversation.
Barman: From the two gentlemen at the bar.
A: Oh my God. Boys bought us drinks. Thank you. Thank you so much!
B: Be cool.
A: You be cool. Guys are hitting on us and not just to get to Penny.
B: You're right. Thank you!

It would be a brave teacher who used this in a class, though both Bravo (2008) and Frumuselu, De Maeyerb, Doncheb, and Gutiérrez-Colon Plana (2015) consider that careful use of such comedies as BBT can make ideal material for learners to gain idiomatic and colloquial language within classroom settings (see descriptions of their work in Chap. 5). Perhaps, a student-fan of BBT should present it and flip the classroom. BBT is one of those online programmes, which, along with *How I Met your Mother*, has millions of fans worldwide and is watched, with or without captions, informally to very good effect by non-native speakers of English, particularly viewers aged less than 25 years (as Sockett, 2014, reports). I have heard many anecdotes of substantial informal learning taking place from intensive watching of the many programmes in the series, which is now up to series 9 in the UK.

6.2.7 Soap Operas

Soap operas can be very challenging as the language comes fast, is often very colloquial and a great deal of the plot development as well as the dialogue depends on familiarity with what has gone before and knowing who the characters are. That said, they are usually very well crafted, have lots of rich colloquial language, are culturally important and can provide very good material for teaching and learning. My attempts to use them have not been particularly successful, as they tend to be so closely associated with leisure watching at home.

In the *Teletext 888 Project*, for example, there was general resistance to spending time watching soap operas, no matter how much I might emphasise the value of the colloquial language used and the insights into British (or American and Australian) culture such programmes offered. *Neighbours* (featuring a young Kylie Minogue) was unsuccessful. That said, as with soap operas, the stories of successful learning from intensive watching of soap operas on which language learners have become hooked are so numerous that they cannot be dismissed lightly. Almost every week these days, I am told by an informant that they learnt a great deal of a foreign language and communicated successfully in the language through learning language from soap operas.

These days, continuing drama series such as *Game of Thrones* and *Breaking Bad*, broadcast with captions and with captions in boxed sets, are similar to soap operas with many different threads and episodes that end in cliffhangers. These have tremendous global appeal, making them ideal for flipped classroom use, since viewers can report not only on their viewing of the shows but also on their interactions online with English-speaking fan communities. When non-native speaker viewers become hooked, they compensate for the difficult material through their motivation.

6.2.8 Lifestyle (Direct Address) Programmes

In the past, I have referred to these as "direct address" programmes. They have many of the necessary attributes for good teaching material, while remaining very much authentic broadcast material. These are programmes on cooking, gardening, do-it-yourself, consumer affairs and so on. In my view, they have a substantial claim to be considered as educational and instructional resources, however entertaining they may be. They have the potential to inform, entertain and involve learners. The viewer is encouraged to take action, to phone in, to change behaviour, to write letters, to try one technique or another, frequently receiving explicit instruction in how to perform tasks. In educational terms, they also exemplify, dramatise and supplant. They provide examples of what can be done and how it can be done, whether building houses, changing water valves or frying chickens. They dramatise through providing us with examples of language used authentically in its social context, and they supplant by demonstrating and describing what happens in situations that would be difficult or even impossible for us to see for ourselves—for example, the chemical processes at work in cooking or the interior of a hot water tank.

All these programmes share the same characteristics that make them ideal for language teaching and learning: they have self-contained short sequences, they concentrate on the verbal message with visual support, they are replete with highly specific and useful language, they are rich in potential tasks and spin-off activities, they make a clear point and they are cohesive and textual.

In any one week in the UK, the five main terrestrial channels broadcast many programmes of this type, often with supporting material online or in book or magazine form. Just about all these programmes carry captions. Even for native-speaker viewers, the caption text is useful when needing to remember precise instructions, especially for cooking recipes. Without the captions, the fast pace and highly specific terminology of most programmes of this genre mean that little language is likely to be followed. Comprehension and attention to the language are likely to be lost.

Let us take the example of programmes on cooking. In addition to focusing on students' comprehension of the sequence through some pre-viewing and post-viewing questions, the cross-cultural transferability of cooking language used in the programmes can be easily exploited once the language is made transparent by the captions. I have found that learners love to compare methods of preparing and cooking similar foods in their own cultures, using the appropriate language as revealed in the captions.

Following is a short sequence from one of the most popular TV chefs in Britain, Jamie Oliver. Jamie travels around the world gathering recipes for what he calls his "superfood diet"—low calorie meals with healthy ingredients. In the given sequence, he is cooking "Black rice pudding with mango and passion fruit" for breakfast. As he has a strong Essex accent and rather quirky speech, the captions are doubly helpful.

Jamie: So this my friends is black rice. And get used to it as there's a lot more of it coming into the supermarkets. And it's really, really good for you.

And check this out. This has three times the amount of fibre of your average white rice. If you can't find black you can use brown as well. Cook 200 grams, drain it and set it to one side. Now we want layers, so I'm going do it like a trifle. So I'm going to do a quick puree. It takes no time at all. We're going use mango, a mega-superfood. Just 100 grams contains 112 % of our recommended daily intake of vitamin C. All I do is, I put the skin and the flesh in like that against a glass. Let's get that in the liquidiser. For a classic tropical vibe, I'm going to add mango's best mate, lime. And then simply puree it, it'll take seconds. So that's done. Now what I want to do is almost dress that rice. Convince it that it's sweet and delicious. So to do that I'm going to make a kind of smoothie. In go two bananas, packed with potassium, followed by 200 ml of hazelnut milk fortified with calcium and containing vitamin B12 which helps us stay alert. Whizz this up and add a tablespoon of vanilla extract. Then add three-quarters of the rice and blitz that. Right, let's go in here with the rest of the rice. What I get here is incredible texture. I mean, look at that. …

And so he goes on, chatting his way through the cooking. This is just a couple of minutes of the programme, but already it is easy to see that his language has a wide variety of colloquial expressions along with some technical and non-technical cooking language. So while we have "liquidiser," we also have the slang for "liquidise," which is "blitz." We have the very common cooking instruction: "Cook 200 grams, drain it and set it to one side." And what is a "tropical vibe"? Jamie has credibility, and his English is pretty regular vernacular speech these days.

6.2.9 Learning About Culture

Many language courses include teaching about the local and national culture. Once we have made programmes accessible to language learners through captions, we can exploit rich sources of language and cultural material. In my courses on British culture and society, described in an article on British Studies and captioned viewing (1997), students were shown or were expected to watch a wide variety of programmes on such topics as Legal Systems in England, Wales and Scotland, Education, Racial and Minority Issues and Monarchy and the Constitution. I used the programmes for self-correcting listening comprehension exercises from audio-only versions of interviews, for providing students with research material for seminar presentations, for examples of discourse in specific settings, for background material for difficult topics such as Northern Ireland (an excellent two-part series by the BBC giving firstly the Protestant/Unionist position, then the Catholic/Nationalist/Republican position) and for providing specific terminology and phraseology on law, education and so on.

A few years ago, a series of programmes broadcast criminal trials in Scotland. Not everyone knows that Scotland has a separate legal system from England and Wales, so even this was an eye-opener. These programmes were immensely popular with my students for the terminology, the authenticity, the drama, the language and the setting. As most of those involved in the trials spoke with strong Scottish accents and frequently with dialectal features (*dinnae, wisnae*), the captions, which usually reported the dialectal feature verbatim, were invaluable in making these social documents accessible and useful in language learning terms.

These days, we are used to seeing many more "fly-on-the-wall" programmes, such as a series on educating secondary school students in different parts of Britain, which provides extraordinary insights into what goes on in British secondary schools. Likewise, there are several series on daily life in hospitals, in police stations, in airports and so on. The common factor in all these programmes is that they contain a great deal of authentic language: the interactions between teachers and students, between nurses and patients and between the police and the public. I have provided a short sequence from *Educating Cardiff*, which will give a flavour of what the captions reveal. At times, the speech is unclear, with many "throwaway" lines and offhand remarks from staff and students of the school. The sequence features Emily, who is disruptive in her class, but also comes across as articulate and reflective when interviewed.

Scene in classroom:

> *Emily*: Stop it. It's getting sore (she and a boy are hitting one another during a lesson).
> *Boy*: Say sorry.
> *Emily*: No
> *Teacher*: Emily., you need to move to that table now. Move now or I'll ring *on call.*
> *Emily*: Why. Cos I won't move. Cos he hit me.
> *Teacher*: Yes, yes. Cos you hit him as well.
> *Emily*: You hit me.
> *Boy*: You hit me. You HIT me!
> Cut to Emily being interviewed
> *Interviewer*: What's the most annoying thing about school?
> *Emily*: The work. It's like when are you ever going to need Pythagoras in your life? Or how to know what a right-angle triangle is? For Music you've got *YouTube*. For Geography, you've got a globe. For Maths you've got a calculator and for Drama you've got ......life.

6.3 Programmes Speaking for Themselves

In this chapter, with examples of the speech from a variety of programmes, I have illustrated how television really is a very verbal medium in order to bolster my argument that we need to make use of captions if we are to fully exploit the potential of programmes and let them speak for themselves. Most of the programmes I have highlighted would be virtually incomprehensible and inaccessible without captions to all but the most proficient listeners, but with captions they can become rich language resources for both teachers and learners, and many of the examples given would work well in the "flipped classroom." Captions enable us to realise our dream of using foreign language films and TV for language teaching and learning.

7

The EURECAP Project

7.1 Setting Up the Project

> Gist watching can only take you so far. I needed the captions to reach a good level (EURECAP participant).

As I reported in Chaps. 4 and 5, the bulk of research, to date, on the value of captions has involved learners watching relatively short clips rather than whole programmes or films, and being tested on aspects such as comprehension, content recall and vocabulary learning. Controversially perhaps, it has always been my contention that most questions about the value of captions in terms of vocabulary and comprehension were largely answered by Price and Dow's study back in 1983, and the meta-analysis carried out by Maribel Montero Perez and colleagues (Montero Perez, Van Den Noortgate, & Desmet, 2013) further confirmed what we have always known about captioned viewing. What remains largely unanswered is the value in developmental terms (confidence, tuning in, correct perception/reception, speed of following/understanding/reading, transferability, change in behaviour) of prolonged watching for learners who are able to choose what they watch, are in control of the pace of viewing and can apply a range of strategies appropriate for the type of film or programme they are watching, their level of interest and their own level of proficiency in the foreign language.

At the end of my plenary talk at the conference in Pavia, I announced that I would be taking research forward with multilingual captioning through a project involving DVDs with captions in different languages. The first hurdle for the project came when I found on my return to Oxford that it was not easy to buy DVDs with captions in foreign languages in the UK. The main distributor only imported DVDs with English translation subtitles, claiming that there was no market for those with captions.

Eventually in Spring 2015, with a small amount of funding to buy DVDs from local Amazons and with participants who were learning French, German, Italian and Spanish at Oxford University, either as specialists or non-specialists, I started the EURECAP (European Research on Captioning) pilot project, seeking to gather data on the benefits, affordances and downsides for individuals watching a range of foreign language DVDs with captions over a period of 5 or 6 weeks. Participants were recruited from among second-year Modern Languages students, those taking Oxford University Language Centre courses for non-specialists and members of an independent language learning project called *LAMBDA* (http://www.lang.ox.ac.uk/lambda.html). Those who signalled interest were sent a document outlining the project, its objectives and what was required of them in terms of viewing and feedback. Around thirty replied, giving their informed agreement to take part. Some agreed to watch films in two languages, and one agreed to watch in three languages.

Each participant completed a self-assessment questionnaire (developed from one used by Brantmeier, Vanderplank, & Strube, 2012) and C-test in one or more of the four languages (with permission from the University of Bielefeld) to establish a reading and listening self-assessment baseline and general proficiency score before beginning to watch DVDs. From answers to questions 8, 9 and 10 in the questionnaire at 4 or 5 (shown below on p. 189), it was evident that the participants were fluent readers in the foreign languages they chose to watch:

8. I can understand texts written in a very colloquial style and containing many idiomatic expressions or slang.

1	2	3	4	5
Strongly disagree	Disagree	Neutral	Agree	Strongly agree

9. I can recognize different stylistic means (puns, metaphors, symbols, connotations, ambiguity) and appreciate and evaluate their function within the text.

1	2	3	4	5
Strongly disagree	Disagree	Neutral	Agree	Strongly agree

10. I can read a variety of factual and literary texts and am able to understand the content (main topics and the different points of view).

1	2	3	4	5
Strongly disagree	Disagree	Neutral	Agree	Strongly agree

All participants also indicated that it was an important goal for them to be able to watch TV programmes and films confidently.

DVDs with optional captions for deaf and hard-of-hearing people were purchased from Amazon in France, Germany, Italy and Spain. It was difficult to obtain a wide range of DVDs with captions from Germany (and indeed, as mentioned in Chap. 2, currently, Germany lags behind other large EU countries in captioning for deaf and hard-of-hearing people on broadcast TV). For example, a film, *Phoenix*, which was released in 2014, starring a leading German film star, Nina Hoss, was only available with German language captions at double the price of the one with English translation subtitles Many other German films had no version with German captions, and were available with only English subtitles. Eighteen DVDs in French, 17 in German, 12 in Italian and 16 in Spanish were obtained, and participants were encouraged to change DVDs about every three or four days. In the end, this proved too rapid a turnover for most participants, and the average number watched by participants was closer to six, with a range of three to eleven (Table 7.1).

Table 7.1 Films with captions watched during the project

French	German	Italian	Spanish
Les beaux jours	Diplomatie	Pane e tulipani	Los amantes pasajeros
Respire	Indien	Lo sono Li	10.000 Km
Elle s'en va	Gold	Anime nere	No tengas miedo
8 femmes	Der Junge im gestreiften Pyjama	La grande bellezza	El cuerpo
3 coeurs	Das Wilde Leben	Il giovane favoloso	La lengua de mariposas
Quai d'Orsay	Hell	Venuto al mondo	Vivir es fácil con los ojos cerrados
Les Intouchables	Rosa Luxemburg	Benvenuti al sud	Futbolín
La fleur de l'âge	Der Untergang	Il capitale umano	Volver
Yves Saint Laurent	Phoenix	Il Vitelloni	El hijo de la novia
Qu'est.-ce qu'on a fait au bon Dieu?	Nirgendwo in Afrika	La bestia nel cuore	El niño
Il était une fois, une fois	Sophie Scholl	La prima cosa bella	Los ojos de Julia
Samba	John Rabe	Sole a catinelle	Balada triste de trompeta
Entre les murs	Der Baeder-Meinhof Komplex		Relatos salvajes
Les saveurs du palais	Die Verlorene Zeit		Ocho apellidos vascos
Une village français	Nichet mein Tag		Carmina y amén
Sous le figuier	Rubbeldiekatz		Séptimo
Diplomatie	Der Krieger und die Kaiserin		
Le roi danse			

Several films were watched by several participants in a language group. For example, *La grande bellezza* was popular in Italian, *Entre les murs* in French, *Diplomatie* in German/French and *El cuerpo* in Spanish.

Participants were required to keep either hard copy or online diaries of the films they watched, with a checklist of questions to bear in mind:

- **The quality of the captions** (how faithful they are to the sound, differences between the sound and text, if this is positive/negative/disturbing/useful and so on)
- **The use made of the captions** (e.g., pausing and replaying to match sound and text when there are difficult passages, making a note of useful words and phrases or letting the film run and enjoying being able to follow what is being said, or looking up words and phrases that are unknown/unfamiliar in context—if so, with some striking examples)
- **Whether using the captions over time has any effect on viewing behaviour** (Becoming less or more reliant on them over time, gaining confidence in listening, forgetting about them while watching, being aware of whether the sound or the text is being used to follow, seeing if it's possible to manage without the captions from time to time—since they can be switched off)
- **How useful the availability of captions is for each film on a scale of 1 to 10** (1 = not useful, 10 = invaluable). For example, do the captions help in following jokes or complicated plots?
- **Confidence in being able to watch each film with or without captions on a scale of 1 to 10** (1 = not confident without them/highly dependent, 10 = totally confident/can watch happily without them). For example, some films may have a lot more dialogue than others and require much more effort.

One participant, Shiree, devised a template for her own use, which she shared with other participants

Captioned Media in Foreign Language Learning and Teaching

Title:	Viewed previously:	Y/N	# times:

I. Pre-viewing check:
Confidence in viewing this film w/out captions
(1 = not confident, 10 = totally confident)   1 2 3 4 5 6 7 8 9 10
Confidence in viewing this film with captions   1 2 3 4 5 6 7 8 9 10
(1 = not confident, 10 = totally confident)

II. Viewing behaviour
Phase 1 (watched w/   Y/N   Time taken to watch (excl. note
out captions)   taking):
Plot summary:

Jokes, idioms or other notable points:

Did I...	pause and replay	Y/N	# times:
	make a note of useful words and phrases heard	Y/N	# times:
	look up words and phrases—give examples	Y/N	# times:

**Phase 2 (watched with   Y/N   Time taken to watch
X captions)   (excl. note taking):**
How much did I miss from the plot (check summary):   1 2 3 4 5 6 7 8 9 10
What else did I miss—e.g., jokes, idioms or other points: 1 2 3 4 5 6 7 8 9 10

Did I...	pause and replay	Y/N	# times:
	make a note of useful words and phrases	Y/N	# times:
	look up words and phrases—give examples	Y/N	# times:

Phase 3 (watched with English subtitles, if available)   Y/N
How much did I miss from the plot (check summary):   1 2 3 4 5 6 7 8 9 10
What else did I miss—e.g., jokes, idioms or other points: 1 2 3 4 5 6 7 8 9 10

III. Quality of captions
Faithful to dialogue? (1 = unfaithful/10 = verbatim)   1 2 3 4 5 6 7 8 9 10
Any differences noted:
Effect: positive/negative/useful/distracting   1 2 3 4 5 6 7 8 9 10
(1 = not very/10 = very)

IV. Overall utility of captions for this film?   1 2 3 4 5 6 7 8 9 10
(1 = not useful, 10 = invaluable)

V. Effect of captions over time on viewing behaviour:

| Did I... | feel less or more reliant on them over time | Y/N | gain in confidence listening | Y/N |
| | notice if I was following the sound or the text | Y/N | forget about them as I watched | Y/N |

VI. Post-viewing check:
Confidence in viewing next film w/out captions
(1 = not confident, 10 = totally confident)   1 2 3 4 5 6 7 8 9 10
Confidence in viewing next film with captions   1 2 3 4 5 6 7 8 9 10
(1 = not confident, 10 = totally confident)

7.2 Results

7.2.1 Questionnaires and C-Tests

Eighteen participants completed all parts of the project, taking the initial and final tests, completing the final questionnaire and returning their diaries or sending online diaries. As expected, the scores on the C-tests remained largely stable within a few points, and it was not expected that there would be large gains on the C-tests. The retests provided a reliability check on the C-tests as a measure of general proficiency. Scores were also used to consider differences in the viewing behaviour, strategies, use of captions and changes in confidence at different levels. The range of scores (out of 100 for each language) was wide on both initial and final tests. Modern Languages students, not surprisingly, had the highest scores. French: 56–93; German: 43–88; Italian: 41–88; Spanish: 65–88.

Both the initial and the final questionnaires probed attitudes to watching films with captions. The final questionnaire asked for responses to the following statements:

1. I still prefer to watch films and programmes without captions—they are a distraction.
2. I have liked having the captions and have referred to them when the listening became difficult.
3. I have found them very useful for learning new or unfamiliar language.
4. It has varied according to the film or programme. With some, I didn't need them, with others, they were essential.
5. Even when they weren't essential, I liked having them as they helped me focus on the words and phrases spoken.

Even if they still preferred to watch without captions, participants might also have circled 2 and 3. Most circled 4, and additional comments frequently mentioned that if a film was regarded as just entertainment or general interest, they did not need them, but if they felt it was a very good film and they wanted to be properly engaged in it, they would make full use of the captions. This aspect of adjusting viewing behaviour to their perception of the film in terms of its quality was a frequent comment.

All felt their confidence had increased, but added comments suggested that some had become more aware of what they needed to do to become fully confident. One participant remarked that she had only "scratched the surface." The same participant provided the insightful comment that she had had confidence at a certain level of understanding before the project, so was less dependent; however, the captions had made her more aware and more dependent initially.

Another participant noted that even when she was comfortable with the language of the film, the captions were useful to fall back on (cf. Pujolà, 2002). Again, we see a paradox similar to the one identified by Salomon in the perception of films and understanding the language. A learner may be quite confident at general gist watching with low effort when captions are not present and may be resigned to this level of understanding (since more effort may not be productive). But the accessibility to the language provided by the captions may have the effect not only of increasing the effort put into watching but also of creating more or less dependency on the captions, depending on a number of factors.

This feeling that the participants had of becoming more aware of the language they needed to know to have a full grasp of plot and dialogue was repeated in an interesting shift in some responses to one of the questionnaire items:

21. It doesn't bother me that I can't follow everything as long as I feel I am understanding generally what is going on in a TV programme or film

1	2	3	4	5
Strongly disagree	Disagree	Neutral	Agree	Strongly agree

There was a shift to the right from initial to final completion of this item. Participants might shift their responses from '4 Agree' in the initial questionnaire to either '3 Neutral' or '2 Disagree' in the final version. Over the course of the project, some participants appeared to have become less willing to tolerate gist listening than they were initially.

Indeed, in response to the question about being more or less dependent on the captions by the end of the project, while all were either less dependent or about the same as when they started, some added that they still liked having the captions. This is not surprising considering how non-native speakers who have lived in Britain for years and in all respects appear to be "native users" of English still like to have captions on when watching television. It could be that participants just appreciated having the technology.

There were few substantial gains in C-test scores. However, one participant, Sean, who gained nine points (74–83), was a Modern Languages student and spent much of his time studying Italian for his degree. His final questionnaire indicated a very positive attitude to captioned films: he had thrown himself into the project, was a fan of captions and subtitles, had watched six films, liked watching with captions and while he could watch without them, found they helped him to follow speech he might otherwise not have caught.

The participant with one of the lowest initial C-test scores, Martha, who achieved the same score in the final test (43), watched five German films, and while gaining in confidence felt she was still dependent on the captions by the end and that they were essential for all the films that she had watched, especially for following dialogue. Another lower-level participant, Nahal, watched eleven German films and was very positive about the boost to her confidence and the need for the captions. One of the films was *The Boy in Striped Pyjamas* dubbed in German, and she commented that the captions did not match the speech and were very distracting. I had noticed the same when watching *The Descendants* (starring George Clooney) dubbed in French with French captions. At times, there appeared to be a parallel script, so different was the speech from the captions. A plausible explanation, as suggested by Nahal, was that the caption script is the translation subtitle script of the original film, whereas the script of the dubbed version spoken by the actors has to take into account that there must be synchronisation between the script and the movement of the speaker's lips. Nahal also indicated that in some films when the dialogue was particularly fast, she could not follow at all and had to rely on reading the caption text quickly, though she could have used the pause button to good effect.

Another linguist, a graduate student, Myrtle, with high C-test scores (88 and 89) watched seven German films at an average of 6 hours per week for four weeks and felt that she had definitely gained in confidence by being able to keep up with rapid speech and unfamiliar accents, and had become less dependent on captions, though it varied from film to film.

While the questions in the questionnaire covered both reading and writing, the main purpose of the reading questions was to ensure that participants had a high-enough level in reading comprehension to read and follow the captions confidently. The questions on listening were designed to indicate any changes from initial to final completion of the questionnaire. As with the C-tests, there were few major changes apart from Item 21, which has been discussed earlier. Notebooks were collected and typed up along with *Sharepoint* diaries kept online.

7.3 Data from Diaries

Participants were asked to provide feedback on their viewing within the following categories. In this section, some general comments are made before drawing on examples from specific individuals whose diaries reported complex behaviours.

1. Confidence in viewing with/without captions

A major aim of the project was to assess changes in viewing confidence levels over the period of film watching. As mentioned earlier, there was huge variation in how essential captions were for viewing either whole films or sections of films. While the final questionnaires indicated that most participants had gained in overall confidence over the period of the project, the major effects appeared to be while viewing individual films or series. As they "tune in," their confidence grows. Several issues come out clearly. Firstly, many participants are aware they are reading a lot and not giving so much attention to the sound at times. Secondly, while confidence appears to grow steadily, they also become aware that the captions make the films so much more intelligible that they like to keep them on for "reassurance" or because it makes watching "less tiring."

For example, Felicity notes the following on watching *El cuerpo*:

I realised I was reading a lot rather than listening. I think this is quite a lot to do with habit, as I use captions a lot anyway, and partly a lack of faith in my listening skills. But when I remembered to make the effort to read less and shift my attention to listening, I felt I was doing well and noticing the things that give depth to character, their speech patterns and relationships, rather than just the fact and plot points—but I already knew what to listen out for!

- I had a go at turning the captions off for 5 mins or so, but even though I was familiar with it, I still found it a bit difficult and didn't catch every word. I'm not sure I could give a reliable estimate, but I think I would have understood about 70 % without captions if I hadn't seen it before.
- I think my listening has improved a lot, but I don't think my grammar or vocab have gained much.

Violet stresses how her listening confidence grew both during watching an individual film, *Sous le figuier,* and as she watched more episodes of a series, *Un village français*:

Sous le figuier
As I became familiar with the actors and their ways of speaking, it became easier to rely less on the captions. However—they were important when speech was too quick for me to follow—or when elderly/very young actors were speaking, as this often sounded muffled, if they were speaking particularly quietly.

In time, I do gain more confidence in listening yet I didn't turn the captions off this movie, perhaps I had become too used to them.

Un village français
Lots of the dialogue was also spoken quite quickly, so sometimes it became easier to simply read the captions as opposed to tuning in and trying to completely follows the conversation.

The language overall was relatively easy to understand, and I didn't feel like I had to pause the film or replay sections to get a better grasp of the plot, for example. The main difficulties in language were potentially any of the more technical terms, but I didn't think these specific terms were

100 % crucial to my immediate understanding or appreciation of the film, therefore I didn't stop watching to look them up. I preferred to simply continue watching the film.

I definitely gained in listening confidence as I watched this series and became used to the characters' voices. However, I was never confident enough to turn the captions off.

The importance of having captions in the early stages of watching a film is mentioned by Lana in her notes on *3 coeurs*:

> As the film went on I definitely felt that I relied less on the captions. The dialogue in this film was never too rapid so I could actually understand most of what was being said. There was one particular character who mumbled quite a lot when he spoke so I found it helpful to have the captions for when he was speaking.

Despite their growing confidence, in most cases the captions stay on (remember that they can turn them on and off), and only rarely does the participants' confidence without captions match their confidence with captions.

Nahal, who watched eleven German films, was quite clear that by the time she watched her seventh film, *Nirgendwo in Afrika*, her confidence in listening had grown:

> I feel it is getting easier for me to follow movie plots—especially when they involve a non-political set-up [she had had a hard time following *Rosa Luxemburg*].

By her eleventh film, *Die verlorene Zeit*, she felt able to write.

> After having watched so many films, I felt confident enough to watch it even without captions; that would not have been possible earlier.

Shiree, one of the most strategic participants, who made detailed notes on each film she watched, wrote two reports on her progress, one after three weeks, and the other at the end of the project when she had watched six films:

After three weeks:

Have generally noticed growth in confidence watching w/out captions (Usual habit is to always watch with Italian captions and never try without). However, wouldn't have noticed this without having written detailed notes of films (without the notes, I wouldn't have remembered if I'd caught things 1st time or not).

Post-project thoughts:

Leaving aside the final film (which I think was to some extent anomalous), I would say that as the project progressed, I definitely felt less reliant of the captions over time and gained a lot of confidence in listening without using captions. I don't think I was ever confident enough to forget about the captions altogether but the immediate checking of listening comprehension was, overall, a positive experience. It was also very reassuring to note that the things I missed without captions were things I missed with the Italian captions (e.g. new vocab, more complex structure or idea, idiom/poss. dialect, or fast conversation). Overall, a very positive experience.

2. Viewing behaviour and strategies

Few studies have looked at individual viewing behaviour and strategies in the context of language learning, or at how learners use captions when they have control of the pace of viewing and to turn captions on and off. Pujolà's (2002) study on students using the "Help" option in computer-based watching of audiovisual material is a rare example of looking at this behaviour, and the findings of this present project are quite similar to his findings. Notes from diaries showed a very wide range of viewing behaviour depending on factors such as the genre of the film, amount of speech, quality of speech (clear vs. rapid, naturalistic), listening ability and confidence, tiredness, attitude to captions and topic/film familiarity.

Participants frequently made extensive notes on how they watched with captions, and there was a spectrum of behaviour from the non-strategic behaviour of letting the film run and pausing only very occasionally to check a word, to the highly strategic behaviour of Shiree—of which more is given here.

For example, Lana was typical in writing for almost every film that she watched (6) that she let the film run but occasionally looked up words on an app. Naomi and Harry also said they did not like to stop the flow of a film so did not pause and replay, but made notes of new and unfamiliar words and looked them up afterwards. For *Respire* (French), a film about high school students with a lot of colloquial youth language and slang, Naomi made a note of 20 words and phrases, while Harry noted the same number for *El Niño*.

Some participants, such as Violet, became adept at shifting their attention between more listening and more reading, as and when needed. For example, in watching *La grande bellezza*, she writes:

> I replayed to match sound and text. I paused to look up words I couldn't understand just in case they proved key. I became more confident in my listening ability as I watched the film yet relied heavily on captions. They were instances where I had to concentrate solely on reading the captions as the characters were speaking too quickly. Also, the film is set in Rome, many have Roman accents—often I needed the captions in order to understand the Roman accent.

Similarly, Felicity, who began watching without any strategies other than pausing occasionally to look up an unfamiliar word, becomes more strategic by her sixth film, *El hijo de la novia*, even making use of English subtitles at difficult points:

> I struggled with this film, I think because it is Argentinian and the accents are a bit different. Also the main character has lots of stressed and rapid phone calls in the first section.
>
> - The vocabulary was a bit harder too, I thought, though this may be Argentinian differences too, and I struggled to understand some of the captions. This film also had English subtitles, and a couple of times I switched to re-watch a section and make sure I got it all—for example, I could tell the mother with dementia was saying rude and embarrassing things, but I didn't know exactly what (again, my lack of knowledge of swear words was holding me back!).

- Because the film wasn't very action-driven, it was easy to understand what was going on, but the meaning came from the relationships between characters and the subtleties of dialogue, so I probably missed a fair bit. I was very reliant on the captions, and couldn't really understand much when I tried to listen more than read.

Felicity, an experienced watcher of captioned TV, was strategic in her viewing from the first film, *El cuerpo*, as it had parts that were essential to following the plot, but were particularly difficult:

I used the pause button quite a lot. Sometimes I would rewind a few seconds to see it again, but this was a crime thriller with quite a few interview scenes and several rapid phone conversations between two characters, and in those bits I paused at most of the individual 'screens' of captions because they changed slightly more quickly than I was able to read them. I wasn't exactly reading every word, but during the rapid speech I still needed a bit longer.

And, again in watching *La lengua de mariposas*:

Speech was generally clear and not at such a frenetic pace as in *El cuerpo*, but there were far fewer visual clues as to what was being spoken about, so it was difficult in a different way. There were two passages of about 30 seconds each that I felt were significant and that I might not have understood the full sense of what was happening, so I switched to the English subtitles and watched again. In both cases I was pleased to find that I had been correct in what I had understood from the Spanish. Once again, the only word I looked up because it was used several times turned out to be a swearword!

An experienced independent learner, Davis, wrote about how he watched a French film, *Samba*, as follows:

Watched *Samba*. The French wasn't too hard. I enjoyed watching it a lot, because my ability to make do with just French captions was better than I had expected. I paused quite often to look up words I didn't know, mostly slang and nouns. One actress spoke very quickly, so sometimes I reversed the tape to hear a phrase again. I liked how the captions condensed the actual amount of words, giving me a puzzle & insight into the structure of spoken French. Favourite new expression: "tu es un chaud lapin". I look up words using *Reverso* for normal words, and *Wiktionary* or *Google* for slang. This is very quick.

Lizzie also made very thoughtful notes about her viewing strategy when watching *Le roi danse*:

I noticed that when reading the captions, I missed the value of the visuals (because concentrating on reading). It was more successful to listen and check, but more time consuming and it was better to get an overview of the film first. I listed and checked a lot of vocabulary. Some words were very 'popular' (or rude!—not sure I'd want to learn them!). The film was highly visual and not particularly complex verbally. I think I reached a different level by watching several times. I could see the plot links, themes etc. by the 3rd or 4th time. It became a different experience and I used it in a presentation.

Gist watching can only take you so far. I needed the captions to reach a good level

The ultimate in a planned and strategic approach certainly came from Shiree, a very experienced Italian learner with a collection of Italian films at home. Shiree devised her own viewing template (shown on p. 191–192 – though this should be changed to be all on one page) and procedure for viewing films, which involved viewing, firstly, without captions, then with captions and then, if necessary, with English subtitles. Her diary begins:

Having thought about this, I think the only way I can measure the utility/quality of the captions is if I watch the films first without them and then make a note of what I didn't pick up without the captions in Italian. Then, really, I'd need to watch again with English subtitles to see what I didn't pick up with the Italian captions. This is going to reduce the total number of films I can see, if I'm watching each one 3 times. We'll see.

Shiree, as we have seen, a very organised and independent-minded participant, watched six Italian films. Her entries for three of them are as follows:

L'ultima ruota del carro
Not seen before. Watching w/out any captions, missed most of the plot (thought title was "last roll of the wheel"; thought friend was protagonist's boss—not vice versa; thought 2nd medical opinion was severance pay). Did understand he was offered a partnership; didn't understand friend was a jailbird. Difficult to follow fast dialogue (e.g. argument). Watching with Italian captions, still missed meaning of title, why he was given cooking cert (got joke about washing hands but not the nepotism of his in-laws), reason for his abusive phone call to hospital, and some cultural references (son recites Rome football team but not the backbenchers), details of fight with wife, the word "siren" (winning image in lotto ticket). Watching with English subtitles, still missed some cultural refs (e.g. assassination by Red Brigade; weird dance competition on TV).

Quality of captions: faithful to the dialogue, but distracting because I couldn't read quickly enough—and had to stop and replay a few times. Was conscious of reading the text, not listening to sound. Confidence in viewing next file w/o sub-titles fell from 4/10 to 1/10 and with captions fell from 9/10 to 7/10.

Shiree is similarly detailed in her next viewing and again stresses quite how hard it is to follow without captions and how essential the captions are to making any real sense of an authentic film:

Il giovane favoloso
Not seen before. Watching w/out any captions, missed important parts of the plot: e.g. details of opening scene (characters' names!); illness, conversation in courtyard, conversation with uncle and father (I thought Uncle was advising father to let J. go into the clergy—not vice versa); poetry (I thought he was reciting bits of Dante, not his own poem about Dante). Got conversation between J & Giordani but missed why he tore up his letter; thought Giordani was his tutor & that Ranieri was his brother. Completely missed his move to Rome/Florence; reason why he burns Ranieri's letter from mistress; that he had his clothes altered (I thought they were new).

Watching with Italian captions, still missed good portion of dialogue: J's complaints of how he is treated; details of his Uncles criticisms; why he is collecting letters/autographs for Fanny; dialogue with nature; visits to Uncle in Rome, criticism of bad poet at dinner; doctor advises against ice cream (thought he had advised it!).

Poetry and background conversations were most difficult to follow, compounded by complete ignorance of who he was (though film made infinitely more sense after a quick read of wikipedia—e.g. text and themes of his poems & philosophical works).

Quality of captions: very faithful to the dialogue, but very fast and complex sentences/ideas. They were essential to following the story. Confidence in viewing next file w/o captions rose from 1/10 to 4/10 and with sub-titles rose from 6/10 to 7/10.

After three weeks, Shiree reviews her strategies:

I suppose, if I were a more confident listener, I would write different notes. For example, the first few films, I noted non-verbal plot advancement; now, I've noticed that I note only conversation, but am recording more details. (Though, for lack of time, am not recording phrases which are not understood—I think are mostly expressions or idioms). I have also noticed that I'm noting the occasional word in Italian—because faster than trying to translate and more effective as an aide memoire. Have also begun to note down unfamiliar words but not yet systematically looking them up! Might be more effective, note-wise, to break the films into scenes.

Other thoughts:

Each film seems to have its own listening challenges:

- *La prima cosa bella* had lots of different types of muffled dialogue—children as narrators, character speaking through respirator or microphone, whispering or multiple dialogues.
- *Giovane favoloso* had narrative recitation of poetry (disembodied poetry over vistas, recreation of poetic dialogue with Nature), and philosophical dialogue (I would probably have picked up much more of the story had I been at all familiar with Leopardi's work.)
- *Sole a catinelle* had song lyrics (specific to the film), jokes & puns ("laundering", importance of "aspiration"), bits of southern dialect, and mistaken pronunciation (son corrects father). However, had very little difficulty following child narrator (as opposed to *La prima cosa bella*).

Other changes:

- Have begun recording names of characters
- Am still having trouble disambiguating: negatives (don't eat gelato)

- interrogatives (mistook narrative questions for statements in conditional)
- blind narration (i.e. w/out seeing speaker—but have this trouble in English too so prob going a bit deaf)
- fast dialogue during arguments
- There is a reduction of basic errors/misunderstanding (I'm getting at least 60 %–70 % of plot if not more w/out captions).
- The things I miss in 1st viewing are usually the same things I miss in using Italian captions—i.e. I can't read fast enough to make sense of it so, usually either: new vocab, more complex structure or idea; idiom/poss. dialect; or fast conversation
- Also, sometimes, captions aren't true to the dialogue (paraphrasing instead of verbatim)

The last film Shiree watches is a disappointment in several respects (though others thought it was a very good film):

La grande bellezza
Not seen before but had listened to a student presentation about the film in class. Watching w/out any captions, missed virtually all the plot/dialogue. Watched it twice with Italian captions and wasn't much the wiser (unfamiliar dialect, slang, cultural references). Watched it with English subtitles some days later and realised it actually was as fatuous as I'd thought. Very disappointing.

Shiree ends with more reflections as follows:

Post-project note
Unfortunately, due to pressures of work, I wasn't able to continue with the project after the first week of June. It seems unfortunate to have ended on a disappointing film (*la Grande Bellezza*) but, overall, I think it was a very helpful exercise (though the commitment to watch each film 3 times—without captions, then with captions in Italian, then with subtitles in English—meant fewer films watched in total). Writing up the detailed notes of films watched without captions was a very positive demonstration of a higher level of comprehension than I would have credited. (Yes, I didn't get everything and I misunderstood some things but I followed more than I thought I would have been able to do, so that was a very positive and helpful thing to take away from the project.) It was also useful to note the varying levels of quality of the captions—not something I'd thought much about.

Every project needs a Shiree, a standout participant who is able to both describe her or his behaviour and also reflect on it. Shiree stands in contrast to those with higher C-test scores (hers were 64 and 59), especially the Modern Languages students, who wanted to watch the films as enjoyable entertainment or cultural artefacts rather than as opportunities to develop their knowledge and skills intensively. In this sense, she placed an entirely different value on the enterprise compared to many other participants.

3. Quality of captions

Many of the comments in participants' diaries were about the quality of captions. Most participants appreciated the need for captioners to edit spoken language to accommodate the text, and, for many, this often presented an interesting exercise in itself when there were changes of words and phrases. At other times, comments were less positive, and, beyond a certain point, substantial differences between sound and text became distracting or confusing. The tendency of some producers to use the script of translation subtitles for captioning has already been mentioned. In some films, captions were almost verbatim much of the time; at the other extreme, in some films, they cut substantial amounts of speech and changed many words. Some participants made constructive use of the differences, whereas others found differences slightly, or even greatly, distracting. Some of the comments on the quality/nature of the captions included:

La grande bellazza
Quality of captions was good i.e. the text separate from the sound made sense, however:

 A) Often, the captions would condense two sentences into one.
 B) The captions would rearrange the syntax of what was said, for no obvious reason.
 C) The captions would make us of a different word (synonym) than what was spoken without, obvious reason again.

All of which somewhat confused me whilst I watched the film and made it slightly difficult to simultaneous use speech and text to understand the film.

Several mentioned the captions that were inserted to give background information for the deaf, such as the sounds of birds or music. Violet mentions the following:

> …it was interesting to read the captions not related to dialogue but to the other general noise, for example; (*suono di campane*) (*tintinnio*) (*cinguettio di uccelli*) as I wouldn't have been exposed to this vocab without the captions.

In one case, for the film, *Il était une fois*, she noted that:

Captions don't match!

- It is really distracting! + big gaps. Text w/o captions is considerable
- Stopped after 15 minutes
- Movie not interesting + poor captions meant there was little reason to continue.

Comments about the faithfulness of captions were much more positive for Spanish films than for French films. For example, for *Carmina y amén*, the captions are "Captions: very accurate, no differences noted, fairly confident in watching, next film without captions," and for *La lengua de las mariposas*, "Quality of captions: Completely accurate" and for *Relatos salvajes,* "Captions: faithful to dialogue, no differences noted."

Beth's comments on the captions in *Les beaux jours* sum up what many wrote about differences between captions and speech:

> Captions very useful for clarifying/focussing attention
> More scenes where I struggle to understand dialogue, so captions useful in making it clearer what goes on.
> Captions not always accurate – small phrases such as "je n'en sais rien" and "de toute facon" do not appear, especially when the dialogue is faster.
> Sometimes I find myself getting distracted by inaccurate captions then get lost as I seem to focus on relationship between sound and words and forget to look at meaning.

4. Value of captions

The majority of participants wrote that they would not have been able to follow most films with full understanding without the captions. They tended to comment that they would have gained a general understanding of the plot and characters but would probably or certainly have missed key elements and language without the captions. Several participants gave examples of where they would have missed vital dialogue.

Beth, in watching *3 coeurs* (French) comments in her diary:

> I can understand a lot without reading captions but still tend to use them- they focus my attention more on what is being said, and are particularly helpful when there are more than two people having a conversation.

Sean spoke for many when he wrote:

> Even if I could follow most of the film without them, they were a reassuring and often helpful presence.

Many of the participants wrote about using the captions to "tune in" to the sound during the first 10 or 15 minutes of a film, especially when there are unfamiliar accents. Myrtle, in writing of the German film, *Gold*, says even more:

> I found that I definitely became less and less reliant on the captions as the film progressed, and could have switched them on without missing much of the film, but found it a lot less tiring to leave them on, as it helped me understand characters when they mumbled or spoke too quickly. Moreover, I found that I became aware, through the captions, of a couple of new expressions that I was previously not familiar with and would have missed without the captions. For example, the female character tells one of the men courting her, "Hör auf, mich wie ein rohes Ei zu behandeln." I would have probably missed the part "ein rohes Ei", as it is metaphorical and I would not have automatically associated it with the context. This would have meant that I would probably have misunderstood the interaction between the two characters. I looked it up on an online dictionary (dict.cc)

to see how else it can be used. I also found that having the captions on meant that I was paying attention to nouns' genders about which I may have had doubts. Finally, as the captions are designed for people with hearing difficulties and included descriptions of intra-diegetic sounds other than the dialogues (background noises, types of music, different types of breathing such as panting, sighing, etc.), I found that I became familiar with the names of some unusual noises that I wouldn't have been familiar with, as for example, "Grillengezirpe" for "the chirping of crickets."

Felicity in watching *El cuerpo* reports:

I found the first few minutes (of *El cuerpo*) very difficult and was worried I had over-estimated my ability, but then I both 'got my ear in', and relaxed, accepting that I wouldn't understand every phrase. I made the decision in the first few minutes not to stop and look words up, or I would never have got through it. (in fact I looked up one that seemed to be used a lot and I thought it might be related to 'fear/miedo', of course it turned out to be a swearword!) I used the pause button quite a lot. Sometimes I would rewind a few seconds to see it again, but this was a crime thriller with quite a few interview scenes and several rapid phone conversations between two characters, and in those bits I paused at most of the individual 'screens' of captions because they changed slightly more quickly than I was able to read them.

Sally reinforces the value of captions in the early stages in writing about *Nicht mein Tag*:

This was a comedy, so the dialogue was fairly straightforward. I needed the captions more at the beginning until I got my ear in to the particular speech patterns. Thereafter I relied on them less. Only really needing them when the speech was particularly rapid or mumbled. I paused a couple of times for complicated sentences, to read the caption fully and absorb and I looked up 5 or 6 words. All bar one were abuse or swear words! I only looked up words that were repeated and I wanted to be sure I got it right.

The value of captions in being able to follow a difficult plot is emphasised by Arthur writing about *La lengua de mariposas*. He tells us.

I would have understood the story overall without the captions, but would have missed some details. For example, the scene where the old man explains why the Chinese girl living with him cannot speak. The actor's speech was not as clear or articulate as the others. Also, maybe his deep voice also made it harder to understand. I certainly wouldn't have understood what he was talking about without the captions.

Shiree, on the other hand, had very definite views on the value of the captions in *La grande bellezza*:

I can't judge how faithful they were to the dialogue because I couldn't follow most of the dialogue. They were essential to get any sense out of the film but unhelpful insofar as I couldn't recognise most of the vocab (and very much resented taking time to look up what turned out to be slang for "I'm going to f*** you"). Life is too short.

Arthur stresses the value of the captions in adapting to unfamiliar accents:

Relatos salvajes
Confidence in watching film without captions: 7/10
   It was a bit difficult getting used to the Argentinian accent at first, so the captions were very useful. I got quite used to the accent by the end of the film. However, the film consists in a series of stories about people's taking revenge. The accent seemed somewhat different or stronger depending on the actor. Thanks to the captions, I could get used to each individual accent quite quickly, but often, when I had got used to an actor's accent to the point what I could watch without looking at the captions, that would be when the film would switch to another story with other actors, and I had to get used to the accents all over again. But that was quite stimulating.

5. Effect of captions over time on viewing behaviour

On reading the diaries, it was striking to see changes in behaviour as participants became increasingly aware of the opportunities offered by the presence of the captions. One might say that what unfolded was a shift from primarily "viewing" behaviour to more "learner" behaviour as they realised how much greater their self-efficacy was in following and understanding films and in having their awareness of the language of the film raised by the presence of the captions.

Not all participants kept a full diary answering all questions for each film, but a fairly typical set of diaries entries was provided by Violet. Violet was an interesting case, a second-year Modern Languages student, who scored 76 in the French C-test and 69 on the Italian C-test, a confident reader in both languages but less confident in watching films, as evidenced by her questionnaire answers, though a confident speaker and listener in interactions in both languages. Violet also commented that the films provided her with more listening practice than she was used to in her degree studies and that she had gained in confidence. Some extracts from films watched earlier and later show her development:

Sous le figuier
As I became familiar with the actors and their ways of speaking, it became easier to rely less on the captions. However—they were important when speech was too quick for me to follow—or when elderly/very young actors were speaking, as this often sounded muffled, if they were speaking particularly quietly.

In time, I do gain more confidence in listening yet I didn't turn the captions off this movie, perhaps I had become too used to them.

In this film I didn't pause in order to look up vocab I didn't immediately understand, because I never felt individual words were crucial to my general understanding/appreciation of the film, which itself flowed a relatively simple premise. I just let the film run and enjoyed watching it without interruption.

Availability of captions: 6/10—because I did need them to follow fast speech, characters with difficult speech, but I think I could have still enjoyed the film without captions.

Confidence without: 8/10

Entre les murs
Quality of the captions was good, and faithful to the sound/speech. Only issue was that often speech was condensed i.e. from two spoken lines there might have been only one written line. I replayed occasionally out of curiosity to read words that I had never seen before in order to learn them. There's a lot of slang, so a lot of unfamiliar vocab. Also,

speech was quite fast so replays allowed me to get a better grasp of what was being said.

I became more confident in my listening ability as I watched the film and stopped relying heavily on the captions. It became gradually easier to understand each character's speech without the use of captions.

3 coeurs

It's helpful in this film to have different colour captions when an actor is speaking that's not the one pictured on screen.

With this film, I didn't often pause of replay in order to re-read the captions or look up unusual vocab. For the most part, the speech/text was quite slow as rarely did the actors speak very quickly. Also it seemed to be mostly always quite informal, regular vocabulary that I was familiar with. The hardest vocabulary (for me) was the captions that dealt with the extra, background noise i.e. 'vrombissement d'un aspirateur'.

Un village français

Captions were well-matched to the sound and appeared faithful. This is a series with a lot of different characters, a lot of dialogue etc. so I often relied on the captions to be able to keep up with what was being said.

Lots of the dialogue was also spoke quite quickly, so sometimes it because easier to simply read the captions as opposed to tuning in and trying to completely follows the conversation.

Having watched other films with captions I would say that the font of the captions in this series wasn't as sharp or as clear as it could have been. However, this doesn't strike me as a truly important issue.

Again, it was useful to have different colour captions.

One issue however was that sometimes the captions condensed what was being spoken aloud, and so some dialogue was lost. I think I was almost always about to understand dialogue however even when the captions might have missed something out.

I definitely gained in listening confidence as I watched this series and became used to the characters' voices. However, I was never confident enough to turn the captions off.

Availability of captions: 6.5/10; Confidence without: Start—6/10, another episode—8/10

It might be argued that Violet is getting herself into a position of being dependent on the captions. I would argue that this is a relative position.

She has only watched five French films and two Italian films and is already growing in confidence in viewing. The captions remain not only a valuable or even essential "crutch" but also a means of identifying many new words.

Lana was a very interesting case of someone who found the captions rather distracting initially, but grew in appreciation over the course of watching six films. Her first viewing was the French film *Yves St Laurent*:

> I like to let the film run so I didn't stop it at all. I used the captions to understand more complex sentences but often it was quite distracting to have them on the screen and largely I would have preferred to just watch the film without them and then try to guess from the context what was being said.

By her last film in Spanish, however, she was writing:

> 'No tengas miedo' (Spanish)—The captions were extremely accurate and in sync with the dialogue which made them useful as opposed to distracting.
> I did let the film run but I looked up a few words on wordreference.com on an app on my phone when they popped up and I couldn't guess from the context what they meant (eg. pastañear = to blink and un recado = an errand) I hadn't actually seen these words ever before so it was helpful to look them up.

6. Reservations about captions

As there were so many comments that expressed reservations about films having captions, I have included a section on these. We have already seen earlier how Lana's initial view was that they could be useful but were a distraction, and others with similar views also reinforce the sense that some participants thought that watching foreign films should be a visual and listening experience, not a reading one.

Davis, for example, put this perceived downside well:

> For both films I've watched, I notice that I'm quite reliant on the captions. I grew up in Holland, where I watched lots of subtitled TV-shows as a kid, so I'm used to it. I think that the captions are extremely useful for gaining vocabulary, but because they give meanings away it detracts from the function of the film as a listening task. If I didn't have captions, I might be more motivated to learn to make do with what I do understand. Still, the captions are hugely helpful at this point in my learning and it's very enjoyable!

Felicity also expressed a common reservation:

> I felt very reliant on the captions, and although I was conscious of listening throughout, I was aware that I was picking up more from reading than listening.

Harry, likewise, feels rather guilty: "I try to not look at captions for a while (when watching *Balada triste de trompeta*) but always end up glancing if I'm not a 100% certain I heard right."

For some, there is still a sense that they are somehow cheating in what should be a listening exercise. Harry puts the dilemma well:

> *Balada triste de trompeta*
> Captions—glanced at them for most of the film. Weren't vital, but possibly helpful. Hard to tell if they served as a crutch or impediment this time—I try to not look at captions for a while, but always end up glancing if I'm not a 100 % certain I heard right.

7. Quality of films

While this was not an explicit category, many participants made comments on the quality of the films they watched. In many cases, this was a deciding factor in whether they watched the whole film or not, and how much effort they put into watching. For example, for some well-made thrillers, such as *El cuerpo*, participants were prepared to put considerable effort into getting the plot and characters right. While *Nirgendwo in Afrika* was highly rated by several participants, one of whom called it a "captivating film," *La grande bellezza* divided opinions. Sean found it "a great film," whereas, as Shiree thought, "life was too short" to bother with it after watching for a short time.

Another film, *Der Krieger und die Kaiserin*, received a very bad review from Sally, but it was partially redeemed as a German language exercise by the presence of the captions:

> This was a drama, but an arty-farty one. It was shockingly bad, I would not have sat through it in English! Honestly, I could fill this whole book on what I didn't like about this film!

There were lots of silences, but I still needed the captions, because the dialogue was often quiet or mumbled. It also didn't necessarily follow from the pictures. I looked up 3 or 4 words, but most of the last hour I just wanted it to end. I don't think the captions were verbatim of the dialogue, but had everything that was important.

I absolutely needed the captions to be sure I wasn't just missing the point. I'm pretty sure I wasn't. It was one of those films where the filmmaker no doubt thought they were being terribly clever, but forgot other people have to watch it.

I like thoughtful, intelligent films. This wasn't.

Without captions, I wouldn't have passed 20 mins. At least I could practise my German!

8. Differences across levels

As mentioned earlier, there was a wide range of C-test scores. The C-test is designed to capture general proficiency (Eckes & Grotjahn, 2006), so, in this case, the C-tests for each language provided little precise information about listening ability or confidence in viewing. Entries in the diaries from the two participants with the lowest scores and the two with the highest scores suggest that the lower proficiency participants made more use of the pause and replay functions and were active strategically in learning from the films. The higher proficiency participants wrote that they let the films run and occasionally noted words, which they looked up afterwards (cf. Zamoon, 1996). Their notes also frequently mentioned that they wanted to enjoy the films as films. However, as observed under changes of behaviour, even these participants made more use of the captions and control available as time went on and they watched more films.

The main obvious difference between, say a high proficiency participant, Myrtle (C-tests 87/90 [French] and 88/89 [Italian]), and a lower proficiency one, Martha (C-tests 43/43 [German]), was that while both commented on the need for captions in the initial part in order to tune in, Myrtle felt that she needed them less and less as films progressed and could usually give a confidence rating of 8/10 for watching without captions. Martha, in contrast, continued to rely on captions for following the films, not just for reassurance or because it made watching "less tiring," as Myrtle put it. These findings are exactly in line with Pujolà's (2002) findings, where lower and higher proficiency learners use the "Help" option for captions for different reasons. Similarly, with mid-range C-test scores (57/60), Sally treated films very much as language learning opportunities, admitting that she could not manage without the captions.

One tentative implication that might be drawn from the behaviour of the high-level Modern Languages students is that they are, perhaps, missing opportunities in their desire to watch as L1 viewers might (or as long-term expatriate L2 viewers), and are more like the Brazilian class-based learners described by Cole (2015 and Ch. 8, pp. 230–233) than the autonomous learners who engage very actively in valued activities such as watching TV and films in English. It is the non-specialists, with lower general proficiency, who appear to be exploiting most actively the opportunities for developing language knowledge and skills through captioned viewing.

7.4 A Complex Matrix of Factors

As we have seen, the diary entries produced a complex matrix of factors, some concerned with the film, others about the captions and most related to the viewing behaviour and perceptions of the participants. As the numbers in the project were small, there was little value in running any statistical tests on the data gathered, but for a future, larger project, with so many key factors now identified, it would be useful to express the factors in scales, which could be used to see patterns with each participant across films, captions, languages and proficiency levels and explore the relative influence of the different factors. In Table 7.2, below, the scales may appear to overlap at times, but I felt this was essential as the participants chose to use highly specific language in their entries. So, one participant might describe the captions as supporting or distracting, whereas another might say they were useful or not needed but not distracting and easily ignored. The "distracting" category tended to be used when the captions were inaccurate and/or poorly edited or contained content different from the speech.

Table 7.2 Film and viewer factors in watching captioned films

Film factors	Viewer factors
Good quality film/poor quality film	Supporting captions/distracting captions
Accurate/complete captions/inaccurate/limited captions	Captions useful/captions not needed
Easy film/difficult film	High confidence (with)/low confidence (with)
Complex content/simple content	High confidence (without)/low confidence (without)
Fast/difficult speech/slow/simple speech	Complex viewing/simple viewing
Strong local/regional	Positive attitude to captions/negative attitude to captions
	High proficiency score/low proficiency score
	Less dependent/more dependent
	More listening/more reading

7.5 Discussion

In Chap. 2, I outlined Salomon's concept of AIME and the paradox that the perception of TV and films as easy media turns out to be a constraint on effective learning from these media. At the same time, for foreign language learners, print is regarded as the easier medium and TV and films as the more difficult, with full, confident comprehension of TV programmes usually a distant and unreachable goal. The consequence of such perceptions is that, just as with the less able learners in Salomon's study, perceived self-efficacy in watching TV programmes and films may be relatively lower than reading printed material, and the opportunities for making use of audiovisual media as language learning resources are severely constrained.

As we have seen in the experiences of EURECAP participants, the accessibility offered by the captions transformed their usual viewing experience of partial understanding or just being able to follow the general lines of the plot, to full or nearly full understanding of plot, characters, complicated dialogue, rapid speech and accents. Even jokes may be laughed at for the right reasons.

At the level of psychomotor skills (see Simpson (1966) and Chap. 5), there was substantial feedback to indicate that the captions helped participants to "tune in" to unfamiliar accents in the foreign language, supporting Mitterer and McQueen's (2009) contention that captions provide for lexically-guided retuning of perceptual categories of sounds. An obvious limitation to this project is that there were no initial and final tests or delayed post-tests, which might have captured gains (or lack of them) in specific areas such as improved phonetic perception or "tuning in." The captions appear valuable at a "local" level, as Mitterer and McQueen (2009) also found with distinctive Scottish and Australian accents. However, the evidence for a wider "global" value is not clear from this pilot project. Arthur puts the issue very well in noting, after having watched *Relatos salvajes*:

> Thanks to the captions, I could get used to each individual accent quite quickly, but often, when I had got used to an actor's accent to the point that I could watch without looking at the captions, that would be when the

film would switch to another story with other actors, and I had to get used to the accents all over again. But that was quite stimulating.

All participants saw film watching as a valued activity in Cole's (2015) terms, whether for the language, the culture or for appreciation of a particular film or director. Yet, all were aware that this valued activity had hitherto been lacking to some extent, as they could not engage fully with films they thought worth watching. All participants also made it clear in their questionnaire responses that one of their goals was to be able to watch films and TV programmes with confidence. The presence of captions increased their confidence and sense of self-efficacy and, in many cases, brought about a switch from general viewing to viewing that also focused on the language of the film or even to viewing for enjoyment being replaced by conscious learning, with some regret, it should be said in some cases. Certainly, the diaries show that all participants were able to appreciate many of the films in ways that they would not have been able to without the captions. Many participants mentioned that the presence of the captions changed the very nature of viewing, as they kept being drawn to the language shown in the captions and paying attention to it. Time and again, the diaries contained comments about switching off the captions for a while as participants checked their listening, then switching them back on just for "reassurance." One participant, Jonathan, summed up his experience as follows:

> For me, it is mostly about the intentions, the mindset. You can watch a difficult (fast, dialect) film with captions and even pause to look at the captions and still be learning informally, since learning language is secondary to following the film (and, perhaps, feeling like you are a real, authentic viewer, understanding the film as it was meant to be understood, seeking to learn the culture fully (rather than the language) etc.).

Yet, again, this is exactly what was meant about the issues with OU programmes, reported in Chap. 2, which were being watched more as entertainment than as serious programmes, designed to change behaviour and thinking. In the results of the project, we again see the paradox identified by Salomon emerging. Remember that according to Salomon, people will invest greater effort in processing material (and hence learn better) when they encounter complex, ambiguous or new material that cannot be easily fitted in to their existing mental schema. This was meant to apply to native speakers, but if we consider this perspective in terms of watching a foreign film, the results of the project suggest that it is not those with the highest scores and relatively nearer to their goal of completely confident viewing who make most use of the captions, but those with relatively lower proficiency (but not low proficiency). The higher-level participants, particularly some of the Modern Languages degree students, felt self-efficacious enough not to put much effort into viewing compared to the others, although to do so would certainly have helped them towards their goal, as Cole's fully autonomous learners (2015 and Ch 8) make clear. In a future, larger project, it would be worth considering setting some participants tasks to orientate their viewing while leaving others free to watch as they choose, in order to compare the effects on viewing behaviour and language learning focus.

Did the project achieve its objectives? I wanted to see the effects of regular viewing of captioned films, under the choice and control of the participants, on confidence, tuning in, correct perception and reception, speed of following, understanding and reading, transferability and changes in behaviour. Although in most cases, the number of DVDs watched was fewer than participants had agreed to watch at the outset, the evidence from the diaries suggests strongly (1) that captioned viewing did help build their confidence, (2) that through the captions, they were enabled to tune in to the dialogue of films, especially those with fast speech and complex plots and (3) that they became used to using the captions flexibly, blending listening and reading as and when required by the nature of the film as it progressed. The diaries also provided evidence for a steady improvement in comprehension, depending, of course, on specific films, and for a change in behaviour, as resistance to captions gave way to appreciating their value in multiple ways—from following a complex plot, to getting used to dialects and accents, or learning colloquial language they had never come across before.

So, how do the findings of the project move us forward from the *Teletext 888 Project* and research up to 2015 on captioned viewing? The most important findings involve perceptual changes and changes in level of confidence, behaviour, perceived self-efficacy and strategies for learning and self-regulation over time. Also, in terms of the valued activity for the individual, there were changes from valuing the film viewed as a cultural artefact in the foreign language, to a greater focus on its value for language acquisition. The importance of the quality of the film also emerged as an important finding in the case of some participants. Some participants decided, within a short time, that a film was not to their taste or was of poor quality and not worth watching for any reason, whereas for others, the quality of the film was a determining factor in how often it was viewed, in what conditions and for what purposes. There were many cases to illustrate the importance of the mindset of the individual participants, and how this varied from film to film. In some cases, a film was watched three times, and by the third time, intensive viewing for language acquisition was taking place as more and more language was taken out.

All this adds to the case for the prime value of captioned viewing being in informal settings where learner-viewers have choice and control, a theme I shall develop in the next chapter, drawing on recent research.

8

The Developing Environment for Language Learning: A New Audience and the Revised Model of Language Learning with Captions

8.1 Pavia and Beyond

8.1.1 The "Subtitles and Language Learning" Project

In his chapter in the proceedings of the Pavia conference (Gambier, 2015), Yves Gambier, a key figure in translation and subtitling research in Europe for many years, writes in answer to the question, which the project set out to answer: Can we learn a foreign language while watching TV?

> There is no question of letting anyone believe that learning a language from scratch is possible by only watching subtitled audiovisuals. Nobody has learned Chinese just by watching subtitled audiovisuals on TV… (p. 68).

I would beg to differ. I have run a project on guided independent learning in French and German at Oxford University called *Lambda* for about

18 years and have interviewed hundreds of applicants for the project, collecting their language learning histories, strategies and motivations. While I have yet to come across a learner of Chinese who has done what Gambier suggests, I have come across many learners who began their French and German learning from scratch by watching television and gained a great deal, in particular, from watching TV advertisements in French or German.

In contrast, as Gambier reports, according to *Eurobarometers* surveys carried out every six years (2000, 2006, 2012), few people considered that they learnt language by watching TV or listening to the radio, and most respondents still preferred programmes and films dubbed in their L1 in many European countries. Yet, politically, the European Commission has been emphasising through its communications, such as *Multilingualism: An asset for Europe and a shared commitment* (2008), that it wishes to see the media as an informal source for language learning, while a number of European governments are also clear in their support for subtitling and its potential for assisting language learning. In their research and reports, the theme is constantly and consistently one of seeking to change the habits of those in countries where dubbing is the norm (e.g., Germany) and making maximum use of the new possibilities for multilingual audio-visual translation afforded by new technologies.

As Gambier tells us, the "Subtitles and Language Learning" project aimed at testing and confirming that subtitles, as used in cinemas, on TV channels and on DVDs, allowed:

> The development of motivation for language learning, making people aware of language diversity and the similarities between certain languages, thus making them easier to acquire;
> The development of competences in a given foreign language, the basic foundations of which are already mastered. ... (p. 68)

There were ten partners in the project (Universities in Turku [Finland], Patras [Greece], Pavia [Italy], Vilnius [Lithuania], Poznan [Poland], Faro [Portugal], Ljubljana [Slovenia], Barcelona [Spain], Castello de la Plana [Spain] and Ramat Gan [Israel]), and each followed two complementary strategies in gathering data:

1. Relying on the opinions and self-evaluations of three distinct groups: learners in non-formal settings, language students and foreign language teachers, and
2. Defining a set of learning activities related to the use of subtitled audiovisual material.

The scale of the project was impressive and aimed to increase the number of training courses, especially in "small" languages and those that were not cognates (e.g., Italian and Finnish), to include the broadest possible range of learners, from those with little or no exposure to those close to being immersed in the foreign language, and to develop a common methodology for collecting data across Europe, which would allow for comparisons and correlations. Their work was to involve promoting the use of subtitled material in formal and non-formal settings, and promoting language learning policies in different settings that would favour this approach, as well as identifying useful activities involving subtitled material that would not only speed up the language learning process but also help our understanding of how subtitles contribute to learning.

Six questionnaires, which aimed to tap into aspects such as learners' motivation, the influence of subtitles and the development of language skills, were distributed, three at the beginning of the project and three when informants appeared to have stopped using subtitled material. The questionnaires also established profiles in learners' age, reading habits, level of education, current knowledge of the foreign language, exposure to subtitles, time spent in front of screens and features of subtitles watched.

Gambier and colleagues correctly identified the changes going on not only in Europe but globally in language learning in informal contexts and the way in which independent learners are now "flipping the classroom," accessing foreign language media sources in their own time for their own valued activities, and in doing so, are acquiring foreign language skills in ways which would have been almost unheard of even twenty or thirty years ago.

8.1.2 The Findings of the Survey

In her chapter, "A Survey on Stakeholders' Perceptions of Subtitles as a Means to Promote Foreign Language Learning" (Mariotti, 2015),

Cristina Mariotti, one of the key members of the project, provides an excellent overview of the questionnaire survey mentioned earlier. Mariotti reports the findings of this massive, multicountry survey on the perceived value of subtitles (translation/interlingual) and captions (same-language/intralingual) among a large population of class-based learners, independent learners and teachers. Mariotti, as Gambier before her, uses the term "subtitles" to cover both captions and subtitles, so, at times, it is not clear whether the one or the other or both are being referred to (see Note 1). The findings of the survey had important implications for my own further research, and as its methodology and findings deserve to be widely known, I am reporting it in some detail here.

Those involved in the survey set out to answer two questions:

1. What are the stakeholders' attitudes towards the use of subtitles as used in public and commercial TV channels, on DVD and on the Internet as a means of promoting foreign language learning, and
2. In the opinion of stakeholders, what foreign language competences can benefit the most from using subtitled audiovisual material?

The "stakeholders" included foreign language teachers, secondary and university students and independent adult learners. Teachers who agreed to take part were asked to view subtitled audiovisual material at least once every two weeks, and could choose the type of material they used. The independent learners, who had been contacted personally by the researchers, were supposed to watch subtitled audiovisual material in their free time regularly and at least once every two weeks.

The data were gathered using questionnaires given at two time points to 45 teachers, 481 secondary school students (aged 15), 893 university students attending foreign language classes at least once a week and 555 adult learners (average age 30). The data were gathered from Finland, Italy, Lithuania, Poland, Slovenia and Spain. The adult learners had a very wide variety of L1s, and many were migrants who wished to learn the language of the country without the guidance of a teacher. Not all informants completed both questionnaires.

The first questionnaire was given out at the start of the survey (in September 2010) when informants started viewing subtitled audiovisual material for the project, and the second one at the end of the viewing period for different populations (May 2011 for students and teachers, October 2011 for autonomous adult learners). The first questionnaire for teachers included biographical information and their familiarity with using subtitled audiovisual material in the classroom. The second questionnaire for teachers focused on identifying factors such as the criteria that guided choices of audiovisual material, the combinations of subtitles (intralingual, interlingual or reversed), the reasons for the choices, frequency of watching, language areas that benefited most and the benefits and drawbacks of using subtitled material. The two student/adult learner questionnaires had a similar structure, with the first focusing on biographical information, attitudes towards foreign languages and viewing habits, whereas the second one (with many open questions) aimed to gather data on their experience of subtitles and language learning, whether and how watching subtitled material had changed their language learning habits and their opinions on using subtitles to promote foreign language learning.

Most of the teachers were familiar with using subtitled material for language teaching, though the amount of use by teachers varied a great deal, from 38.5 % who used it a lot to 15.4 % who said they never used it. The variations across countries tended to reflect the national availability of subtitled material. Motives for using them were varied and predictable: as a supplement to normal activities, developing reading and listening skills, aiding memorisation and/or motivation, student preference and teacher preference. Drawbacks tended to be concerned with training, technological or organisational complications. Choice of materials was influenced primarily by student motivation, along with level and ease of use, compatibility with other materials, length of video clips and how easy they were to obtain. Interestingly enough (and in great contrast to recommendations from video-use recipe books), teachers used mostly full-length feature films (18), with short feature films (8), documentaries (7), episodes of TV series (7) and cartoons (5) trailing behind. Of particular relevance to the present book, teachers preferred using translation subtitles with lower levels or challenging material, and captions with intermediate/advanced learners or gifted, fast and well-motivated classes.

The uses made were also quite predictable: The teachers thought that subtitles were most useful for listening comprehension, vocabulary retention and pronunciation as well as their intercultural knowledge. Most of the time, it seems, teachers focused on using films for general listening comprehension or for stimulating oral production. In general, teachers appeared to consider that subtitled audiovisual materials provided useful input and exposure to the foreign language. There was some criticism of the nature of film subtitles, as almost half thought that they went too fast and there should be subtitles specifically for language learning. Teachers also complained about having to develop self-made exercises to integrate the audiovisual material into the classroom (and we know that this can be very time-consuming).

Most of the students in formal learning situations watched video material to improve their competence in English (73.5 %), and just over half stated that their preferred activity in the classroom was watching videos. Similarly, over half were familiar with viewing with subtitles and were satisfied with the audio–subtitle combination chosen by their teachers. A total of 858 informants in this category completed the second follow-up questionnaire, and 65 % of these were positive about their viewing experiences during the project, with 69.1 % thinking it was time well spent. They were also positive overall about how much the activities with subtitles had helped in their foreign language learning, especially listening and speaking skills.

The project also had an effect on their viewing habits outside the classroom, and almost 70 % reported that they had started watching more subtitled programmes in their free time as a result of the project. Most of the negative comments concerned the quality of the subtitles, especially discrepancies between sound and text and the speed of the subtitles as they found it difficult to listen to one language and read subtitle text in another.

In terms of my own research, the findings with the third group, the learners in non-formal settings, are of most interest, and it is certainly a major achievement that the researchers were able to gather data from 555 learners in this category across Europe. In all, 55 % viewed subtitled films and programmes to learn English, 23 % Spanish, 20 % French and 12 % Italian. The most important reason for wanting to learn another language was communication with L2 native speakers, whereas employment reasons came second. Respondents tended to prefer material with L2 audio and subtitles in their L1 or in a language they could fully understand, especially if they were watching primarily for leisure. However, putting responses about attitudes to L2 learning and responses about subtitle combinations together, L2 learners much preferred the option of L2 audio with L2 captions. Learners proved to be very independent in their choices of material, despite offers of help from the research group, and watched freely selected material either broadcast, on DVD, PC or the Internet. Only 258 respondents completed the second questionnaire; just over 76 % reported a positive experience with subtitled programmes and films being very useful for language learning and over 60 % feeling that watching these was time well spent.

Respondents' answers to questions about the benefits of viewing subtitled material indicated that they liked to watch because they felt the subtitles could help them improve their listening skills and understand foreign dialogues and foreign accents. They also felt more confident in using the foreign language; they started to watch subtitled programmes and films more often and became more active in conversations. Not surprisingly, they also felt that their reading skills as well as their knowledge of the foreign language had improved.

As my own earlier research had found, the informal learners liked watching with subtitles, as it was more fun and a relaxing way of learning a foreign language. Again, as with the formal learners, they felt that the quality of subtitles was poor at times and that they often went too fast. Some reported the difficulty of watching images and paying attention to language at the same time. Unsurprisingly, those who watched most enjoyed the experience and had positive attitudes towards subtitles, they thought that watching subtitled material was time well spent and also believed that the more they watched, the more they learnt.

I suggested in my chapter in the publication of the proceedings (Vanderplank, 2015) that the rich data for understanding the potential of captions and language learning almost certainly lie outside the classroom and in informal situations, probably with adult learners, especially those who have reached an intermediate level or higher, and can make use of captions. The data from this survey provide confirmation for this position, while there is little new to learn from what teachers and their students tell us: audiovisual material is popular with learners, but it is time-consuming for teachers to prepare activities; subtitled material is useful for listening comprehension, vocabulary retention and pronunciation and provides good learning resources for oral skills, though the potential of subtitles for improving written productive and receptive skills appears to be largely unexploited.

The chapter concludes with a very pertinent comment that the increasing accessibility of subtitled audiovisual material may well have an impact on the practices of teachers, class-based learners and informal learners, and a future study would be needed to see this effect. Already, only a few years after the survey, the world may seem a different place in terms of the availability of audiovisual material, especially streaming films, programmes and clips on YouTube and other Internet sources, as well as access on the move.

I will now turn to some research on this informal audience, which uses TV programmes and films actively to develop their language skills.

8.2 Autonomous Learners and Informal Learning in Captioned Viewing

In my talk at the Pavia conference (Vanderplank, 2016), I suggested that we may have been looking in the wrong place for answers to our questions about language learning from TV, video and films. Have we been too narrow in focusing on the high-school or higher education student population we sample from when captions are used every day by mature post-formal education adults? In Chap. 5, I reported the research carried out by Sarah Rose Zamoon (1996) surveying the informal watching of captioned and uncaptioned TV programmes by international students at her university in the USA. Many students watched captioned programmes in their homes for a wide variety of reasons, using a wide range of strategies. Her findings tended to indicate that the main users of captioned programmes for language learning were those lower level learners who had not yet been formally admitted to degree programmes at the university, as they had to pass an English language test at a high enough level. Higher level students who were already students at the university tended to be only occasional users.

What evidence is there for the benefits of captioned viewing in informal contexts and with adult learners? The research reported in Chap. 5 by d'Ydewalle and by Pavakanun (d'Ydewalle & Pavakanun 1996, 1997, Pavakanun & d'Ydewalle 1992) and later by their colleagues (Van Lommel, Laenen, & d'Ydewalle, 2006) suggested that viewers could indeed pick up language from watching a foreign language film, though this was mainly vocabulary items, and the favoured condition appeared to be reversed subtitling where the programme was in the L1 and the subtitles were in the L2.

There is also a relevant study by Joan-Tomás Pujolá focusing on the use of Help options/strategies in language laboratory and multimedia settings in a non-formal self-study programme for developing reading and listening skills (Pujolá, 2002). Twenty-two adult Spanish learners of EFL at the Escola Oficial d'Idiomes in Barcelona at about B2/C1 and C1/C2 levels of the CEFR took part. TV, radio and newspaper texts were used as source language input and Help options included online optional captions, dictionaries, transcripts, replay/rewind, cultural notes and feedback with explanations. Pujolá found that students at different levels behaved in varied, idiosyncratic ways. In general, the higher levels saw captions as "backup," whereas lower levels saw them as a necessary tool for understanding. Overall, though, there appears to be very little relevant research, as it is so difficult to capture informal learning out of educational contexts for obvious reasons.

Further examples of research evidence, which offer encouragement for the future, include the work carried out by Pemberton, Fallahkhair, and Masthoff (2005) and Fallahkhair, Masthoff, & Pemberton (2004) at the University of Brighton, who reported on an assessment of the potential for interactive TV (iTV) technologies in language learning (rather than language teaching) using a focus group of twenty-one subjects to gather information on viewer behaviour in foreign language learning. As they say, where learners are independent and adult, issues of acceptability and "fit" into everyday life become critical. In general, participants were very positive about the potential of iTV for scaffolding incidental language learning as part of entertainment viewing, especially through optional captions or subtitles.

The authors present the possible scenario and profile of a typical mature, motivated, autonomous learner: a well-educated woman named Martha, who is in her 40s, is learning French, and has found a French TV channel that broadcasts its programmes with French captions. She finds it difficult to keep up with the captions, as she is usually doing something else while watching (such as preparing food). The authors then go on to describe a possible future in which viewers can opt for subtitles or captions in the language of their choice and can adjust the speed and quality of subtitles/captions to their level and needs. The progress made since digital TV arrived in the UK suggests that the scenarios are now close to being realised.

Another example is the research by Geoffrey Sockett and colleagues reported in Chap. 2, in which they look at the informal learning of English by non-native speakers, with particular reference to the role of virtual communities (Sockett & Toffoli, 2012). Using data collected from diaries, they investigated how a small group (5) of non-specialist language learners at the University of Strasbourg used the Internet in their spare time for two months to read and listen to English, and also communicate in English, notably in online communities through social networking websites. The striking aspect of this study is that it suggests that we need to move from the current mainstream model of the teacher-driven learner-autonomy paradigm, in which the learner only makes decisions about learning and choices of method, to one in which the learner is a "language user" and "social actor." The only activities that involved all five users were social networking (often with other nationalities in English) and watching video content, usually streamed or downloaded, and sometimes with informally contributed French subtitles. One participant watched at least 2 ½ hours a day!

I should also mention again the work of Jason Cole (2015), with specific reference to the group of autonomous learners watching captioned films and TV programmes in informal settings in Brazil. Sixty-seven participants in his study comparing autonomous learners (FASILs) with classroom-trained learners (CTLs), 94 % of all interviewees, responded that they watched English television in some form or other. A major difference between the FASILs and the CTLs regarding television use was the level of engagement with language that participants in each group reported. FASILs were more likely than CTLs to mention that television led to attention to linguistic detail, and they tended to be the participants who described more fully how this happened.

Though participants in both groups talked about how they used subtitles or captions, a larger percentage of FASILs, than of CTLs, mentioned that they used these for support when watching shows with technical vocabulary or unusual dialects (e.g., *House*). For example, one FASIL, Adriano, stated that he generally watched television and films without subtitles, but when watching a film that dealt with "gadgetry," for example, James Bond films, or when there were "whispered words," he turned to English captions. Oyama expressed the same sentiment when discussing why he sometimes turned to English captions:

> Nowadays I use subtitles only for shows and movies with technical vocabulary or when I know the characters talk very fast and use a lot of slangs [sic]. (2015, 296)

Participants used both English captions and Portuguese subtitles as a way of scaffolding their listening, though it was primarily FASILs who reported this strategy. One reported the following:

> I don't look at the subtitles all the time, I listen, listen, listen. If I don't get something then I go to the subtitles, so I like having it as a crutch. Well I didn't get it so I lean on it, and I ... 'oh that's what he said' and usually that's when I learn new words (2015, 296)

FASILs were much more likely to offer responses that indicated they independently sought to understand language structures due to their practical value in helping to decipher content that interested them. Several participants mentioned that they were sensitive to bad translations, which led them to attempt to figure out jokes and metaphorical language on their own. Cole reports that one student, Oyama, felt that imperfect translations led him to engage more deeply with the language,

> You start noticing that the subtitle doesn't quite match what the-the person's saying. Some jokes are off [...] Probably it's because uh, because it's a wordplay in the original language, so I notice that sometimes, and that made me want to-to learn more. (2015, 297)

Both CTLs and FASILs mentioned the positive effect of repeated viewing of scenes or whole films, but, again, it was more often FASILs who went into more detail about this process. Again, Cole provides a telling quote from one student, Viviane, whose description was one of several that showed the level of engagement with language that FASILs sometimes were capable of:

> I memorize what the actors say. I think it helps because you see the film the first time and you might understand but you can't repeat what they say. When you see it several times you are going to be able to repeat because you are going to understand more exactly what they were saying. (2015, 298)

Cole suggests that the apparent difference between FASILs and CTLs in terms of engagement with the English used in programmes cannot be attributed to less interest or use of television. CTLs were just likely to watch English language television shows regularly as FASILs were. CTLs were also as likely as FASILs to report extensive viewing: the heavy number of hours they watched television per day or week. Participants from both groups mentioned binge watching, short periods of time (weeks/months) when they devoured full seasons of shows (accessible through downloading) for many hours a week before sliding back into a less extensive viewing pattern. His conclusion is (2015, 298) that the differences between FASILs and CTLs in the use of English language television programmes and films had less to do with time spent with the content than with the way the participants engaged with the films and programmes.

Cole's FASILs, while relatively numerous, may, nonetheless, be a fairly restricted population, willing to devote substantial time and effort to achieving their goals, only one of which may be proficiency in a foreign language. Perhaps closer to the norm these days are Sockett's informal learners who watch TV programmes online and engage in other activities that bring language learning benefits. I frequently come across experienced, informal learners who are able to access a wide range of media of their own choosing and develop their language skills. While the autonomy agenda in SLA research for some time has been firmly anchored in teacher-advised or teacher-directed activities (Little, 2004; Lantolf, 2013), the truly independent or autonomous learner outside the classroom has exploited the affordances of the Internet and other media to enhance their foreign language skills through informal means.

8.3 Effects "of," "with" and "through" Technology

Another of my themes at the conference talk was how technology has been changing not only the way we live but increasingly the way we learn in general, and learn languages in particular. I picked up a theme, which I had originally come across in the 1990s, and which now seemed more relevant than ever, especially as it had been developed still further.

Towards the end of the *Teletext 888 Project*, I became increasingly attracted to the idea that what I was interested in was conceptually different from what most other researchers involved in captions were interested in. Drawing on ideas developed by Gavriel Salomon (Salomon, 1993) in the collection, *Distributed Cognitions*, regarding how we use technological innovations, and how technological innovations in turn enable us to develop new ways of tackling tasks, I tried to characterise the differences in approaches in terms of those that were interested in the effects OF captions on watching video material and my own approach as being primarily interested in looking at effects WITH captions when watching video material. Comparing the two terms, the implications for research questions using effects of' research arguments are generally: "what does inserting captions or subtitles do in terms of language-learner behaviour and how can we measure this?" This is analogous to asking, "what does literacy do to people?" (Answer: It enables them to read books, learn new vocabulary and write essays—and text their friends). This "effects of'" question is also the one asked by most researchers in the field of captions and foreign language learning. "What is the effect of adding captions?" (Answer: "It increases comprehension and vocabulary recognition.") However, I came to the conclusion that this approach had a strong constraining effect on caption research. What matters is what learner-viewers do with captions. "Effects with" technology concerns how we may perform a particular task better once we are experienced and skilled users of a tool or piece of technology such as a personal computer, smartphone or DVDs with captions. For captions on films and TV, "effects with" are being able to freeze-frame subtitle text, locating key spoken sequences, elimination of the need for a transcript, ease of identifying unknown and familiar words, "hearing" and "tuning in" to difficult speech and accents and so on. In other words, "effects with" captions are linked to learners having choice and taking control if they wish!

At the time, I was unable to put this new framework of thinking into practice or explore its implications fully. However, the growth in autonomous language learning, fuelled by the availability (and accessibility) of media sources via the Internet, has in many respects validated the notion of "effects with" technology in general, and captions in particular. Indeed, I wish to go further. Since talking about "effects with" technology in my talk at the Pavia conference, I have found that Salomon and his co-researcher David Perkins (2005) have developed their thinking further and proposed the notion of "effects through" technology.

When we talk about "effects through" technology, we have in mind activities that would not be possible without the application of technological resources. While there may be alternatives to many technological aids (pen and paper as an alternative to word processing, printed maps and atlases as an alternative to *Google* maps), there are many situations and activities these days that have been made possible only through technology. The most obvious and frequent example given by Salomon and Perkins is certainly mathematical calculation, but in language learning, there are also activities that have only in the recent past become possible, thanks to technology. Take, for example, the experiences of the FASILs in Brazil described by Cole and Sockett's informal learners in Strasbourg. Yes, in the past some of these might have become autonomous English learners through using books and listening to English language tapes and broadcasts on the radio. I used to estimate that the real autonomous learner was a rare person indeed, and over the past 20 or 30 years, the direction of studies of autonomy within SLA research towards a weak form of autonomy, directed by teachers and advisers, suggests that the field in general thought so too. Yet, both in the survey reported by Mariotti in this chapter and in Cole's and Sockett's research, far larger number of autonomous informal learners than one might have expected were found, so there is no reason to think that, given access to the same technological affordances and valued activities as those in the research reported, they do not exist in large numbers these days all over the world.

8.4 A Revised Model of Language Learning Through Captioned Viewing

Drawing together the findings of research into captioned viewing and informal, independent language learning, along with the insights providing by psychologists such as Bandura, Salomon, Mayer and Moreno, it is possible to develop a revised model of my original 1990 model, taking into account a range of factors reported.

The original model, as presented in Pavia, is similar to the ones given in Figs. 8.1, 8.2 and 8.3:

In the model in Fig. 8.3, learners attend to the input provided by the captioned film or programme consciously, systematically and reflectively—all three being components of watching attentively. Both ATTENTION and ADAPTATION are included in TAKING OUT, as is ADOPTION, the stage at which the learner produces correct and appropriate language. However, this model underplays the role of selection and grading factors in the early stages and how learner-viewers actually behave. My revised model, Fig. 8.4, combines Figs. 8.2 and 8.3 into one, and provides for loops within the selection and grading process for the learner-viewer to have choice and control, as well as adding boxes that capture the perceptual aspects of captioned viewing.

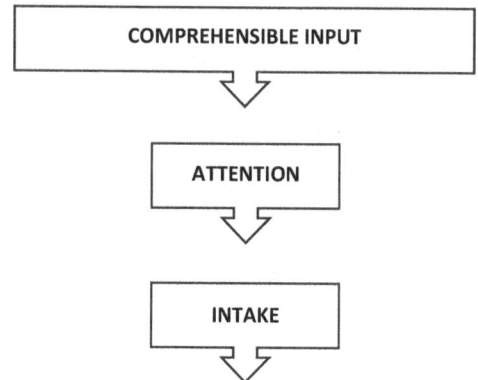

Fig. 8.1   The basic model

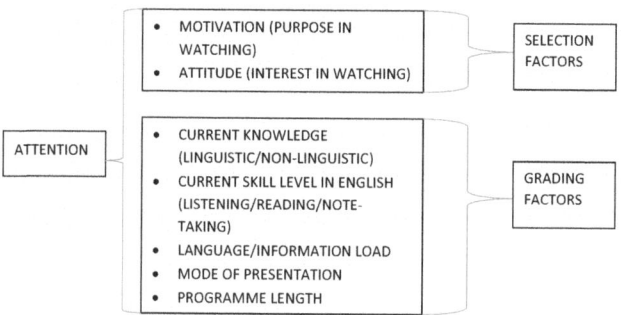

Fig. 8.2   Attention with selection and grading factors

8.5   Applying the Model

It may be objected that the model presented in Fig. 8.4 is overly complex for something as seemingly simple as watching TV. Yet, the evidence from the research reported in this book indicates that it is indeed complex and deserves to be treated as such given the large number of variables at play. I have included loops for possible rejection of the choice of a programme or film before serious and engaged viewing gets under way. A programme or film may be rejected for a wide variety of reasons, for selection reasons or grading reasons, and a new choice made. It may be as simple as surfing channels and watching for no more than a minute or so, or, as in the case

8 The Developing Environment for Language Learning

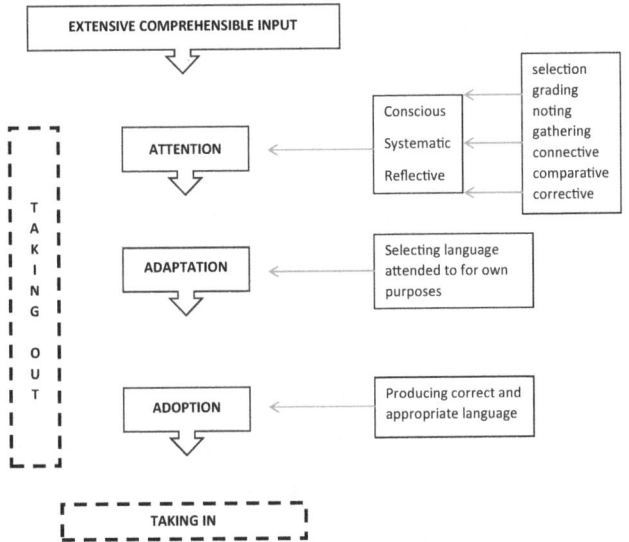

Fig. 8.3 The original 1990 model of "paying attention to the words"

of some of the films watched in the EURECAP project, we may give a DVD a good try before abandoning it and selecting another. It is both at the grading level and at the Adaptation level that the psychomotor aspect of perceptual tuning in is captured in the model. If the text initially provides sufficient support for lexically-guided tuning in, the learner-viewer will continue. If not, perhaps because the captions are inaccurate and distracting, the film or programme may be rejected.

In particular, in the revised model, ATTENTION is given a key role as an important stage, though as part of the process, not as an end. In this respect, my model expands on the position taken by Winke, Gass, & Sydorenko (2013), in which the authors' theoretical position is to focus on the notions of "attention" and "noticing," linking the use of captions to SLA research, which still frequently relies on Schmidt's *Noticing Hypothesis* (Schmidt, 1995, 2001).

It should be said, though, that "noticing" may be fleeting, as may "attention," and may produce little of value. In terms of the cognitive and affective taxonomies described in Chap. 6, "attention" is located at the bottom of the affective pyramid, before "responding" and "valuing,"

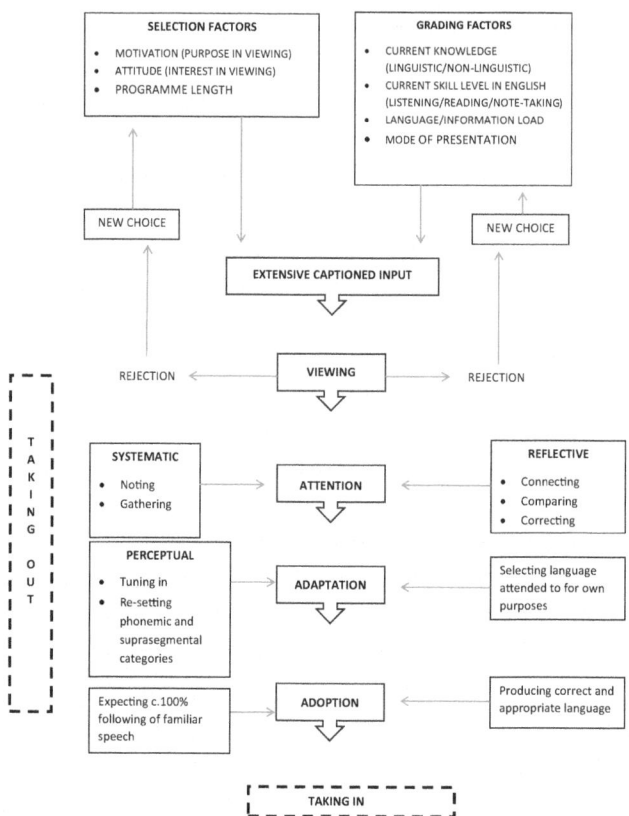

Fig. 8.4 A cognitive-affective model of language learning through captioned viewing

as I illustrated in my list of these factors in Chap. 6 (page 169) when discussing the importance of affective and cognitive objectives in viewing captioned documentaries. These were as follows:

Cognitive Objectives

1. Recall and recognition of knowledge
2. Comprehension of knowledge
3. Skill in application of knowledge apprehended

4. Skill in analysis of situations involving this knowledge; skill in synthesis of this knowledge into new organisation
5. Skill in evaluation in that area of knowledge to judge value of materials and methods for given purposes

Affective Objectives

1. Receiving and attending to stimuli
2. Responding (on request, willingly or enthusiastically)
3. Valuing what has been responded to so as to respond voluntarily and seek ways of responding
4. Conceptualisation of each value responded to
5. Organisation of these values into a system and finally organising the value complex into a single whole; a characterisation of the individual.

In the model in Fig. 8.4, learner-viewers attend to the extensive captioned input, systematically and reflectively. Both ATTENTION and ADAPTATION are included in TAKING OUT. New boxes have been added at both the ADAPTATION and ADOPTION stages to take account of perceptual tuning in, as mentioned in my own articles, and by researchers in captioning such as Bravo (2008) and Mitterer and McQueen (2009). For production, the learner may then adopt language that has been adapted by producing appropriate spoken or written language. Adopting (or "taking on") someone else's language does not mean that it is taken in, in the sense of being absorbed or assimilated into one's linguistic competence, though it does indicate that the language has value to the learner in some way ("ah, that's how you say it, I can use that!"). An example of ADOPTION in the research literature would be Bravo's (2008) follow-up written task for her learners who have watched a captioned programme, then performed a captioning exercise themselves and, finally, selected, adapted and then adopted colloquial expressions which have been used in the programme in their own text production. On "taking in," my position remains that real and genuine regular use is the only guarantee of "taking in" and fully internalising a new language.

Why is it important to have a model? Firstly, the model is an attempt to capture and describe the processes that have been observed or reported in captioned viewing by learners. In particular, the very elaborate processes in the ATTENTION stage reflect the complexity of much of the feedback given by EURECAP participants and informants in studies such as Cole's (2015) and Bravo's (2008). The ADAPTATION and ADOPTION stages were also seen in Cole's informants and have been reported to me in numerous anecdotal reports by participants in the *Lambda* independent language learning project at Oxford.

In psychological terms, I also wished to capture the insights offered by Roxanna Moreno (2006) and Moreno and Mayer (2007) in bringing motivation, attitude and other affective factors to bear in second language viewers benefiting from captioned viewing for language learning. As I have said before, just because a programme or film has captions does not mean that a second language viewer will attend consciously, systematically and reflectively to take out language. This is evident from the millions of second language speakers with normal hearing who watch TV programmes with captions every day and who do so to increase their enjoyment of programmes by being able to check on their understanding occasionally when speech is very rapid or unclear. The other side of motivation and attitude belongs to the level of engagement with the film or TV programme itself. So much of the research reported has taken "interest" as a given, whereas, in reality, the quality of a film or interest in watching a programme is a key factor in engagement and attention.

Lastly, when yet another article to be reviewed arrives comparing captioned and no-captioned viewing for listening comprehension (as it did last week) and/or vocabulary acquisition, it is really time for a change in research questions. My model offers research "spaces" for exploring new research questions that are appropriate for the new environment for language learning. Apart from questions testing the validity of the model as a whole, at each stage or level in the model, there are possible questions related to the learner, the film or programme and the technology. Questions concerning the learner and the film or programme are probably quite obvious, but those exploring the technology are less so and concern both "effects of" and "effects through" technology. For example, the latest research reported by Montero Perez (Montereo Perez,

2013, and Chap. 5) indicates that glossing captions is hugely popular with learners. Just as some e-book readers now offer translations per word at a touch, such a feature with captions may not be far off and will benefit from research into its applications. The ATTENTION space may also offer multiple research questions, particularly in classroom contexts where the teacher can set tasks to be carried out outside class, which may enhance learning with captions (or not), as suggested in Chap. 6. Similarly, both ADAPTATION and ADOPTION lend themselves to task-based approaches where learners view captions programmes or extensively clips and extract language that they can use in fulfilling tasks related to programme themes or language. On the perceptual side, research following up Mitterer and McQueen's findings is urgently needed to test how much exposure to captioned viewing is needed and in what circumstances before there is significant retuning of perceptual categories on more than a limited local level. And what about TAKING IN? Only longitudinal studies will be able to show whether language has really been taken in for personal use. An important aspect of future research drawing on this model will be to try and design experiments that can assess the extent to which those using captions to assist them in developing their listening skills make gains without so limiting the experience as to call the ecological validity of an experiment into question. As Mitterer and McQueen (2009) have shown, it is possible to design naturalistic experiments using standard captions on popular programmes.

Note 1 The confusion, however, is widespread. In the UK, we talk freely about "subtitles" when we mean subtitles for the deaf and hard-of-hearing on broadcast English language programmes and "subtitles" when we mean translation subtitles, also in English, for a French or Danish crime thriller.

9

Conclusion

So this is the end of my story. From hopes and dreams thirty years ago to reality and disillusionment ten years later, and then a recent reawakening in a different world where the same hopes and dreams are being realised by learners through technologies, some of which were not even thought of in the world of 1980s viewing.

9.1 A Changed and Changing World of Language Learning

Although much of this book has been taken up with covering the key milestones and issues in using captioned TV and films for language learning over the past thirty years, the reader will certainly have noted that significant research and changes have taken place in the past five years or so, which help to make a strong case for captions in second and foreign language learning in this new world of learner agency and empowerment. If it had been a matter of simply reviewing key research in the

© The Author(s) 2016
R. Vanderplank, *Captioned Media in Foreign Language Learning and Teaching*, DOI 10.1057/978-1-137-50045-8_9

past five years, I would, perhaps, have written another state-of-the-art article or book chapter, but the aim of this book has been to set out the case for captioned viewing as an area of second language acquisition and applied linguistics which deserves recognition and which embodies the changes happening in language learning with regard to effects both with and through technology.

There is also still widespread ignorance and prejudice about captions, and many of those who might gain most from watching with captions are unlikely to read publications on caption research in academic journals. There will continue to be many teachers, for example, who still regard the use of captions as somehow "cheating," since, in their view, using TV programmes and films should be all about listening with visual support. One reason for this prejudice is probably that there are far too few practical articles on the use of captions in teaching foreign languages. Throughout the 1990s, I tried to promote their use as much as possible with articles in a wide variety of teacher-orientated journals, but I have not seen much evidence of promotion at this level in recent years. As the findings from the EURECAP pilot project also showed, teachers are not alone in these feelings, which are often shared by learners at a variety of levels. What the project also showed, though, is that with regular, systematic and reflective use of captions, this sense of cheating disappears, as learner-viewers become steadily more sophisticated in using them according to their particular needs, such as a sequence involving strong accents or rapid and unclear speech. At least there is substantial evidence now, as reported in this book, that among younger users of social and broadcast media, we are seeing a high level of awareness not only of their availability but also of their usefulness.

In 1999, in a book chapter entitled "Global medium – global resources? Perspectives and paradoxes in using authentic broadcast material for teaching and learning English," I wrote:

> The suggestion that English language television broadcasting remains relatively undeveloped in global terms compared to the spread of English as the language of international communication and as a chosen language of publication in the arts and sciences may appear absurd at first sight. After all. we were told that Saddam Hussein kept himself informed by watching

CNN during the Gulf War; American comedies and soap operas such as *Friends* and *Baywatch* have kept viewers throughout the world hooked. Yet, a glance at the television pages of newspapers in countries where English is a foreign language shows that English language channels broadcast by cable and satellite are just a few products among many in the global broadcasting marketplace. American programmes with their huge global reach are invariably dubbed or subtitled for consumption by local audiences.

It is the contention of this paper that in both general educational terms, and, more specifically, in pedagogical terms, many of the promises of television as an aid to language teaching and learning remain unfulfilled. It is certainly true that Anglo-American TV production and content values have helped to shape the conventions and grammar of programme making on a global scale. However, it remains far from certain that authentic programmes broadcast in English have achieved anything like their potential as rich and varied linguistic and cultural resources. (1999, 259–260)

What a difference fifteen years or so and *YouTube* can make. The change, I would suggest, has been largely a "bottom-up" change, driven by individual users, though it should be said that many teachers of foreign languages do promote and encourage the use of multimedia sites and tools for language learning outside school, language schools and university courses as the methodology of the flipped classroom steadily gains support. Bravo's (2008) work with Portuguese high-school students, for example, suggests that teachers can use captioned films and programmes very effectively to raise language awareness, train learners in productive viewing strategies involving active processing of target vocabulary and even getting learners to caption clips of episodes themselves in order to provide intensive listening practice.

The spread of captioning in Europe in flexible forms and formats certainly gives us hope for the future, even if there are major challenges, many of them put there by the broadcasters and producers themselves. In the UK, for example, not only have TV programmes been captioned in English for many years, but the same is true in Wales, where the TV channel, S4C, broadcasts much of its output in Welsh with Welsh captions, which are widely used by the hearing community for accessing Welsh language programmes, and captions are even provided on online repeat services such as *BBC iPlayer*. Yet, we still have a long way to go.

On a recent visit to France, for example, I was able to watch French programmes, with high quality captions in French. However, on my return home, I was not able to continue watching, as captioned TV programmes are still not widely available across borders, either broadcast or on repeat services. This is not something that can be left to market forces and producers. It has only been through legislation, rules on funding and strong pressure from authorities that, even now, we see broadcasters and producers providing captions in different languages for deaf and hard-of-hearing people. In a strongly market-driven world, the incentives coming from the additional market of second language viewers and learners may be small. Yet, as reports have shown, we have seen steady improvements in captioning across Europe and elsewhere, and we can feel optimistic that the captioning of programmes and cross-border viewing of TV programmes will continue to increase on a global basis.

9.2 Where Next for Captioned Viewing for Language Learning and Teaching?

The demise of broadcast television has been prophesised for many years as technology advances and we acquire new means of receiving information in its various forms. Yet, what we find, in reality, is that there are more broadcast outlets for our consumption than ever, as new entrants to the market, such as *Amazon*, become producers and broadcasters. Certainly, how we watch, when we watch and what we do with our watching may be in a state of constant change as televisions become ever more like huge computer screens and tablets and other mobile devices become larger and smarter, but the fact is that television remains a large component in the lives of many, worldwide. In our own field, this recognition is slowly growing. A good example is Geoffrey Sockett's book, *The Online Informal Learning of English* (2014) in which the index has thirty "television" references, and six of these are multipage references. The second most frequent word in the index is "series," with twenty-six referring to broadcast series such as *How I Met your Mother*.

The case for the value of captioned viewing in informal language learning is clear, but its use in teaching remains to be fully developed. In the same book chapter as the one quoted earlier, I suggested, somewhat rudely perhaps, that the perspective offered by publications on teaching using clips from TV programmes saw language learning as something of a game show, with the teacher as the game show host. I would still maintain that serious use of the language of uncaptioned TV clips for intensive or extensive language learning in the language classroom remains a relative rarity, as nothing has changed as far as the issue of access to the language of programmes is concerned. In contrast, the uses of captioned programmes I have proposed are very different from what might be called "traditional" uses of video clips in the language classroom. I have stressed how captioned programmes and films liberate the teacher and help create greater engagement and autonomy for the learner. I have made suggestions in my chapter on different programme genres as to how different genres may be exploited for different purposes. The findings of researchers such as Mitterer and McQueen's (2009), reported in Chap. 5, also have implications for teaching with captioned viewing, especially for intensive pronunciation and listening practice. I have emphasised that captioned viewing fits well into the notion of the flipped classroom where the teacher asks learners to watch a programme out of class, with questions and tasks set, which the learners work on in their own time on devices which they control. Class time can then be spent not on simple viewing and comprehension but on intensive follow-up work, depending on the task set and the nature and content of the programme.

9.3 Making a "Splash" with Captioned TV

So, can we learn a foreign language while watching TV? Is this a Disney fantasy or do captioned DVD and films hold the key to developing confident listening skills, which lag behind the other skills in a foreign language? Originally, I had thought about starting this book by writing about the film *Splash*, released in 1984, in which a mermaid, Madison, (played by Darryl Hannah) leaves the sea in search of her long lost love, Allen (played by Tom Hanks). I revised this idea as I felt I should build my case before telling the reader about Madison. She surfaces in New York, is arrested and then finds herself in the care of Allen. Unable to speak

English, she learns it very quickly from watching TV. It is striking that she calls herself Madison (after Madison Avenue, where she watches a TV programme in a shop window—Madison Avenue is the centre of the advertising industry in the USA) and relies a great deal on broadcast advertisements to pick up English. Advertisements, after all, usually carry a great deal of text, frequently also spoken, in order to get their message across. In language learning terms, she appears to have been going through a silent period, all the while absorbing language before active use, paying attention to the words as she watched. Her experience takes me back to Valerian Postovsky's (1974, 1977) research into a delayed oral response, which indicated that this period, free from pressure to produce spoken language, can be of great value to learners.

While *Splash* may, of course, be dismissed as pure fantasy, over the years, I have heard many stories from fluent speakers of foreign languages who claim to have acquired a great deal of their fluency and ability to understand (and even speak) the foreign language from watching TV programmes—notably advertisements and series—in the country where the language is spoken. In one account, the person told me that she had not gone out of her flat much in her first three months in Berlin, and had spent a lot of time picking up words and phrases from advertisements and TV programmes. For her, the largely silent period, watching and taking in from this source, was key to her language development. In another, more recent account, a German student told me how she had watched captioned comedies, soap operas and advertisements while house sharing with British students in order to be able to take part in conversations with them and become friends. No doubt, there will be readers of this book who will think of their own anecdotes and cases of similar language learning. If other readers have not experienced captions, my last words are to urge you to try them out and see for yourselves the transforming potential of this add-on designed to be of benefit to deaf and hard-of-hearing people, which is also an invaluable resource for millions of foreign language learners worldwide. Help spread the word!

References

Anderson, L. W., & Krathwohl, D. R. (Eds.). (2001). *A taxonomy for learning, teaching, and assessing: A revision of Bloom's taxonomy of educational objectives.* New York: Longman.

Armes, R. (1988). *On video*. London: Routledge.

Baddeley, A. D. (2007). *Working memory, thought and action*. Oxford: Oxford University Press.

Baker, R. (1985). *Subtitling television for deaf children*. Southampton: Department of Teaching Media\University of Southampton.

Baker, R., Downton, A., & Newell, A. (1980). Simultaneous speech transcription and TV captions for the deaf. In P. A. Kolers, M. E. Wrolstad, & H. Bouma (Eds.), *Processing of visible language* (pp. 445–457). New York: Plenum Press.

Baltova, I. (1999a). Multisensory language teaching in a multidimensional curriculum: The use of authentic bimodal video in core French. *The Canadian Modern Language Review/La Revue canadienne des langues vivantes, 56*(1), 31–48.

Baltova, I. (1999b). *The effect of subtitled and staged video input on the learning and retention of content and vocabulary in a second language*. Unpublished doctoral dissertation, University of Toronto. Retrieved from http://www.collectionscanada.ca/obj/s4/f2/dsk3/ftp04/nq41096.pdf.

Bandura, A. (1995). Exercise of personal and collective efficacy in changing societies. In A. Bandura (Ed.), *Self-efficacy in changing societies* (pp. 1–45). New York: Cambridge University Press.

Bandura, A. (2001). Social cognitive theory: An agentic perspective. *Annual Review of Psychology, 52*, 1–26.

Bandura, A. (2002). Growing primacy of human agency in adaptation and change in the electronic era. *European Psychologist, 7*(1), 2–16.

Bean, R. M., & Wilson, R. M. (1989). Using closed captioned television to teach reading to adults. *Reading Research and Instruction, 28*(4), 27–37.

Benson, P., & Chan, N. (2010). TESOL after YouTube: Fansubbing and informal language learning. *Taiwan Journal of TESOL, 7*(2), 1–23.

Bianchi, F., & Ciabattoni, T. (2008). Captions and subtitles in EFL learning: An investigative study in a comprehensive computer environment. In A. Baldry, M. Pavesi, & C. Taylor Torsello (Eds.), *From Didactas to Ecolingua: An ongoing research project on translation and corpus linguistics* (pp. 69–90). Trieste: Edizioni Università di Trieste.

Bird, S. (2005). Language learning edutainment: Mixing motives in digital resources. *RELC Journal, 36* (3), 311–339.

Bird, S. A., & Williams, J. N. (2002). The effect of bimodal input on implicit and explicit memory: An investigation into the benefits of within-language subtitling. *Applied Psycholinguistics, 23*(4), 509–533.

Brantmeier, C., Vanderplank, R., & Strube, M. (2012). What about me?: Individual self-assessment by skill and level of language instruction. *System, 40*(1), 144–160.

Bravo, M. C.C. (2008). *Putting the reader in the picture: Screen translation and foreign language learning.* Unpublished doctoral dissertation, Universitat Rovira I Virgili, Tarragona, Spain. Retrieved from http://tdx.cat/handle/10803/8771.

Bravo, C. (2010). Text on screen and text on air: A useful tool for foreign language teachers and learners. In J. Díaz Cintas, A. Matamala, & J. Neves (Eds.), *New insights into audiovisual translation and media accessibility: Media for all* (pp. 269–283). Amsterdam, The Netherlands: Rodopi.

Brett, P. (1997). A comparative study of the effects of the use of multimedia on listening comprehension. *System, 25*(1), 39–53.

Brett, P. (1998). Using multimedia: A descriptive investigation of incidental language learning. *Computer Assisted Language Learning, 11*(2), 179–200.

Brett, P. A. (2000). Too many media in my multimedia? A study of the effects of combinations of media on a recall task. In P. A. Brett (Ed.), *CALL in the 21st century: Proceedings of the ESADE*. IATEFL conference, June/July, 2000, Barcelona, Spain.

Buck, G. (2001). *Assessing listening*. Cambridge: Cambridge University Press.

Caimi, A. (2006). Audiovisual translation and language learning: The promotion of intralingual subtitles. *The Journal of Specialised Translation, 6*, 85–98.

Chai, J., & Erlam, R. (2008). The effect and the influence of the use of video and captions on second language learning. *New Zealand Studies in Applied Linguistics, 14*(2), 25–44.

Chandler, P., & Sweller, J. (1991). Cognitive load theory and the format of instruction. *Cognition and Instruction, 8*, 293–332.

Chang, S. (n.d.). *The interaction between schemata and subtitles*. Retrieved from www.ntut.edu.tw/~wwwoaa/journal/39-1/39-1-14p.pdf.

Chapple, L., & Curtis, A. (2000). Content-based instruction in Hong Kong: Student responses to film. *System, 28*(3), 419–433.

Charles, T., & Trenkic, D. (2015). Speech segmentation in a second language: The role of Bi-modal input. In Y. Gambier, A. Caimi, & C. Mariotti (Eds.), *Subtitles and language learning* (pp. 173–197). Frankfurt: Peter Lang.

Chung, J.-M. (1999). The effects of using video text supported with advance organizers and captions on Chinese college students' listening comprehension: An empirical study. *Foreign Language Annals, 32*(3), 295–308.

Chung, J.-M. (2002). The effects of using two advance organizers with video texts for the teaching of listening in English. *Foreign Language Annals, 35*(2), 231–241.

Cole, J. (2015). *Foreign language learning in the age of the internet: A comparison of informal acquirers and traditional classroom learners in Central Brazil*. Unpublished doctoral dissertation. Department of Education, University of Oxford.

Cooper, R., Lavery, M., & Rinvolucri, M. (1991). *Video*. Oxford: Oxford University Press.

Corder, S. P. (1960). *English language teaching and television*. London: Longmans.

Cross, J. (2009). Effects of listening strategy instruction on news videotext comprehension. *Language Teaching Research, 13*(2), 151–176.

d'Ydewalle, G., & Pavakanun, U. (1996). Le sous-titrage à la télévision facilite-t-il l'apprentissage des langues? In Y. Gambier (Ed.), *Les transferts linguistiques dans les médias audiovisuels* (pp. 217–223). Paris: Presses universitaires du Septentrion.

d'Ydewalle, G., & Pavakanun, U. (1997). Could enjoying a movie lead to language acquisition? In P. Winterhoff-Spurk & T. Van der Voort (Eds.), *New horizons in media psychology* (pp. 145–155). Opladen, Germany: Westdeutscher.

d'Ydewalle, G., & Van de Poel, M. (1999). Incidental foreign language acquisition by children watching subtitled television programs. *Journal of Psycholinguistic Research, 28*(3), 227–244. Reprinted as Van de Poel, M., & d'Ydewalle, G. (2001). In Y. Gambier & H. Gottlieb (Eds.), *(Multi) media translation: Concepts, practices, and research.* (pp. 259–273). Amsterdam, Germany: John Benjamins.

Danan, M. (1992). Reversed subtitling and dual coding theory: New directions for foreign language instruction. *Language Learning, 42*(4), 497–527. Reprinted as Danan, M. (1995). Reversed subtitling and dual coding theory: New directions for foreign language instruction. In B. Harley (Ed.), *Lexical issues in language learning.* (pp. 253–282). Ann Arbor, MI: Language Learning/John Benjamins.

Danan, M. (2004). Captioning and subtitling: Undervalued language learning strategies. *Meta, 49*(1), 67–77.

De Bot, K., Jagt, J., Janssen, H., Kessels, E., & Schils, E. (1986). Foreign television and language maintenance. *Second Language Research, 2*(1), 72–82.

Eckes, T., & Grotjahn, R. (2006). A closer look at the construct validity of C-tests. *Language Testing, 23*, 290–325.

European Federation of Hard of Hearing People. (2011). *State of subtitling access in EU, 2011 Report.* Retrieved from http://ec.europa.eu/internal_market/consultations/2011/audiovisual/non-registered-organisations/european-federation-of-hard-of-hearing-people-efhoh-_en.pdf.

European Federation of Hard of Hearing People. (2015). *State of subtitling access in EU, 2015 Report.* Retrieved from http://media.wix.com/ugd/c2e099_0921564404524507bed2ff3648781a3c.pdf.

Fallahkhair, S., Masthoff, J., & Pemberton, L. (2004). Learning languages from interactive television: Language learners reflect on techniques and technologies. In L. Cantoni & C. McLoughlin (Eds.), *Proceedings of World Conference on educational multimedia, hypermedia and telecommunications 2004* (pp. 4336–4343). Chesapeake, VA: AACE.

Fisher, B., Lynch, D., & Allen, C. (1995). *Satellite television in the classroom.* London: Centre for Information on Language Teaching.

Frumuselu, A. D., De Maeyerb, S., Doncheb, V., & Gutiérrez-Colon Plana, M. del M. (2015). Television series inside the EFL classroom: Bridging the gap between teaching and learning informal language through subtitles. *Linguistics and Education, 32*(B), 107–117.

Gallagher, M. (1978). Good television and good teaching: Some tensions in educational practice. *Educational Broadcasting International, 11*(4), 203–206.

Gambier, Y. (2015). Subtitles and language learning (SLL): Theoretical background. In Y. Gambier, A. Caimi, & C. Mariotti (Eds.), *Subtitles and language learning* (pp. 63–82). Frankfurt: Peter Lang.

Garza, T. J. (1991). Evaluating the use of captioned video materials in advanced foreign language learning. *Foreign Language Annals, 24*(3), 239–258.

Geddes, M., & Sturtridge, G. (1982). *Video in the language classroom*. London: Heinemann.

Goh, C. C. (2000). A cognitive perspective on language learners' listening comprehension problems. *System, 28*(1), 55–75.

Goldstein, B., & Driver, P. (2015). *Language learning with digital video*. Cambridge: Cambridge University Press.

Graham, S. (2006). Listening comprehension: The learners' perspective. *System, 34*(2), 165–182.

Guichon, N., & McLornan, S. (2008). The effects of multimodality on L2 learners: Implications for CALL resource design. *System, 36*(1), 85–93.

Guillory, H. G. (1998). The effect of keyword captions to authentic French video on learner comprehension. *CALICO Journal, 15*(1–3), 89–108.

Halliday, M. A. K. (1989). *Spoken and written language*. Oxford: Oxford University Press.

Hayati, A., & Mohmedi, F. (2011). The effect of films with and without subtitles on listening comprehension of EFL learners. *British Journal of Educational Technology, 42*(1), 181–192.

Herbert, M. (2004). *The use of DVD in foreign language learning: Strategies used by learners for meaning focused and form focused tasks*. Final year project, Trinity College, Dublin.

Hernandez, S. S. (2004). *The effects of video and captioned text and the influence of verbal and spatial abilities on second language listening comprehension in a multimedia learning environment*. Unpublished doctoral dissertation, New York University, New York.

Herron, C., Cole, S. P., Corrie, C., & Dubreil, S. (1999). The effectiveness of a video-based curriculum in teaching culture. *The Modern Language Journal, 84*(4), 518–533.

Herron, C., Corrie, C., Cole, S. P., & Henderson, P. (1999). Do prequestioning techniques facilitate comprehension of French video? *The French Review, 72*(6), 1076–1090.

Herron, C., Dubreil, S., Corrie, C., & Cole, S. P. (2002). A classroom investigation: Can video improve intermediate-level French language students' ability to learn about a foreign culture? *The Modern Language Journal, 86*(1), 36–53.

Herron, C., Dubreuil, S., Cole, S. P., & Corrie, C. (2000). Using instructional video to teach culture to beginning foreign language students. *CALICO Journal, 17*(3), 395–429.

Herron, C., York, H., Corrie, C., & Cole, S. P. (2006). A comparison study of the effects of a story-based video instructional package versus a text-based instructional package in the intermediate-level foreign language classroom. *CALICO Journal, 23*(2), 281–307.

Holobow, N., Lambert, W. E., & Sayegh, L. (1984). Pairing script and dialogue: Combinations that show promise for second or foreign language acquisition. *Language Learning, 34*(4), 59–74.

Huang, H.-C. and Eskey, D.E (1999–2000) The effects of closed-captioned television on the listening comprehension of intermediate English as a foreign language (ESL) students. *Journal of Educational Technology Systems, 28*(1), 75–96.

Hwang, Y. (2003). *The effect of the use of video captioning on English as a Foreign Language (EFL) on college students' language learning in Taiwan.* Unpublished doctoral dissertation, The University of Mississippi, Mississippi.

Independent Television Commission. (1999). *ITC guidance on standards for subtitling* London: Independent Television Commission. Retrieved from http://www.ofcom.org.uk/static/archive/itc/itc_publications/codes_guidance/standards_for_subtitling/index.asp.html.

Keddie, J. (2014). *Bringing online video into the classroom.* Oxford: Oxford University Press.

Koolstra, C. M., & Beentjes, J. W. J. (1999). Children's vocabulary acquisition in a foreign language through watching subtitled television programs at home. *Educational Technology Research & Development, 47*(1), 51–60.

Kothari, B. (1999). Same language subtitling: Integrating post literacy development and popular culture on television. *Media and Technology for Human Resource Development, 11*(3), 111–117.

Kothari, B., Pandey, A., & Chudgar, A. (2004). Reading out of the 'idiot box': Same-language subtitling on television in India. *Information Technologies and International Development, 1*(3), 23–44.

Kothari, B., Takeda, J., Joshi, A., & Pandey, A. (2002). Same language subtitling: A butterfly for literacy? *International Journal of Lifelong Education, 21*(1), 55–66.

Kramsch, C., & Andersen, R. W. (1999). Teaching text and context through multimedia. *Language Learning & Technology, 2*(2), 31–42.
Krashen, S. D. (1981). *Second language acquisition and second language learning*. Oxford: Pergamon.
Krashen, S. D. (1985). *The input hypothesis: Issues and implications*. New York: Longman.
Krathwohl, D. R., Bloom, B. S., & Masia, B. B. (1964). *Taxonomy of educational objectives: The classification of educational goals. Handbook 2: Affective domain*. London: Longmans Green.
Kusyk, M., & Sockett, G. (2012). From informal resource usage to incidental language acquisition: Language uptake from online television viewing in English. *ASp. la Revue du GERAS, 62*, 45–65.
Lambert, W. E., Boehler, I., & Sidoti, N. (1981). Choosing the languages of subtitles and spoken dialogues for media presentations: Implications for second language education. *Applied Psycholinguistics, 2*(2), 133–148.
Lambert, W. E., & Holobow, N. E. (1984). Combinations of printed script and spoken dialogues that show promise for beginning students of a foreign language. *Canadian Journal of Behavioural Science, 16*(1), 1–11.
Lantolf, J. P. (2013). Sociocultural theory and the dialectics of L2 learner autonomy/agency. In Benson, P., & Cooker, L. (Eds.), *The applied linguistic individual: Sociocultural approaches to identity, agency, and autonomy* (pp. 17–31). Sheffield, UK & Bristol, CT, USA: Equinox.
Laurillard, D. (1991). Mediating the message: Programme design and students' understanding. *Instructional Science, 20*(1), 3–24.
Lavery, M. (1982). *Active viewing*. Canterbury: Pilgrims Publications.
Leveridge, A. N., & Yang, J. C. (2013). Testing learner reliance on caption supports in second language listening comprehension multimedia environments. *ReCALL, 25*(2), 199–214.
Little, D. (2004). Constructing a theory of learner autonomy: Some steps along the way. In Mäkinen, K., Kaikkonen, P., & Kohonen, V. (Eds.), *Future perspectives in foreign language education* (pp. 15–25). Oulu, Finland: Publications of the Faculty of Education in Oulu University 101.
Liversidge, G. B. (2000). *The role of captioning in second language acquisition*. Unpublished doctoral dissertation, Temple University Philadelphia, Philadelphia.
Lonergan, J. (1984). *Video in language teaching*. Cambridge: Cambridge University Press.
Lonergan, J. (1991). A decade of development: Educational technology and language learning. *Language Teaching, 24*(1), 1–10.

Lowry, D. T. (2014). Analyzing verbal narratives in TV news and commercials. In R. P. Hart (Ed.), *Communication and language analysis in the public sphere* (pp. 244–261). Hershey, PA: Information Science Reference.

MacKnight, F. (1983). Video in English language teaching in Britain. In J. McGovern (Ed.), *Video applications in English language teaching* (pp. 1–16). Oxford, England: Pergamon Press\The British Council (ELT Documents 114).

Mariotti, C. (2015). A survey on stakeholders' perceptions of subtitles as a means to promote foreign language learning. In Y. Gambier, A. Caimi, & C. Mariotti (Eds.), *Subtitles and language learning* (pp. 83–104). Frankfurt: Peter Lang.

Markham, P. L. (1989). The effects of captioned videotapes on the listening comprehension of beginning, intermediate, and advanced ESL students. *Educational Technology, 29*(10), 38–41.

Markham, P. L. (1993). Captioned television videotapes: Effects of visual support on second language comprehension. *Journal of Educational Technology Systems, 29*(3), 183–191.

Markham, P. L. (1999). Captioned videotapes and second-language listening word recognition. *Foreign Language Annals, 32*(3), 321–328.

Markham, P. L. (2000–2001). The influence of culture-specific background knowledge and captions on second language comprehension. *Journal of Educational Technology Systems, 29*(4), 331–343.

Markham, P. L., & Peter, L. A. (2003). The influence of English language and Spanish language captions on foreign language listening/reading comprehension. *Journal of Educational Technology Systems, 31*(3), 331–341.

Markham, P. L., Peter, L. A., & McCarthy, T. J. (2001). The effects of native language vs. target language captions on foreign language students' DVD video comprehension. *Foreign Language Annals, 34*(5), 439–445.

Mayer, R. E. (2009). *Multimedia learning* (2nd ed.). Cambridge: Cambridge University Press.

Mayer, R. E., Lee, H., & Peebles, A. (2014). Multimedia learning in a second language: A cognitive load perspective. *Applied Cognitive Psychology, 28*, 653–660.

Mayer, R. E., & Moreno, R. (1998). A split-attention effect in multimedia learning: Evidence for dual processing systems in working memory. *Journal of Educational Psychology, 90*, 312–320.

McGovern, J. (Ed.). (1983). *Video applications in ELT.* Oxford, England: Pergamon Press\The British Council (ELT Documents 114).

Mills, N., Herron, C., & Cole, S. (2004). Teacher-assisted versus individual viewing of foreign language video: Relation to comprehension, self-efficacy, and engagement. *CALICO Journal, 21*(2), 291–316.

Mitterer, H., & McQueen, J. M. (2009). Foreign subtitles help but native-language subtitles harm foreign speech perception. *PLoS One, 4*(1), e7785. doi:10.1371/journal.pone.0007785.

Montero Perez, M. (2013). 'Watch and Learn?! Five studies into the use and effectiveness of captioned video for L2 listening comprehension and vocabulary acquisition.' Unpublished doctoral dissertation, KU Leuven, Belgium.

Montero Perez, M., Peters, E., & Desmet, P. (2014). Is less more? Effectiveness and perceived usefulness of keyword and full captioned video for L2 listening comprehension. *ReCALL, 26*(01), 21–43.

Montero Perez, M., Peters, E., & Desmet, P. (2015). Enhancing vocabulary learning through captioned video: An eye-tracking study. *The Modern Language Journal, 99*(2), 308–328.

Montero Perez, M., Van Den Noortgate, W., & Desmet, P. (2013). Captioned video for L2 listening and vocabulary learning: A meta-analysis. *System, 41*(3), 720–739.

Montero, Perez M., Peters, E., Clarebout, G., & Desmet, P. (2014). Effects of captioning on video comprehension and incidental vocabulary learning. *Language Learning & Technology, 18*(1), 118–141.

Moreno, R. (2006). Learning with high tech and multimedia environments. *Current Directions in Psychological Science, 15*, 63–67.

Moreno, R., & Mayer, R. E. (2007). Interactive multimodal learning environments. *Educational Psychology Review, 19*, 309–326.

Nation, I. S. P. (1990). *Teaching and learning vocabulary.* Boston: Newbury House.

Nation, I. S. P. (2001). *Learning vocabulary in another language.* Cambridge: Cambridge University Press.

Neuman, S. B., & Koskinen, P. S. (1990). *Using captioned television to improve the reading proficiency of language minority students.* Falls Church, VA: National Captioning Institute.

Neuman, S. B., & Koskinen, P. S. (1992). Captioned television as 'comprehensible input': Effects of incidental word learning from context for language minority students. *Reading Research Quarterly, 27*, 95–106.

Ofcom. (2005). *Subtitling: An issue of speed.* London: Ofcom—Office of Communications. Retrieved from http://stakeholders.ofcom.org.uk/binaries/research/tv-research/subt.pdf.

Paivio, A. (1986). *Mental representation: A dual-coding approach*. New York: Oxford University Press.

Paribakht, T., & Wesche, M. (1993). Reading comprehension and second language development in a comprehension-based ESL program. *TESOL Canada Journal*, 11 (1), 9–29.

Park, M. (2004). *The effects of partial captions on Korean EFL learners' listening comprehension*. Unpublished doctoral dissertation, University of Texas at Austin, Austin, TX.

Pavakanun, U., & d'Ydewalle, G. (1992). Watching foreign television programs and language learning. In F. L. Engel, D. G. Bouwhuis, T. Bősser, & G. d'Ydewalle (Eds.), *Cognitive modelling and interactive environments in language learning* (pp. 193–198). Berlin: Springer.

Pemberton, L., Fallahkhair, S., & Masthoff, J. (2005). Learner-centred development of a mobile and iTV language learning support system. *Educational Technology & Society*, 8(4), 52–63.

Pew Research Center. (2014). *State of the News Media 2014*. Retrieved from http://www.journalism.org/2014/03/26/state-of-the-news-media-2014-overview/.

Pew Research Centre. (2010). *Americans Spending More Time Following the News*. Retrieved from http://www.people-press.org/2010/09/12/americans-spending-more-time-following-the-news/.

Postovsky, V. A. (1974). Effects of delay in oral practice at the beginning of second language learning. *The Modern Language Journal*, 58, 229–239.

Postovsky, V. (1977). Why not start speaking later? In M. Burt, H. Dulay, & M. Finocchiaro (Eds.), *Viewpoints on English as a second language* (pp. 17–26). New York: Regents.

Price, K. (1983). Closed-captioned TV: An untapped resource. *MATESOL Newsletter, 1–2,* 1–8.

Pujolà, J.-T. (2002). CALLing for help: Researching language learning strategies using help facilities in a web-based multimedia program. *ReCALL, 14*(2), 235–262.

Rieh, S. Y., Kim, Y.-M., & Markey, K. (2012). Amount of invested mental effort (AIME) in online searching. *Information Processing and Management, 48*, 1136–1150.

Rodgers, M. (2013). *English language learning through viewing television: An investigation of comprehension, incidental vocabulary acquisition, lexical coverage, attitudes and captions*. Unpublished doctoral dissertation, Victoria University of Wellington, New Zealand.

Rybak, S. (1983). *Foreign languages by radio and television: The development of a support strategy for adult home-learners*. Unpublished doctoral dissertation, Brighton Polytechnic, Brighton, England.

Salomon, G. (1981a). Introducing AIME: The assessment of children's mental involvement with television. In H. Kelly & H. Gardner (Eds.), *Viewing children through television* (pp. 89–102). San Francisco: Jossey-Bass.

Salomon, G. (1981b). *Communication and education*. Beverly Hills, CA: Sage.

Salomon, G. (1983a). The differential investment of mental effort in learning from different sources. *Educational Psychologist, 18*, 42–50.

Salomon, G. (1983b). Using television as a unique teaching resource for OU courses. *IET Papers on Broadcasting No. 225*. Milton Keynes, England: The Open University.

Salomon, G. (1984). Television is 'easy' and print is 'tough': The differential investment of mental effort in learning as a function of perceptions and attributions. *Journal of Educational Psychology, 76*(4), 647–658.

Salomon, G. (1993). No distribution without individual's cognition: A dynamic interactional view. In G. Salomon (Ed.), *Distributed cognitions* (pp. 111–138). Cambridge: Cambridge University Press.

Salomon, G., & Leigh, T. (1984). Predispositions about learning from print and television. *Journal of Communication, 34*(2), 119–135.

Salomon, G., & Perkins, D. (2005). Do technologies make us smarter? Intellectual amplification with, of and through technology. In R. J. Sternberg & D. D. Preiss (Eds.), *Intelligence and technology: The impact of tools on the nature and development of human abilities* (pp. 71–86). Mahwah, NJ: Lawrence Erlbaum.

Sanders, D. A. (1977). *Auditory perception of speech: An introduction to principles and problems*. London: Prentice-Hall.

Schmidt, R. (1995). Consciousness and foreign language learning: A tutorial on attention and awareness in learning. In R. Schmidt (Ed.), *Attention and awareness in foreign language learning*. (pp. 1–63). Honolulu, HI: University of Hawai'i, National Foreign Language Resource Center.

Schmidt, R. (2001). Attention. In P. Robinson (Ed.), *Cognition and second language instruction* (pp. 3–32). Cambridge: Cambridge University Press.

Sharples, M., Adams, A., Ferguson, R., Gaved, M., McAndrew, P., Rienties, B., et al. (2014). *Innovating Pedagogy 2014: Open University Innovation Report 3*. Milton Keynes, England: The Open University.

Shea, P. (2000). Levelling the playing field: A study of captioned interactive video for second language learning. *Journal of Educational Computing Research, 22*(3), 243–263.

Simpson, E. (1966). *The classification of educational objectives: Psychomotor domain*. Office of Education Project No. 5-85-104. Urbana, IL: University of Illinois. Retrieved from http://files.eric.ed.gov/fulltext/ED010368.pdf.

Smith, J. J. (1990). *Closed captioned television and adult students of English as a second language*. Arlington, VA: Arlington Refugee Education and Employment.

Smith, E. E., & Shen, C-W. (1992). The effects of knowledge of results Feedback of captioning on listening comprehension of English as a second language in interactive videodisc system. In M. R. Simonson, & K. A. Jurasek (Eds.), *14th Annual Proceedings of Selected Research and Development Presentations at the 1992 Convention of the Association for Educational Communications and Technology.* (pp. 718-742). Ames, IA: Iowa State University.

Sockett, G. (2014). *The online informal learning of English*. Basingstoke, England: Palgrave Macmillan.

Sockett, G., & Toffoli, D. (2012). Beyond learner autonomy: A dynamic systems view of the informal learning of English in virtual online communities. *ReCALL, 24*(2), 138–151.

Stempleski, S., & Tomalin, B. (1990). *Video in action: Recipes for using video in language teaching*. New York: Prentice Hall.

Stewart, M. A., & Pertusa, I. (2004). Gains to language learners from viewing target language closed-captioned films. *Foreign Language Annals, 37*(1), 438–447.

Sweller, J. (2005). Implications of cognitive load theory for multimedia learning. In R.E. Mayer (Ed.) *The Cambridge Handbook of Multimedia Learning* (pp. 19-30). Cambridge: Cambridge University Press.

Sydorenko, T. (2010). Modality of input and vocabulary acquisition. *Language Learning & Technology, 14*(2), 50–73.

Taylor, G. (2005). Perceived processing strategies of students watching captioned video. *Foreign Language Annals, 38*(3), 422–427.

Thompson, G. (1979). Television as text: Open University case study programmes. In M. Barrett, P. Corrigan, A. Kuhn, & J. Wolff (Eds.), *Ideology and cultural production* (pp. 160–197). London: Croom Helm.

Toffoli, D., & Sockett, G. (2010). How non-specialist students of English practice informal learning using web 2.0 tools. *ASp. la Revue du GERAS, 58*, 125–144.

Umino, T. (1999). The use of self-instructional broadcast materials for second language learning: An investigation in the Japanese context. *System, 27*(3), 309–327.

Van Lommel, S., Laenen, A., & d'Ydewalle, G. (2006). Foreign-grammar acquisition while watching subtitled television programmes. *British Journal of Educational Psychology, 76*(2), 243–258.

Vanderplank, R. (1988a). The value of teletext subtitles in language learning. *ELT Journal, 42*(4), 272–281.

Vanderplank, R. (1988b). Implications of differences in native and non-native approaches to listening. *British Journal of Language Teaching, 26*(1), 32–41.

Vanderplank, R. (1990). Paying attention to the words: Practical and theoretical problems in watching television programmes with uni-lingual (CEEFAX) subtitles. *System, 18*(2), 221–234.

Vanderplank, R. (1993). A very verbal medium: Language learning through closed captions. *TESOL Journal, 3*(1), 10–14.

Vanderplank, R. (1994a). Resolving inherent conflicts: Autonomous language learning from popular broadcast television. In H. Jung & R. Vanderplank (Eds.), *Barriers and bridges: Media technology in language learning* (pp. 119–134). Frankfurt: Peter Lang.

Vanderplank, R. (1994b). Subtitles: Silent films to teletext. In R. E. Asher & J. Y. M. Simpson (Eds.), *The encyclopaedia of language and linguistics* (pp. 4398–4399). Oxford, England: Pergamon.

Vanderplank, R. (1996a). Really active viewing with teletext subtitles and closed captions. *Modern English Teacher, 5*(2), 32–37.

Vanderplank, R. (1996b). *Effects of and effects with television in education: Towards a strong hypothesis for the value of teletext subtitles/closed captions.* Paper given at the CETaLL Symposium, AILA Congress, Jyväskylä, Finland, August, 1996.

Vanderplank, R. (1997). Television, teletext subtitles and British studies. *British Studies Now, 8*, 15–16.

Vanderplank, R. (1999). Global medium—global resource? Perspectives and paradoxes in using authentic broadcast material for teaching and learning English. In C. Gnutzmann (Ed.), *Teaching and learning English as a global language: Native and non-native perspectives* (pp. 253–266). Tübingen: Stauffenberg.

Vanderplank, R. (2010). Déjà vu? A decade of research on language laboratories, television and video in language learning. *Language Teaching, 43*(1), 1–37.

Vanderplank, R. (2015). Thirty years of research into captions/same language subtitles and second/foreign language learning: Distinguishing between 'Effects of' subtitles and 'Effects with' subtitles for future research. In Y. Gambier, A. Caimi, & C. Mariotti (Eds.), *Subtitles and language learning* (pp. 19–40). Frankfurt, Germany: Peter Lang.

Vanderplank, R. (2016). 'Effects of' and 'effects with' captions: How exactly does watching a TV programme with same language subtitles make a difference to language learners? *Language Teaching, 49*(2), 235–250. Orginally published online 2013.

Vanderplank, R., & Dyson, P. (1999). Who is in The Learning Zone?: Evaluating the impact of Italia 2000. In G. Hogan-Brun & U. O. H. Jung (Eds.), *Media multimedia omnimedia* (pp. 125–138). Frankfurt: Peter Lang.

Vulchanova, M. D., Aurstad, L. M. G., Kvitnes, I. E. N., & Eshuis, H. (2015). As naturalistic as it gets: Subtitles in the English classroom in Norway. *Frontiers in Psychology, 6*, 122–124.

Webb, S., & Rodgers, M. P. H. (2009a). The lexical coverage of movies. *Applied Linguistics, 30*, 407–427.

Webb, S., & Rodgers, M. P. H. (2009b). Vocabulary demands of television programs. *Language Learning, 59*(2), 335–366.

Wesche, M., & Paribakht, T. S. (1996). Assessing second language vocabulary knowledge: Depth versus breadth. *The Canadian Modern Language Review/La Revue canadienne des langues vivantes, 53*(1), 13–40.

Weyers, J. R. (1999). The effect of authentic video on communicative competence. *The Modern Language Journal, 83*(3), 339–349.

White, C., Easton, P., & Anderson, C. (2000). Students' perceived value of video in a multimedia language course. *Educational Media International, 37*(3), 167–175.

Williams, H., & Thorne, D. (2000). The value of teletext subtitling as a medium for language learning. *System, 28*(2), 217–228.

Winke, P., Gass, S. M., & Sydorenko, T. (2010). The effects of captioning videos used for foreign language listening activities. *Language Learning & Technology, 14*(1), 66–87.

Winke, P., Gass, S. M., & Sydorenko, T. (2013). Factors influencing the use of captions by foreign language learners: An eye-tracking study. *The Modern Language Journal, 97*(1), 254–275.

Yüksel, D., & Tanriverdi, B. (2009). Effects of watching captioned movie clip on vocabulary development of EFL learners. *The Turkish Online Journal of Educational Technology, 8*(2), 48–54.

Zamoon, S. R. (1996). *Closed captioned television: A perceived means to self-help in second language learning*. Unpublished M.A. thesis, Iowa State University.

Index

A

advance organizer, 82
affective, 5, 48, 59, 69, 100, 145, 162–170, 173, 239, 241–243
affective filter, 30, 53, 54
affordances, 159, 188, 235, 237
Amount of Invested Mental Effort (AIME), 35–37
assessment, 33, 82, 188, 231
attention, 25, 38, 57–64, 69, 88, 94, 110, 112–114, 135–142, 151, 160, 166, 170, 182, 200, 209, 238, 239, 242, 243
attitude(s), 3, 5, 19, 20, 29, 32, 33, 53, 54, 59, 67–69, 121, 122, 166, 169, 170, 173, 175, 193, 199, 226, 227, 229, 242
audiovisual, 3–5, 26, 31, 32, 34, 39, 41, 118, 129, 134, 150, 151, 199, 218, 223, 226–228, 230
autonomous learners, 40, 55, 69, 216, 230–235
autonomy, 150, 153, 235, 237, 249

B

Bandura, A., 3, 38, 39, 237
bimodal, 79, 88–90, 127, 128, 144
bimodal input, 79, 88, 89, 111, 127, 128, 143, 145–146
Bravo, M. de C.C., 103, 117–120, 124, 134, 135, 180, 241, 242, 247

C

Caimi, A., 131

Index

classroom, 5, 20, 22–25, 28, 32, 33, 47, 55, 72, 124, 126, 129, 130, 149, 158, 162, 164, 176, 180, 185, 227–229, 235, 243, 249
cognitive, 48, 68, 72, 100, 106, 142, 145, 147, 162–170, 172, 173, 175, 239–241
   cognitive-affective model, 240
   cognitive load theory, 142, 146
   cognitive theory of learning, 147
Cole, J., 27, 28, 32, 40, 93, 216, 232–234, 236
communicative approach, 20
communicative competence, 93
comprehensible input, 30–32, 53, 58, 63, 95, 238
comprehensible input hypothesis, 30
Cross, J., 25
cultural artefact, 206, 221
cultural resource(s), 19, 20, 22, 38, 40, 61, 129–130, 150, 154, 158, 167, 177, 185, 247
culture, 1, 4, 26, 27, 52, 158, 181, 183–185, 219

D

Danan, M., 88–89, 132, 144–146
d'Ydewalle, G., 89, 231
diary studies, 5, 144, 202, 208, 211, 216
discourse(s), 4, 26, 34, 48, 65, 170–175, 184
documentary(ies), 4, 18, 21, 33, 48, 52, 59, 64, 71, 84, 89, 94, 127, 128, 139, 151, 152, 161–168, 170, 173–175, 240
Dow, Anne, 3, 43–47, 76, 78, 81
dual-coding theory, 75, 76

E

education, 33, 34, 38–39, 129, 230
educational level, 45, 125
educational potential, 68, 161
Educational Recording Agency (ERA), 150
educational resource(s), 19, 34–40, 129–130

F

fansubs (fansubbers, fansubbing), 16, 17, 133, 136
flipped classroom, 4, 33, 159, 181, 185, 247, 249
Frumuselu, A., 103, 124, 146, 180

G

Gambier, Y., 223–226
Gass, S.M., 77, 84, 110, 139, 239
genre, 4, 14, 31, 48, 82, 117, 118, 126, 139, 149–185, 199, 249
grading, 57, 103, 136, 237–239. *See also* selection
grammar, 8, 28, 60, 90, 93, 247

H

Herron, C., 23, 27, 28, 93

I

incidental, 30, 83, 102–104, 108, 109, 115, 121, 122, 172
independent learners, 2, 5, 32, 69, 95, 150, 156, 225, 226
informal learning, 31, 180, 230–235

input, 3, 25, 26, 30–32, 43, 55, 58, 79, 87, 89, 92, 95, 107, 111, 127, 128, 143, 228, 231, 237
input hypothesis, 30
intentional, 87, 112, 115, 172

K

Koskinen, P.S., 77, 78, 80, 102
Kothari, B., 130
Krashen, S., 30, 32, 53
Krathwohl, D.R., 164, 165, 167

L

Lambert, W.E., 88, 143, 144
language acquisition, 2, 20, 45–47, 105, 221. *See also* second language acquisition
language learning resources, 59, 61, 161, 176, 218
lifestyle, 4, 18, 48, 152, 181–183
listening comprehension, 4, 26, 50, 54–56, 75–104, 118, 121, 131, 138, 184, 199, 228, 242
literacy, 4, 11, 14, 104, 130–131, 142
longitudinal studies, 4, 26, 81, 106, 117–126, 243

M

Mariotti, C., 226, 237
Markham, P., 77, 78, 86, 87, 90, 93, 129, 151
Mayer, R.E., 146, 147, 242
meta-analysis, 3, 53, 75–81, 83, 102, 106, 187

Montero-Perez, M., 3, 53, 75–76, 78, 79, 81, 85, 105, 106, 108–116, 187, 242
Moreno, R., 147, 166, 237, 242
motivation, 23, 38, 39, 53, 130, 147, 166, 224, 225, 227, 242
multimedia, 2, 26, 27, 39, 75, 76, 146, 231, 247
multimodal(ity), 73

N

Neuman, S.B., 77, 78, 80, 102

O

online, 17, 20–23, 31, 32, 37, 109, 136, 150, 157, 176, 181, 182, 191, 208, 232, 234, 247
Open University, 32–34

P

Paivio, A., 89, 145, 146
Postovsky, V., 250
Price, Karen, 3, 43–47, 55, 76, 78, 81, 187

Q

questionnaire, 29, 65, 66, 93, 101, 103, 107, 109, 111, 117, 188, 193–196, 211, 219, 225–228

R

register, 134, 168, 178
reversed subtitling, 88, 89, 143, 144, 231

Rodgers, M., 30, 103, 120, 122–124, 151

S

Salomon, G., 3, 34–41, 64, 176, 194, 218, 235–237
same-language subtitles, 7, 9, 130
satellite, 247
scaffolding, 231, 233
schema/schemata, 35, 92, 93, 220
Schmidt, R., 239
second language acquisition, 2, 20, 30, 242. *See also* language acquisition
selection, 29, 57, 85, 103, 116, 136, 237, 238. *See also* grading
self-efficacy, 24, 35, 36, 38–40, 54, 62, 64, 211, 218, 221
series (TV), 8, 12, 17, 23, 27, 29, 31, 59, 65, 66, 82, 93, 99, 102, 108, 114, 116, 121, 122, 124, 129, 146, 151, 159, 160, 162, 177, 179–181, 184, 197, 210–212, 248, 250
sitcom(s), 18, 41, 71, 177–180
situation comedy(ies), 134, 151, 161, 177–180
soap opera, 13, 14, 18, 51, 52, 134, 151, 152, 180–181, 247, 250
Sockett, G., 31, 40, 234, 236, 237, 248
speech (segmentation), 111, 127–129
strategy(ies), 4, 5, 24–26, 48, 51, 55, 71, 72, 83, 86, 92, 103, 107, 108, 117, 120, 124, 131–136, 188, 199–205, 221, 231, 247
streaming, 44, 150, 230

subtitles (Teletext) 21, 43–73, 126
subtitling, 10–17, 88–95, 118, 131, 133, 134, 143, 144, 224, 231
survey(s), 5, 7, 29, 31, 70, 111, 121, 122, 224–230, 237
Sweller, J., 142, 146, 147
Sydorenko, T., 77, 78, 84, 102, 103, 110, 139

T

Tanriverdi, B., 83
task(s), 5, 22–25, 35–39, 50, 59–61, 65, 70, 112, 114, 132, 135, 154, 172, 182, 220, 237, 241, 249
task-based language approaches, 243
taxonomy, 165–167, 169, 170
technological, 9, 124, 227, 235–237
technology, 23, 26, 38, 48, 71, 112, 150, 235, 236, 242, 248
translation, 1, 2, 4, 7, 9, 10, 15, 17, 31, 61, 89, 92, 100, 101, 104, 108, 113–116, 120, 133, 146, 156, 157, 188, 189, 195, 206, 223, 224, 227, 233, 243

V

viewer factors, 217
Vimeo, 22
vocabulary, 30, 31, 40, 50, 60, 76, 79–83, 89–91, 93–95, 102–104, 108–117, 120–124, 176, 178, 187, 200, 212, 228, 247
vocabulary acquisition, 4, 75–104, 122, 242

Vocabulary Knowledge Scale (VKS), 31, 83
Vocabulary Levels Test, 122, 123
Vulchanova, M.D., 30, 93, 101

W

Weyers, J.R., 26
Winke, P., 77, 78, 80, 84, 139, 141, 142, 146, 239

Y

Yüksel, D., 83
YouTube, 9, 16, 17, 19, 22, 136, 150, 177, 179, 185, 230

Z

Zamoon, S.R., 70–72, 215, 230

The manufacturer's authorised representative in the EU is Springer Nature Customer Service Centre GmbH, Europaplatz 3, 69115 Heidelberg, Germany. If you have any concerns regarding our products, please contact ProductSafety@springernature.com

Printed and bound by CPI Group (UK) Ltd, Croydon, CR0 4YY
23/03/2026
02076458-0004